Contents

Exam advice   4

Cognition and behaviour

Chapter 1 Memory   11

Chapter 2 Perception   31

Chapter 3 Development   49

Chapter 4 Research methods   69

Social context and behaviour

Chapter 5 Social influence   95

Chapter 6 Language, thought and communication   115

Chapter 7 Brain and neuropsychology   137

Chapter 8 Psychological problems   157

How this book is organised

Content

On the right-hand side of every spread we have provided the essential content for one topic.

Plus we include some practice questions:

- **Apply it questions** Where you can practise your ability to apply your knowledge to a scenario question.
- **Knowledge Check questions** Where you can see some typical exam-style questions for the spread.

- There is also an **Exam booster** with useful ideas about how to improve your exam performance.

Activities

On the back of each content page are two activities to help you rehearse and process the information.

You can find answers for all the 'Knowledge Check' and 'Apply it' questions as well as the Activities at:

www.illuminatepublishing.com/gcsepsychrgquestionanswers

www.illuminatepublishing.com/gcsepsychrgactivityanswers

In the GCSE level exam there are 2 papers:

Paper 1 Cognition and behaviour

1 hour 45 minutes, each section = 25 marks

Section A: Memory

Section B: Perception

Section C: Development

Section D: Research methods

Paper 2 Social context and behaviour

1 hour 45 minutes, each section = 25 marks

Section A: Social Influence

Section B: Language, thought, communication

Section C: Brain and neuropsychology

Section D: Psychological problems

AO stands for 'assessment objective'

Over the whole exam
35% of the marks are for AO1 Description
35% of the marks are for AO2 Application
30% of the marks are for AO3 Evaluation

APPLY IT – Research Methods

APPLY IT

There are two kinds of application questions:

- Application to research methods.
- Application to other specification topics.

Throughout this book we give examples to help you practise both of these types of questions.

Research methods questions will be in every section of Papers 1 and 2 in addition to the Research methods section on Paper 1.

20%

At least 20% of the marks for your GCSE exam will come from questions on research methods.

Type of exam questions

On all sections of the exam the type of question is unpredictable. You will have combinations of multiple choice questions, short answer questions and extended writing questions. These questions may be description (AO1), application (AO2), evaluation (AO3) or a combination of these. They may be related to research methods. Here are some examples:

AO1 Identify, define (what is meant by), give, explain, briefly outline, describe.	What is meant by 'closed posture'?	[2 marks]
	Identify **one** scanning technique.	[1 mark]
	Briefly outline **two** neural structures in the womb.	[4 marks]
	Explain how depth cues are used to perceive objects in the distance.	[3 marks]
	Describe Piaget's theory of cognitive development.	[4 marks]
AO2 With reference to the example above …	[Stem] Mike remembered breaking his leg as a boy but his sister told him that it was her leg that got broken. [question] How can the theory of reconstructive memory be used to explain the example above?	[4 marks]
AO3 Explain, evaluate, discuss, briefly discuss	Identify and explain **one** criticism of Milgram's research on obedience.	[4 marks]
	The Sapir-Work hypothesis has been criticised. Use your knowledge of psychology to evaluate this hypothesis.	[5 marks]
AO1 + AO3 Extended writing 4 marks AO1 5 marks AO3	Outline and evaluate cognitive behaviour therapy.	[9 marks]
	Describe and evaluate **one** study of conformity. In your description include the method used, the results obtained and the conclusions drawn.	[9 marks]
AO1 + AO2 + AO3 Extend writing + applications 3 marks AO1 3 marks AO2 3 marks AO3	[Stem] Two friends are discussing an accident they saw on the way to school. <Conversation given here> [Question] Outline and evaluate research on bystander intervention. Refer to the conversation above in your answer.	[9 marks]

Examples of research methods questions

AO1	What is an extraneous variable?	[2 marks]
AO2	[Stem] A psychologist planned to compare memory in younger and older participants. [Question] Describe how the psychologist might use random sampling to obtain the sample.	[3 marks]
AO3	Explain **one** difference between quantitative and qualitative data.	[2 marks]
	Explain **one** limitation of using questionnaires in psychological research.	[2 marks]

What to do for a Grade A

Top class AO1 ... includes details and specialist terms.

- This is good → Moore and Frye showed children didn't notice the change if naughty teddy did remove a counter ...
- This isn't good → One study found that children still said the rows were the same if something was taken away...

You don't need to write more you just need to include specific bits of information – most particularly specialist terms but also researchers' names, percentages and so on.

Top class AO2 ... uses text or quotes from the stem of the question.

- This is good → Bill was showing that he disagreed with Tom because he was sitting with his arms and legs crossed.
- This isn't good → When you cross your arms and legs it suggests you are disagreeing, like Bill did.

It's not enough to just mention a few key words – you must really engage with the stem.

This is a skill that needs practice.

Top class AO3 ... is elaborated and therefore effective.

❶ **Beginner level:** State your point: One criticism is ..., This theory is supported by ..., One strength is ....

❷ **Intermediate level:** Add some *context*.

- This is good → One weakness is that the task was artificial. In Asch's study participants were given a trivial task (judging the length of lines) which doesn't reflect everyday situations where people conform.
- This isn't good → One weakness is that the task was artificial. This doesn't tell us about everyday life.

The second example is *generic* – it could be used anywhere.
Context is king.

❸ **Expert level:** Add further explanation to make the point thorough + finish 'This shows that ...

Read the criticisms throughout this book as examples of expert level. We have provided further elaboration and a conclusion for each one.

Whatever you do AVOID a list of beginner level criticisms with no context.

Top class extended writing

Make it organised ... it helps the examiner see the separate elements of your answer. Use paragraphs.

There are more on essays on the next page ...

Describe **FEWER** studies but explain them in detail.

Identify **FEWER** critical points, but explain each one thoroughly.

List-like is bad.

It's actually quite easy to list lots of points – explaining them is challenging.

Context is king.

Good evaluation points must contain evidence.

Your point may be well-elaborated but, if the same elaborated point can be placed in many different essays then it is too **EASY** – everyone can do it.

Good evaluation points have **CONTEXT**.

KNOWLEDGE CHECK

The questions throughout this book should help you identify all the different ways that questions can be asked.

Each GCSE paper has 100 marks and the exam is 105 minutes, which gives you almost exactly 1 minute per mark.

Just because you have written lots doesn't mean you will get high marks.

Students who write long answers often do poorly because ...

- They ramble and may not answer the question.
- They spend too much time on certain questions and have less time for other questions.
- They write too much description in an extended writing question and the maximum mark for description is 4 out of 9 marks.

Research

The term 'research' refers to theories, explanations or studies.

There are lots of little rules

Explain	Questions with the word 'explain' require a bit more than identify or outline – you need to state your point, add some detail (outline) and then offer an example or a reason why.
One or more **Two or more**	Describe **one or more** stages of cognitive development. **[3 marks]** *You can just describe one in detail and/or more than one in less detail – but one is fine for full marks. The same for two or more – just do two.*
Difference between	Explain the difference between open and closed posture. **[3 marks]** *The danger is that you will simply describe each item. You must find a way to contrast them both, for example considering how a person's arms are used.*
Design a study	Imagine that you are going to conduct a study to see if motivation affects perceptual set. Use your knowledge of psychology to describe: • How the study would be carried out. • The way you would measure how much motivation affected perceptual set. • The results you would expect to find in the study. **[6 marks]** *Ensure you explain BOTH conditions of the experiment.* *Ensure that you say what would be found in BOTH conditions.* *Focus on the demands of the bullet points and don't include anything else, such as aims or evaluations.* *It is fine to just copy a study that you have learned about. You don't have to make up a study from scratch. In this question you could describe Gilchrist and Nesburg's study into the effects of food deprivation.*
Questions with extra information	Calculate the range. Show your workings. **[2 marks]** Outline **one** stage of development in Piaget's theory and give **one** application of this stage to education. **[4 marks]** Identify the **two** types of encoding that may be used when revising. Explain your answer. **[4 marks]** Describe Murdock's serial position curve study and evaluate the research methods used in that study. **[9 marks]** *Make sure you satisfy the demands of ALL parts of the question.*

How much should I write?

In general 25 words per mark is a good rule for questions of more than 2 marks – as long as it is focused on the topic. Short answer questions (1 or 2 marks) do not need to be so wordy.

Here are two ways to produce top class extended writing answers:

9 marks	9 marks with a scenario
4 marks AO1, about 100 words *Identify 4-6 things to say and explain each.*	**3 marks AO1, about 75 words** *Identify 4-6 things to say and explain each.*
5 marks AO3, about 125 words *2 or 3 paragraphs/criticisms at expert level.*	**3 marks AO2, about 75 words** *Make 3 links to the stem either from AO1 or AO3.*
	3 marks AO3, about 75 words *1 or 2 paragraphs/criticisms at expert level.*

Effective revision

| Create revision cards | For **description** the amount you need is about 100 words. |

- Identify 4 or 5 points related to the topic.
- Record a trigger phrase in left-hand column.
- Record about 25 words in right-hand column.

An example of just three points:

AO1 trigger	Description
Respect & obey	Authoritarian personalities (AP) have an exaggerated respect for authority, and are more likely to obey orders and look down on people of inferior status. (= 24 words)
Cognitive style	Black and white, rigid style of thinking. They believe in stereotypes and don't like change. (= 15 words)
Childhood	Overly strict parenting, with conditional love. Child identifies with parents but also feels hostility which cannot be directly expressed for fear of reprisals. (= 23 words)

Reduce your cards to the minimum for revision:

AO1 trigger	Description
Respect & obey	Respect for authority, obey orders, look down on inferiors.
Cognitive style	Black and white, rigid, stereotypes, don't like change.
Childhood	Strict, conditional love. Hostility can't be expressed.

For the **evaluation** the amount you need is about 125 words.

- Select 2 or 3 critical points you plan to use.
- For each critical point, record a trigger phrase in left-hand column.
- Record context in middle column.
- If you are doing expert level add a third or even fourth column (as we have in this book).
- A well-elaborated critical point should be about 50 words.

An example of just one point:

AO3 trigger	Intermediate level	Expert level
Correlational	Can't claim AP causes greater obedience.	Other factors may explain the apparent link.

Rehearse the trigger phrases	Cover up all columns except the left-hand one and try to recall what is there using the trigger phrase.
Rehearse the content	When you are standing at a bus stop, see if you can remember all the trigger words for one topic.
Practise writing timed answers	Write an essay answer with just your trigger words in front of you. Give yourself 10 minutes for a 9-mark answer.

If you learn too much you will just try to squeeze it into the exam and you don't have time.

Focus on fewer points and make sure you *explain* them in detail. That's where the marks are.

In this book we have aimed to provide 4 or 5 points of AO1 for each topic, consisting of a trigger phrase and explanations. For example, on page 23 you will find the following AO1 (descriptive) content which has five trigger phrases on the left and an explanation for each on the right:

Description	
The theory	The War of the Ghosts study demonstrated that memory is an active process. People remember overall meaning of events and, when retrieving information, they rebuild.
Memory is inaccurate	We do not have exact recall. Elements are missing and memories are not an accurate representation of what happened.
Reconstruction	We record small pieces of information in long-term memory. During recall we recombine them to tell the whole story. Each time, the elements are combined slightly differently.
Social and cultural influences	The way that information is stored and recalled is affected by social and cultural expectations, like using the phrase 'going fishing' rather than 'hunting seals'.
Effort after meaning	We focus on the meaning of events and make an effort to understand the meaning to make sense of the parts of the story.

No athlete would dream of running a race without doing many practice runs of the right distance and within a set time.

Understanding marking

AO1 question

Describe antidepressant medication as a treatment for depression. [4 marks]

Answer: Antidepressants increase the amount of serotonin that is in the brain so the person feels happier as serotonin makes you feel happy so this gets rid of the person's depressed symptoms.

Serotonin gets passed round the brain more when you take one of these tablets. This leads to improved mood.

An example of an antidepressant is an SSRI which is one of the most popular types of medication as it's easy just to take a pill rather than have to have long therapy as you just take a pill so it is quick.

93 words

AO1+AO2 question

A group of friends have gone out for ice cream. There is a promotion that says that, if they each buy a chocolate ice-cream, they will get a 50% discount. Jack doesn't want chocolate ice cream and wants strawberry instead.

Outline what is meant by 'conformity'. Referring to the conversation above, identify one factor that can influence conformity and suggest how it would have influenced Jack in this situation. [4 marks]

Answer: Conformity is where you change your behaviour because you feel pressure from authority figures. Asch studied conformity with a study using lines where he showed lines and participants had to say which one was the longest.

One factor that can affect conformity is group size. This can affect people because they may feel more likely to conform if there are lots of people there than if there were not many people there. This is because they may feel embarrassed if there are lots of people but feel less embarrassed if there are only a few.

95 words

AO1+AO3 question

Identify and explain one criticism of Piliavin's subway study. [4 marks]

Answer: The people studied were likely to be mainly people who lived in a city. The sample of participants would have been confident in a city environment and were probably used to seeing drunks and smelly tramps in an emergency situation. In a city, especially one like New York, it is probably common to see people who are injured or asking for help. The participants may be more used to ignoring someone in need.

This means that the helping behaviour that was observed may not be typical of all people. This means you can't generalise what you find from just one city.

101 words

Examiner comments

Level and marks	Knowledge and understanding	Accuracy	Detail
2 Clear 3-4 marks	Relevant. ✓	Accurate. ✓	Detail included.
1 Basic 1-2 marks	Present but limited.	May be inaccuracies/ommissions.	✓

Comments: Knowledge and understanding of antidepressants as a treatment for depression is present but limited. The answer doesn't explain in detail how antidepressants treat depression (e.g. mention of the synapse and blocking reuptake).

The answer also includes some evaluation which is not creditworthy in this question as the question says 'describe'.

This is a level 1 basic answer but with some temptation towards the level above as it is accurate and the term 'serotonin' has been used, so 2 out of 4 marks.

To improve this answer more specialist terminology and detail is needed about how the antidepressants treat depression.

Level and marks	Description	Application	Relevant terminology	Substantiated reasoning
2 Clear 3-4 marks	Accurate with detail.	Effective.	Used consistently.	High level, clear, coherent and focused.
1 Basic 1-2 marks	Limited. ✓	A limited attempt. ✓	Used occasionally. ✓	Occasional, may lack clarity, coherence, focus and logical structure. ✓

Marks for this question: AO1 = 2 and AO2 = 2

Comments: This is a basic answer. There is a partial description of conformity which is muddled with obedience. The answer includes a brief description of the Asch line study into conformity although this is not relevant in this answer.

The identification of a factor that affects conformity is correct but this has only limited application to the question without any reference to Jack or the behaviour in context.

The answer is a level 1 answer with no temptation towards the top level (see marking grid above), so would be 1 out of 4 marks.

To improve this answer it should focus more on an explanation for conformity and, most importantly, there should be some application to the scenario.

Level and marks	Criticism	Accuracy	Clarity
2 Clear 3-4 marks	Appropriate. ✓	Accurate. ✓	Clear. ✓
1 Basic 1-2 marks	Appropriate.	Minor inaccuracies.	Muddled.

Marks for this question: AO1 = 1 and AO3 = 3

Comments: It is a good strategy to develop your skills of evaluation by practising elaborating evaluation points and making them relevant and not generic. The skills then become much more automatic in the exam.

This answer fulfils all the top level criteria (see table above) with a relevant criticism of Piliavin's study and a clear and accurate explanation of why the criticism is appropriate, 4 out of 4 marks.

'Substantiated' means providing evidence to support the claims that you make.

Understanding marking

AO1 + AO3 question:

Describe and evaluate von Frisch's bee study. In your description include the method used, the results obtained and the conclusion drawn.

[9 marks]

Answer: He did a study where he put food close and far away from a bee hive. He found that the bees talked to the other bees to show where the food was. There were two dances. The first dance was the round dance which showed the other bees that they had found food that was close. The other dance that they did was called the waggle dance which they did to show the direction of food and the slower they did it the further away the food was. This shows that bees do two different dances so that they can show where food is.

A problem with the study is that it used only bees so you can't generalise what you find to humans.

Another problem is that bees don't always respond to the waggle dance. When the bees see the dancing they don't always respond to it so dancing may not be the only thing that bees use to find food.

A strength of the bee study is that it is very scientific and has made a massive contribution to understanding the way that animals talk to each other and he won a big prize for it.

Another good thing about the study was that the bees were together and were not separated from their bee family so this is ethical as the bees won't be upset and sad.

230 words

Examiner comments

Level and marks	AO1: Knowledge and understanding	AO3: Analysis and evaluation	Relevant terminology	Substantiated reasoning, clear coherent and focused answer
3 Detailed 7-9 marks	Relevant, accurate with detail (method, results and conclusion).	Effective.	Consistently used throughout.	High level.
2 Clear 4-6 marks	Relevant knowledge present. ✓	Some effective. ✓	Usually used. ✓	Frequently. ✓ Though structure may lack some logic.
1 Basic 1-3 marks	Present but limited.	Limited effectiveness.	Occasionally used.	Occasionally. May lack clarity, coherence, focus and logical structure.
0	No relevant content.			

Marks for this question: AO1 = 4 and AO3 = 5

Comments: The answer starts well as the method is described straightaway without any lengthy explanations of who von Frisch was, which just wastes time.

The method is brief and there are omissions. The results are detailed and have been elaborated well with reference to the differences in the bees' dances with a good description of what the dances indicated to the other bees. The conclusion is limited and is just a statement of the results not what the study shows about animal communication.

The evaluation has some effective analysis but it doesn't start well because von Frisch wouldn't have wanted to generalise his results from bees to humans. The second evaluation point is accurate and is reasonably well explained as it is clear why it's an issue but more explanation would have been beneficial. The third evaluation point is correct but it isn't very well or fully expressed. The final evaluation point is not relevant.

Overall comments

The knowledge and understanding of the study has some detail and is accurate but much of it is limited.

There is some effective analysis and discussion of the study but it isn't always well expressed.

Relevant terminology is used though not consistently. However, the answer frequently demonstrates substantiated reasoning but, overall, this reasoning lacks logic as it is not clear what the study is showing.

Overall this is a level 2 response, 5 out of 9 marks

To improve this answer the student should have focused more on explaining just three evaluations and making them each more effective.

Understanding marking

AO1 + AO2 + AO3 question

Two friends are having a conversation about how they just failed their maths test:

Marnie: I am so bad at maths, I am not going to revise again because there is no point as I clearly don't have any talent.

Ivy: I am bad at maths but I am going to put more effort into revising for the next test and I am going to get at least 5 more marks next time.

Outline and evaluate Dweck's mindset theory of learning. Refer to the conversation between Marnie and Ivy in your answer. [9 marks]

Answer: Dweck believes the difference between people who succeed and those who don't is their mindset. She talked about fixed and growth mindsets as a way to talk about success. People with a fixed mindset believe that their abilities are fixed. Winning prizes or doing well in a test is evidence of their ability.

Marnie has a fixed mindset as she believes she doesn't have any talent so gives up trying to do maths. People with a fixed mindset don't believe they should have to work hard at their school work because, if you have to work hard then you can't really be that talented. Because Marnie isn't doing well in maths she might as well give up.

People with a growth mindset believe you can always get a little bit better if you work at it. They believe in effort and they feel good when they are working hard. Ivy has a growth mindset as she is going to put more effort into her revision and thinks if she works at her maths she will get better at it.

An evaluation is there is research that shows people with growth mindsets get better grades. In a study some children were taught a skills session on growth mindsets to see how they did. Another group of children did a session on memory. The researchers found those who had attended the growth mindset session got better grades than the other group, which must have been due to what they were taught.

248 words

Examiner comments

Level and marks	AO1: Knowledge and understanding	AO2: Application of AO1 to scenario	AO3: Analysis and evaluation	Relevant terminology	Substantiated reasoning, clear coherent and focused answer
3 Detailed 7-9 marks	Relevant, accurate with detail. ✓	Clear. ✓	Effective.	Consistently used throughout.	High level. ✓
2 Clear 4-6 marks	Relevant but occasional inaccuracies/ omissions.	Reasonable.	Some effective.	Usually used.	Frequently. Though structure may lack some logic.
1 Basic 1-3 marks	Present but limited.	Limited.	Limited effectiveness. ✓	Occasionally used.	Occasionally. May lack clarity, coherence, focus and logical structure.
0	No relevant content.				

Marks for this question: AO1 = 3, AO2 = 3 and AO3 = 3

The knowledge of fixed and growth mindsets is accurate and reasonably detailed.

The application of Dweck's mindset theory of learning to the conversation is clear – each girl's type of mindset is identified and also the implications are noted.

There is only one evaluation point which is well-elaborated but a bit superficial because the same point could be used in many different essays. It would help to name the researcher to make the point more specific.

Overall comments

The answer scores at the top level for AO1, though towards the bottom. The AO2 is similar in quality. It is the evaluation that lets this answer down as it overall has limited effectiveness.

Relevant terminology is usually used throughout. The answer demonstrates a high level of substantiated reasoning. The clarity is somewhat spoiled by too much emphasis and repetition of the descriptive content.

Taken altogether this makes this a level 2 answer, 6 out of 9 marks as it is very near the top of level 2.

To improve this answer the student should learn how to cut out unnecessary material to leave enough time for more evaluations.

The specification says...

Processes of memory:
Encoding (input), storage and
retrieval (output).
How memories are encoded
and stored.

Description

Encoding	Changing information so that it can be stored in the brain.
Visual encoding	How something looks. For example, 'seeing' your house in your mind and counting the number of windows uses visual encoding.
Acoustic encoding	How something sounds. For example, you can hear the words and music if you think about your favourite song in your head.
Semantic encoding	The meaning of something. For example, if you know what an elephant is and can use 'elephant' in a sentence, you are encoding the word by its meaning.
Other encoding	Tactile encoding is memory of what things feel like to touch and olfactory encoding is memory for smells.

Life was unforgettable at No. 1, Memory Lane.

Encode – store – retrieve

Encoding	The form information takes when we put it into our memory so that it can be held in our brain.
Storage	Holding information in your memory so it can be retrieved at a later point in time.
Retrieval	The process of accessing information that has been stored in your brain and being able to use it.
Different types of retrieval	There are three different types of retrieval: 1. *Recognition* relates to identifying something previously learned from a number of options. 2. *Cued recall* relates to being given a clue to help you remember. 3. *Free recall* is when you remember something without any clue.

Exam booster

Use each other to revise

Revising with other people can be more enjoyable than revising on your own. Work with someone else in your class to test yourself. You don't even have to be with them to do this – two of Mark's students revised over Skype. Revising with someone else means that you are also acoustically encoding the information as you are discussing it with someone else.

APPLY IT

Read the item below and then answer the question that follows.

Jess loves studying languages as she finds that learning words by repeating them back to herself out loud helps her to remember them. She also has a vocabulary list of key words from each topic area for the exam with a definition of what each word means in English. She finds reading through this list useful as understanding words also helps her to remember them.

- Identify the **two** types of encoding Jess uses in the item above. Explain your answer.

[4 marks]

KNOWLEDGE CHECK

1. Outline the difference between storage and retrieval. [2 marks]
2. What is meant by the term 'encoding'? Give an example with your answer. [3 marks]
3. Briefly outline the different processes involved in memory. [4 marks]

Is it true or is it false?

Here are some statements about encoding, storage and retrieval. Add ticks and crosses to the boxes to show which are true and which are false.

True or false?

1	Encoding is about how we get information out of memory.	
2	There are just two main types of encoding.	
3	Thinking about your favourite song and hearing the music in your head is an example of an acoustic memory.	
4	Picturing your house in your mind means you are using visual encoding.	
5	Semantic encoding refers to the meaning of something (such as words).	
6	Being able to use the word 'elephant' so it makes sense in a sentence is semantic encoding.	
7	Tactile encoding concerns our memories of smells.	
8	Storage of information comes before encoding.	
9	Cued recall is a type of retrieval.	
10	Free recall involves identifying something previously learned from different options.	

Mind maps

A mind map (or spider diagram) is a really useful way of organising revision material. It's highly visual and shows how all the parts of a topic are linked. It can give you the best of both worlds – a quick 'at a glance' overview and a closer level of detail as well.

A mind map has a single main idea (topic) in the middle, with lots of branches representing the more detailed elements linked to the main idea. You can add colour, more branches for greater detail, and even little pictures/images. You can use highlighters and felt-tip pens to make each of your mind maps unique – you should aim to make them all look different.

Looking at a mind map is helpful, but creating one is even better because it encourages you to process and restructure the information – and psychological research into memory shows that this is beneficial.

On the right is a mind map representing the information about encoding from the previous page.

Have a go at producing one on encoding yourself.

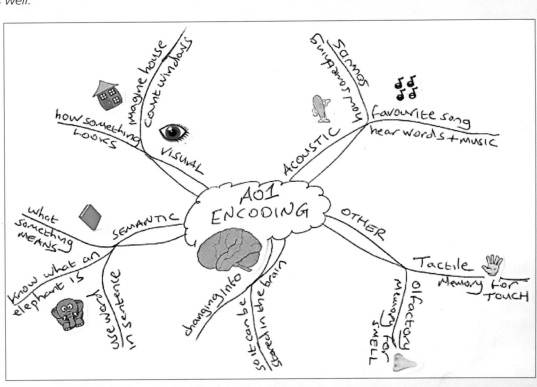

Description

Aim	Baddeley aimed to see if there was a difference in the type of encoding used in short-term (STM) and long-term memory (LTM).
Method	Four groups were given 12 sets of five words to remember.
	Group A had similar sounding words, Group B had dissimilar sounding words, Group C had words with similar meanings, Group D had words with dissimilar meanings (see lists on right).
	Groups A and B were asked to recall their words immediately (testing STM) whilst Groups C and D were asked to recall their words after 20 minutes (testing LTM).
Results	Group A recalled fewer words than Group B. Group C recalled fewer words than Group D.
	In STM words with similar sounds were more poorly recalled than words with different sounds.
	In LTM words with similar meanings were more poorly recalled than words with different meanings.
Conclusion	This shows STM is encoded by sound and LTM by meaning.

Group A	Group B	Group C	Group D
cat, cab	pit, few	great, large	good, huge
can, cad	cow, pen	big, huge	hot, safe
cap, mad	sup, bar	broad,	thin, deep
max, mat	day, hot	long, tall	strong
man, map	rig, bun	fat, wide	foul, old
		high	late

'If vegetarians eat vegetables, what do humanitarians eat?' mused Daisy.

Evaluation

Controlled experiment	One strength is that it is a well-designed laboratory study where extraneous variables were controlled.
	For example, hearing was controlled by giving participants a hearing test.
	Therefore we can be more certain that the type of words used was the factor that affected participants' recall.
STM is sometimes visual	One weakness is that encoding in STM does not always involve sound.
	Other studies (e.g. Brandimonte *et al.*) have found that that if pictures are recalled rather than words then visual encoding is used.
	This suggests that information does not just go into our STM in an acoustic form.
EXTRA: LTM may not have been tested	Another weakness is that LTM may not have been tested in the study.
	Waiting 20 minutes before recall doesn't mean the words are in the LTM.
	This may mean that the conclusion that LTM encodes semantically lacks validity.

Manage your time in the exam

Exam booster

There are 100 marks for each of your exams and they each last 105 minutes. That works out at just about a mark a minute plus a small amount of time to check your answers at the end. It is absolutely vital to practise doing questions under timed conditions so you hit the mark a minute pace and learn to think under time pressure.

APPLY IT – Research Methods

A researcher studied how information is encoded in the short-term memory. Fifty participants were recruited by selecting every 20th person on a school register. Participants were given a list of words to remember.

Group 1: Had 20 words that sounded similar to each other (rolled, bold, fold, tip, sip, kip, etc.).

Group 2: Had 20 words that sounded different from each other (orange, dog, key, car, house, sea, etc.).

After 20 seconds of remembering the words, they had to recall the words in the order of presentation.

1. Identify the sampling method used by the researcher in this study. **[1 mark]**
2. Identify the experimental design used in this study. Explain **one** strength and **one** weakness of this design. **[5 marks]**

KNOWLEDGE CHECK

1. Briefly outline what the participants were asked to do in a study that investigated encoding. **[3 marks]**
2. Describe and evaluate research related to how memories are encoded. **[9 marks]**

Classic study mix up

Exam type question: Describe a study that investigated how memories are encoded.

Below are some sentences that will help you answer the question above.

Unfortunately, the sentences have become jumbled up and are in the wrong order.

Write down the right order in the boxes below so that the answer makes sense.			
Aim	Method	Results	Conclusion

1	In group C, the participants had words with similar meanings.	8	Baddeley used four groups of participants.
2	He gave them 12 sets of five words to remember.	9	Group A was given words that sounded similar.
3	The participants in Group D were given words with dissimilar meanings.	10	Group C recalled fewer words than Group D.
4	Baddeley claimed that the results showed that STM is encoded by sound (acoustically) and LTM by meaning (semantically).	11	Alan Baddeley (1966) wanted to see if there were any differences in the encoding used in STM and LTM.
5	Group B had words that sounded dissimilar.	12	Baddeley found that Group A recalled fewer words than Group B.
6	In LTM words with similar meanings were more poorly recalled than words with different meanings.	13	Participants in Groups A and B had to recall their words straightaway – this tested STM.
7	In STM similar sounding words were more poorly recalled than words with different sounds.	14	Groups C and D recalled their words after 20 minutes – this tested LTM.

Evaluating the study – Fill in the blanks

A strength of Baddeley's research is that it is a _____ study where extraneous _____ were well _____. For example, he controlled hearing ability by giving participants a hearing _____, which was important because the words were _____ out. This is a _____ because we can be more certain that the type of _____ used was the factor that affected participants' recall.

A weakness of the study is that encoding in _____ does not always involve _____. Other studies (e.g. _____) have found that if _____ are used rather than words then the information is encoded _____. This shows that information does not just go into STM in an _____ form.

Another weakness is that _____ may not have been tested in the study. The participants had to wait 20 _____ before _____ but this doesn't mean the words were in LTM. This is a weakness because it could mean the conclusion that LTM encoding is semantic lacks _____.

Here is a cheat list of the words that go in the blanks.

acoustic	recall
Brandimonte et al.	sound
	STM
controlled	
	strength
laboratory	
	test
LTM	
	validity
minutes	
	variables
pictures	
	visually
read	
	words

The specification says...

Processes of memory: Different types of memory; episodic memory, semantic memory and procedural memory.

Description

LTM	These are memories that last a week, month, year or even a lifetime. There are three types of LTM.
Episodic memory	Memory for events from your life and what you have done. For example, your birthday party when you were 10.
Semantic memory	Memory about what things mean (your own encyclopaedia). For example, knowing that the capital of France is Paris.
Procedural memory	Memory of how to do things. We struggle to consciously explain how to perform these skills but can still do them. For example, driving a car.
Declarative and non-declarative	Episodic/semantic memories are called 'declarative memories' because they need conscious recall. Procedural memory doesn't need conscious recall so is called 'non-declarative'.

Evaluation

Specific locations in the brain	One strength of this research is that brain scans show that different types of LTM relate to different brain locations. For example, episodic memory is found in the right prefrontal area whereas semantic memory is associated with the left prefrontal area, and procedural memory is associated with the motor area. This suggests that there are different types of LTM.
Patients with amnesia	Another strength is that this research is supported by the case studies of patients with amnesia. For example, Clive Wearing lost most of his episodic memory but not his procedural memory as he could still play the piano. This again shows that there are different types of LTM.
EXTRA: It's not that simple	One weakness is that distinctive types of LTM are difficult to separate. There isn't a clear difference between episodic and semantic memories because memories are usually a mixture of types. Therefore having separate types of LTM may be an oversimplification.

KNOWLEDGE CHECK

1. Explain the difference between episodic and semantic memories. **[4 marks]**
2. Explain **one** evaluation of different types of memory. **[3 marks]**
3. Using your knowledge of the processes of memory, describe and evaluate different types of long-term memory. **[9 marks]**

Exam booster

Evaluation: Breadth or depth?

Evaluation questions may be written: *Briefly evaluate different types of long-term memory.* [3 marks].

You can either outline **two** criticisms with not much detail (about 20 words each).

Or you can outline **one** criticism in detail (about 40 words) – as we have done below using three separate sentences.

For example: A strength of this research is that brain scans show that different types of LTM relate to different brain locations. A weakness is that distinctive types of LTM are difficult to separate because memories are usually a mixture of the three types.

Motor area

Prefrontal area

The memory cupboard. Where good times and bad are stored.

APPLY IT

Read the item below and then answer the question that follows.

Maddie is learning to drive. She has a very good knowledge about the rules of the road and regularly gets almost full marks in the mock tests she does on theory. She is doing less well in the practical side of driving and constantly forgets how to perform the various skills she needs to know on the road.

- Identify **two** types of long-term memory and explain how each of them relates to Maddie's behaviour. **[4 marks]**

Turbo-charge your AO1

Giving examples is a great way of boosting your descriptions by adding detail. Write down definitions of each type of memory. Add examples to take your definitions further. Try to think of different examples from the ones on the previous page.

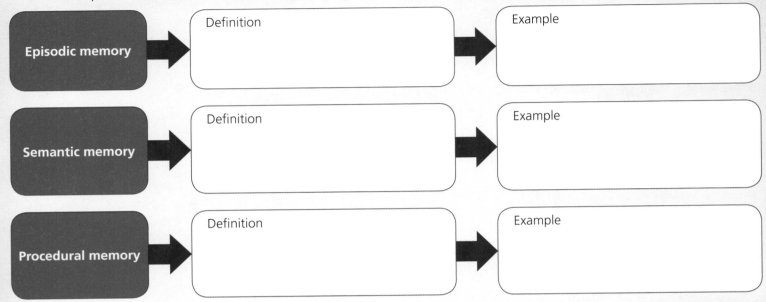

Episodic memory	Definition	Example
Semantic memory	Definition	Example
Procedural memory	Definition	Example

Elaborate your evaluation

Don't waste your AO3 points. Make the most of them by elaborating – develop and explain them fully, just like we do in this book. You can do this by using the trigger phrases in the 2nd, 3rd and 4th columns to help you construct an evaluation.

Specific locations in the brain	Brain scans …	Episodic memory … Semantic memory …	This shows that …
Patients with amnesia	Case studies …	Clive Wearing …	This shows that …
It's not that simple	Types of LTM are …	Episodic and semantic memories …	This shows that …

The specification says...

Structures of memory:
The multi-store model of
memory; sensory, short-term
and long-term.
Features of each store: coding,
capacity, duration.

Description

Multi-store model	States that there are three memory stores and each has different encoding, capacity and duration. Information moves between these stores through either attention or rehearsal.
Sensory memory	Holds information from the senses for a short time and has a large capacity. Paying attention to information transfers it to the STM.
STM	Temporary memory store with a limited capacity of between five and nine items or chunks of information, lasting up to 30 seconds.
Role of rehearsal	Verbal repetition (rehearsal) keeps information in STM. If information is rehearsed for long enough it is transferred into LTM.
LTM	Encoded by meaning, this is a permanent memory store with an unlimited capacity and information can be stored up to a lifetime.

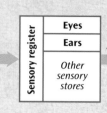

Evaluation

Research support	One strength is that there is support for the existence of different memory stores. Baddeley's study of encoding shows that STM and LTM encode information differently. This shows the two types of memory have qualitative differences.
Simple model	One weakness is the model is too simple suggesting we have one STM and one LTM. Research shows STM is divided into visual and acoustic stores, and LTM into episodic, semantic and procedural memory. So, memory is more complex than the model proposes.
EXTRA: Artificial materials	Another weakness is that research that supports the model used artificial materials. For example, using word lists or consonant syllables. This means that the results would not illustrate all the different ways we use memory.

Exam booster

Don't get your evaluation mixed up

Sometimes you have to evaluate *studies* whilst on other occasions you will need to evaluate *explanations*. Think carefully otherwise you could end up producing evaluation (AO3) that would get you no marks as it is not relevant.

APPLY IT

Read the item below and then answer the question that follows.

A conversation takes place between two students.

Harvey: I don't understand how my teacher can remember everyone's name in the class whereas I still only know the names of a few people.

Muhsin: Maybe it is because he does things like taking the register every lesson and so he has had far more practice repeating their names than you.

- Use your knowledge of the multi-store model to explain why Harvey can't remember all of his classmates' names but his teacher can. Refer to the above conversation in your answer.   **[3 marks]**

KNOWLEDGE CHECK

1. Explain the role of sensory memory in the multi-store model of memory.   **[2 marks]**
2. Outline **one** criticism of the multi-store model of memory.   **[4 marks]**
3. Outline and evaluate the multi-store model of memory.   **[9 marks]**

Magic multi-store model

Here is a diagram of the multi-store model. Below the table is a list of components each with a letter. Place the letters in the right boxes and write one sentence for each component. Put the sentences in the order which makes most sense. Hey presto – you now have a description of the multi-store model.

A	Attention	
B	Short-term memory	
C	Long-term memory	
D	Sensory memory	
E	Maintenance rehearsal	
F	Prolonged rehearsal	

Evaluation match-up

Fill in the blanks and then match up the sentences to make three full evaluation points of three sentences each.

A For example, Baddeley's study found that STM encodes information _____ and LTM encodes _____.	**B** A weakness is that the research supporting the model used _____ materials.	**C** A weakness is that the model is too simple because it suggests we have just _____ STM and _____ LTM.
D For example, many studies used lists of words or _____ syllables.	**E** This means that the results do not show us all the _____ ways we use our memories.	**F** Instead, studies show that _____ is divided into _____ and acoustic stores, and LTM is made up of _____, semantic and procedural memory.
G This shows that memory is more _____ than the multi-store model proposes.	**H** This shows that STM and LTM are qualitatively different.	**I** A strength is that some research supports the existence of _____ memory stores.

The specification says...

Structures of memory: Primary and recency effects in recall; the effects of serial position.
Murdock's serial position curve study.

Description

Primacy and recency effects	Words at the beginning of a list (primacy) are remembered more as they are rehearsed and are in LTM.
	Words at the end of a list (recency) are remembered more as they have been heard recently and are in STM.
Aim	Murdock set out to see if the serial position effect was influenced by the number of words in a list.
Method	Words from the 4000 most common words in English were chosen randomly.
	Participants listened to 20 word lists with between 10 and 40 words on them.
	They recalled the words after each list.
Results	Recall was not affected by the number of words in a list but was related to the position of the word in the list (the serial position effect).
	Murdock found higher recall for the first few words (primacy effect) and for the last few words (recency effect) rather than the middle of the list.
Conclusion	The results confirm the serial position effect, i.e. word position determines the likelihood of recall.
	These findings support the MSM as the first few words were rehearsed, so are in LTM, and the last few words are in STM.

Evaluation

Controlled lab study	One strength of the study relates to it being well-controlled.
	Familiarity of the words was the same throughout each list.
	Therefore, we can be more certain that it was the position of the words that affected recall.
Artificial task	One weakness of the study is the task was artificial.
	Lists of words were used which relates to just one type of memory.
	Therefore, the results don't relate to how we use our memories in other ways, such as for personal events.
EXTRA: Supporting research	Another strength is that research on amnesia supports the conclusions of the study.
	Carlesimo *et al.* found that some people with amnesia can't store long-term memories and do not show a primacy effect but do show a recency effect.
	This shows that the primacy effect is related to long-term memory.

Now, that's my kind of running race! In the primacy-recency effect, it's all about what happens at the beginning and the end.

APPLY IT – Research Methods

Imagine that you are a psychologist and are interested in primacy and recency effects when learning a list of 30 words. Describe how you would conduct this experiment.

You need to include:

- The task you would do to assess the primacy and recency effects.
- What you would measure.
- The results you would expect to find from your experiment. **[6 marks]**

↑↑↑↑ **Exam booster**

Read bullet points in a 'design a study' question.

Some research methods questions ask you to 'design a study'. The 'apply it' question above is an example of such a question – where you are given a scenario and asked to design a study to investigate it.

Most importantly you are also given a list of things you need to include. Make sure that you comment specifically on each of them otherwise you won't get full marks. Some students lose marks as they neglect to mention one or more of these factors.

KNOWLEDGE CHECK

1. Explain how recall is affected by primacy and recency effects. **[4 marks]**
2. What is meant by the phrase 'serial position curve'? **[2 marks]**
3. Describe Murdock's serial position curve study and evaluate the research methods used in that study. **[9 marks]**

Classic study – true or false?

Read the sentences below about the study by Murdock. Indicate whether each is true or false. For the false sentences, rewrite them in the final column so they become true.

		True or false?	
1	Murdock's aim was to support the multi-store model.		
2	Murdock's words were drawn from 4000 common words in English.		
3	Murdock chose every 10th word from the dictionary.		
4	Each participant read 10 word lists.		
5	Each list had between 10 and 40 words on it.		
6	The participants recalled the lists after 20 minutes.		
7	Murdock found a primacy effect because recall of the last few words on each list was relatively high.		
8	Murdock's findings demonstrated the serial position effect.		
9	Unfortunately, Murdock's findings do not support the multi-store model.		
10	The first few words on each list are rehearsed, so are contained in LTM.		

Build your answer

Answering a 9-mark exam question can seem like a big ask when you are first learning to do it. One way to ease into it is to focus on the descriptive (AO1) element. Build your description of Murdock's study by responding to the statements/questions in each box.

What was Murdock's aim?	Explain how he conducted the study (i.e. his method – materials and procedure).	Describe the results of the study.	Explain **two** conclusions you can draw from the results.

Description

Aim	Bartlett investigated how memory is reconstructed when people are asked to recall an unfamiliar story – in particular a story from a different culture.
Method	Participants were shown the War of the Ghosts story. They recalled it after 15 minutes, then after weeks, months and years. Bartlett recorded the recall.
Results	Participants changed the story. They left out information that they were less familiar with. The story was shortened, and phrases were changed to those used in the participants' own culture.
Conclusion	The study shows that we use our knowledge of social situations to reconstruct memory, as details of the story were invented to improve meaning.

Evaluation

Lacks control	One weakness relates to a lack of control. For example, participants were not told that accurate recall was important. Other studies found recall was better when participants were told this. This suggests that recall is more accurate than Bartlett concluded.
The results were biased	Another weakness is that Bartlett's own beliefs may have affected the results. He analysed the recollections himself. His belief that recall would be affected by cultural expectations may have biased the interpretation of the results. Therefore, we cannot fully trust the conclusion.
EXTRA: The story was unusual	A further weakness is that the story was unusual. Recall of the story may not reflect everyday memory processes as these would be less affected by cultural expectations. Therefore, this study tells us little about everyday memory.

KNOWLEDGE CHECK

1. Describe the procedure used in Bartlett's War of the Ghosts study. **[2 marks]**
2. Briefly evaluate Bartlett's War of the Ghosts study. **[3 marks]**
3. Describe and evaluate a study that investigated how memory is an active process. **[9 marks]**

The specification says…

Memory as an active process: Bartlett's War of the Ghosts study.

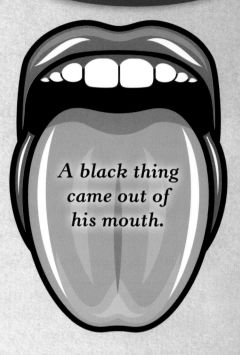

A black thing came out of his mouth.

Exam booster

Remember to evaluate

Exam questions may require you to outline and evaluate a study in a certain area. Students often describe the study in a lot of detail and then either forget to evaluate or just include some brief evaluation. Low marks for evaluation makes a big impact on your mark – make sure you limit your description to about 100 words.

APPLY IT

Read the item below and then answer the question that follows.

Tabitha was unfortunate enough to witness a bank robbery. She was asked to describe the robber to the police. She said the robber was a man wearing a ski mask and he had a gun in his hand. However, when the police checked the CCTV they could see Tabitha was completely wrong – the robber was clearly female, did not have a mask and no gun.

- Use your knowledge of Bartlett's War of the Ghosts study to explain why Tabitha's memory was inaccurate. **[3 marks]**

AO3 – Fill in the blanks

Complete the evaluation by filling in the missing words. Try to avoid looking back at the material on the previous page. But if you do get stuck, the words you need are below the passage.

One weakness of Bartlett's study is that it lacks _____. For example, he did not tell the participants that _____ recall was important. Other studies have found that recall is _____ when participants are told this. This shows that recall is more accurate than Bartlett suggested.

Another weakness is that Bartlett's own _____ may have affected the results. Because he analysed the participants' responses himself, his belief that recall would be affected by cultural _____ might have _____ his interpretation of the results. This means that we cannot fully trust Bartlett's conclusions.

A final weakness is that the War of the _____ was an unusual story. Because it was so unfamiliar, recall of the story may not reflect _____ memory processes as these would not be affected by cultural expectations. This suggests that Bartlett's study tells us little about everyday memory.

Ghosts   **better**   **beliefs**   **biased**

control   **accurate**   **expectations**   **everyday**

The War of the Ghosts cube

This is an activity you can do on your own or with other students. Make a small cube using the template on the right. Roll the cube and give a detailed explanation of whichever phrase or term comes up. If you're with other students you can take turns and explain to each other.

Of course you can use the template to construct cubes for any topic using six terms or phrases.

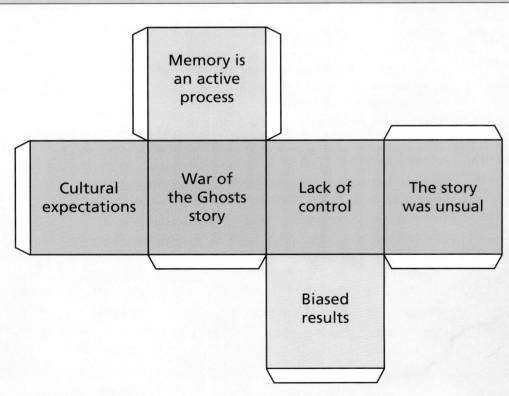

Memory is an active process

Cultural expectations

War of the Ghosts story

Lack of control

The story was unsual

Biased results

Description

The theory	The War of the Ghosts study demonstrated that memory is an active process. People remember overall meaning of events and, when retrieving information, they rebuild the memory.
Memory is inaccurate	We do not have exact recall. Elements are missing and memories are not an accurate representation of what happened.
Reconstruction	We record small pieces of information in long-term memory. During recall we recombine them to tell the whole story. Each time, the elements are combined slightly differently.
Social and cultural influences	The way that information is stored and recalled is affected by social and cultural expectations, like using the phrase 'going fishing' rather than 'hunting seals'.
Effort after meaning	We focus on the meaning of events and make an effort to understand the meaning to make sense of the parts of the story.

Evaluation

More realistic research	One strength of the research is that it reflects how we use memory in our everyday lives. The research doesn't use artificial word lists or consonant syllables but instead uses a story. This makes the findings more relevant to real-life memory processes.
Some memories are accurate	One weakness is that not all memories are reconstructed. For example, in the study participants often recalled 'something black came out of his mouth' because it was quite a distinctive phrase. This shows that some memories are accurate.
EXTRA: Real-world application	Another strength is that reconstructive memory explains problems with eyewitness testimony (EWT). Bartlett's research showed memory is affected by expectations, indicating that people do not always recall accurately. Therefore, EWT is no longer solely relied on as evidence in criminal investigations.

KNOWLEDGE CHECK

1. Outline what is meant by the phrase 'effort after meaning'. **[2 marks]**
2. Describe how memory may be an active process. **[3 marks]**
3. Describe and evaluate how the Theory of Reconstructive Memory has increased our understanding of memory. **[9 marks]**

The specification says...

Memory as an active process: The Theory of Reconstructive Memory, including the concept of 'effort after meaning'.

To be fair, Dianne had been warned that her cosmetic surgeon was 'a bit of a joker'. Memory, like surgery, is reconstructive.

APPLY IT – Research Methods

A study was conducted where participants were taken into a kitchen for 30 seconds and shown objects consistent with what would be found in a kitchen (such as a kettle) and objects not consistent with a kitchen (such as a brick). Participants were then asked to recall the 30 objects they saw in the room. The target population for this experiment was students at Bristol University studying history where 200 students took the subject.

1. Identify the independent and dependent variables in this study. **[2 marks]**
2. Write a suitable alternative hypothesis for this study. **[2 marks]**
3. Explain what is meant by 'systematic sampling' and explain how it might be used in this study to select 20 participants. **[3 marks]**

Exam booster

Answer both parts of the question

Sometimes short answer questions have two parts –for example, *'identify an ethical issue in this study and explain how it could be dealt with'. [2 marks]*. Students can make the mistake of explaining the ethical issue in a lot of detail (e.g. outlining deception) but not saying how it would be dealt with (e.g. by offering a debriefing) and so only gain 1 out of 2 marks.

Fake news

Fake news is everywhere these days, but we're not going to stand for it. Here are some fake headlines about reconstructive memory. Rewrite them so they are true, and then write the first sentence of an imaginary article to explain the headline.

1	Reconstructive memory shows memory is passive, claim psychologists		
2	Memories perfect representation of events, say scientists		
3	**Researchers say how memories are stored is independent of culture**		
4	Details of the event most important thing, reckon researchers		
5	Bombshell: reconstructive memory not like real life		
6	OMG: all memories inaccurate, psychologists opine		

Writing thorough answers

An excellent way to boost your AO3 marks is to make sure your evaluation is thorough. So every time you make a point of evaluation, such as a strength or weakness, you should develop and explain it. The same goes for description – add detail to increase your AO1 marks (using examples is good for this). Fortunately, you can learn these skills with plenty of practice.

Complete the table by responding to the statements in each box. Write your sentences in your own words.

In your own words, THOROUGHLY explain the theory in no more than five sentences – one for each of the main AO1 points.	*THOROUGHLY explain a strength of the theory.*
	Point
	Example
	Conclusion
	THOROUGHLY explain a weakness of the theory.
	Point
	Example
	Conclusion

Description

Interference	If two memories compete with each other, one memory may prevent us from accessing the other memory.
Aim	McGeoch and McDonald aimed to see whether the accuracy of recalling a list of words would be affected by a competing set of words.
Method	Participants learned a list of ten words and then were shown a new list.
	There were five different new lists: words with the same meanings as the first list (synonymns), words with opposite meanings (antonymns), unrelated words, nonsense syllables, three-digit numbers, or no new list.
Results	When participants recalled the initial list of words, memory was affected by the new list (see graph on right).
	The effect was strongest when the new list had words with similar meanings to the first list.
Conclusion	This shows that interference from a second set of information reduces the accuracy of memory.
	Interference is strongest when the two sets of information are similar.

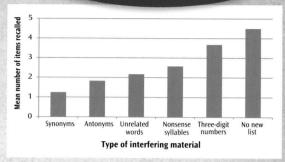

Graph showing results of the study by McGeoch and McDonald.

Exam booster

Outline and evaluate factors affecting the accuracy of memory. [9 marks]

This exam question requires you to write about at least two factors – it is probably best to focus on just two factors because, if you describe three factors you will end up with too much description and leave yourself less time for the evaluation (AO3).

Evaluation

Controlled research	One strength of the study was that there was high control.
	Techniques like counterbalancing were used to reduce the impact that learning the lists in the same order would have on the results.
	This reduced extraneous variables in the study.
Artificial task	One weakness of the study is that it does not reflect real-life memory activity.
	We don't often have to remember lists of words or very similar things.
	This means that the conclusion about the effect of interference is limited because of its artificiality.
EXTRA: Not really forgetting	Another weakness with interference is that it may not be an explanation of forgetting.
	It may be that information is not forgotten but just cannot be accessed because an appropriate cue has not been given (Tulving and Psotka).
	Therefore interference only *appears* to cause inaccurate memory.

Retro style – 'retro' means going backwards. Though as the picture suggests, not everyone can pull off the retro look …

APPLY IT

Read the item below and then answer the question that follows.

Laura is revising for her exams. She finds that when she learns business studies and accounting on the same day she can't recall which topic areas belong to which subject. She thinks it is because they are both to do with money.

- Describe and evaluate **one** factor affecting the accuracy of memory. Refer to Laura's problems with revising in your answer. [9 marks]

KNOWLEDGE CHECK

1. Describe how interference can be applied to using memory in the real world. [2 marks]

2. Explain **one** problem with interference as a factor that affects the accuracy of memory. [3 marks]

3. Outline and evaluate the effect of interference on the accuracy of memory. [9 marks]

Interference theory anagrams

Everyone loves an anagram, apparently. Can you unjumble these words related to interference theory?

#	Anagram		Clue
1	FIERCERENNET		Between two memories = forgetting.
2	HOGMECC		One of the researchers.
3	SCANTNOON SLAYBELLS		A type of stimulus material in the study.
4	IDGIST		Another type of material – numbers.
5	LIARISM		More forgetting if two memories are _____.
6	ATONINGCARBUNCLE		The way to control order effects.
7	DAMNCOLD		Another of the researchers.
8	ITALICFAIR		The environment of a lab.
9	ITVLUNG		Memory researcher keen on cues.
10	SACSEC		Perhaps we forget because we don't have _____ to the memory.

Match them up

How much do you know about interference theory and McGeoch and McDonald's study? Find out by matching the first half of each sentence in the left-hand column with the second half in the right-hand column. Then put the sentences in the correct order.

Left	Right
1. When the participants recalled the first list of words ...	A. ... syllables.
2. After they learned the list ...	B. ... the two sets of information are similar.
3. Another new list contained consonant ...	C. ... if the accuracy of recalling a list of words is affected by a competing set of words.
4. McGeoch and McDonald aimed to find out ...	D. ... the participants were shown a new list.
5. When two memories interfere with each other ...	E. ... their memories were affected by the new list.
6. Another conclusion was that interference is strongest when ...	F. ... numbers.
7. Another list contained three-digit ...	G. ... one memory may prevent us from accessing the other memory.
8. Participants first of all learned ...	H. ... new list.
9. McGeoch and McDonald concluded that ...	I. ... a list of ten words.
10. One new list contained words with the same ...	J. ... interference from a second set of information reduces the accuracy of memory.
11. Some participants were shown no ...	K. ... meanings as the first list.

The specification says...

Factors affecting the accuracy of memory, including context.

Description

Context	Other things that are present at the time of learning act as a cue for recall. This improves the accuracy of memory.
Aim	Godden and Baddeley aimed to see if context improved recall. They used 'underwater' (wet) and 'on the beach' (dry) as the two contexts.
Method	Divers listened to and recalled words in the same or different settings: Same context: dry/dry (DD), wet/wet (WW). Different context: wet/dry (WD), dry/wet (DW).
Results	Recall was highest in the two matching conditions (dry/dry or wet/wet). When a person was in the same environment for learning and recall, their memories were more accurate.
Conclusion	Context of learning acts as a trigger or cue when trying to remember information, and thus improves the accuracy of memory.

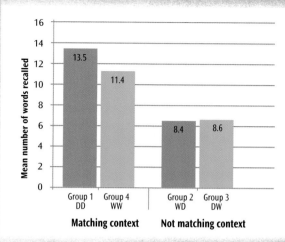

Graph showing results from Godden and Baddeley's study.

Evaluation

Artificial task	One weakness relates to the research using lists of words. Research with more complex materials in real life produced better recall. This suggests that context does not affect memory as much as Baddeley suggested.
Recall was short term	Another weakness is that the study was unrealistic as participants recalled the words almost immediately. This does not relate to scenarios like exams where the gap between learning and recall is longer. Therefore research only tells us about short-term recall.
EXTRA: Similar context	A further weakness with context is that it only acts as a cue for recall if the context at the time of learning and recall are very similar. This rarely happens in real-world situations (Smith). Therefore, context only improves memory recall in limited situations.

Exam booster

However ...

Start some evaluation points with 'However ...' or 'An alternative view is ...' when introducing an evaluation that challenges the previous point you have made. It links your evaluation together and makes your evaluation read more like a discussion (which is ultimately what evaluation is!).

APPLY IT – Research Methods

A teacher wants to see whether context does affect memory. She gives all her students 30 words to learn.

The next day she tests half the class in the same classroom where they learned the list (Group A). She tests the other half of the class (Group B) in a different classroom.

1. Write a set of standardised instructions that could be read to the participants. **[4 marks]**
2. The teacher used randomisation in her study. Briefly explain how she could have done this. **[2 marks]**
3. Identify **one** descriptive statistic the psychologist could use to compare the results from the two groups and explain how it would be calculated. **[3 marks]**

KNOWLEDGE CHECK

1. Outline what is meant by a 'context'. **[2 marks]**
2. Use your knowledge of psychology to describe how context affects the accuracy of memory. **[3 marks]**
3. Describe and evaluate a study that has investigated how context affects the accuracy of memory. **[9 marks]**

AO1 – Fill in the blanks

Try to fill in the blanks in the following passage without looking on the previous page. If you get stuck choose from the word list at the end of the passage to help you out (but only if you really need to).

When we _____ some information, other things are present in the situation at the same time. These can act as

_____ for recall, improving the _____ of memory.

One study into context as a cue was carried out by _____ and _____. They wanted to see if the context of

learning can improve recall. They used '_____' (wet) and 'on the _____' (dry) as the two contexts.

The researchers asked _____ to listen to and recall words in the same or different settings. When the contexts were

_____, divers learned the words underwater and recalled them _____. Or they learned them on the beach

and recalled them on the beach. When the contexts were _____, the divers learned the words underwater and

recalled them on the beach. Or they learned them _____ and recalled them underwater.

The main result was that recall was _____ in the two matching conditions (dry/dry or wet/wet). The researchers

_____ that the context of learning acts as a cue when trying to remember information, so memory is more accurate.

underwater   Godden   **different**   *learn*   **the same**   **cues**   **on the beach**

beach   **accuracy**   **underwater**   **concluded**   **highest**   Baddeley   *divers*

Evaluate with key phrases

Here are some key phrases related to the evaluation of context as a factor affecting the accuracy of memory. First, decide which phrases go together by putting them into pairs. Then try to write a sentence for each pair without looking at your notes or on the previous page. Finally, try to write write a further sentence, to explain why your first sentence is a strength/weakness.

	Write down the pairs	Write a sentence	Strength or weakness
	1		
	2		
	3		

Immediate not delayed

Artificial task

Short-term recall

Learning and recall situations

Lists of words

Contexts must be very similar

Factors affecting the accuracy of memory, including false memories.

Description

False memory	A memory for something that did not happen but a person thinks it is a true memory.
Aim	Loftus and Pickrell aimed to see if false memories could be created in participants through suggestion.
Method	Participants were given four stories about childhood events of which three were true and one false (getting lost in a shopping mall was the false one). The story was created with the help of a relative so that it sounded realistic. Participants read each story and wrote what they remembered.
Results	68% of the true episodes were remembered. Six out of 24 (25%) of participants recalled the false story fully or partially. The rest had no memory of it.
Conclusion	This shows that imagining an event can implant a false memory in a person, reducing the accuracy of memory.

Since he was a baby, Ronan's parents had convinced him he had been to Disneyland. They had even gone to the trouble of photo-shopping fake pictures of Ronan posing with Mickey Mouse for a family album. Sounds harsh? Well, the kid was happy enough and it had saved them the best part of six grand.

Evaluation

Artificial task	One weakness is that the false memory event is not of the same traumatic kind that could be found in therapy. Harmless events might be implanted easily but traumatic events may not. Therefore, conclusions that can be drawn about false memories are limited.
Ethical issues	Another weakness is that the research raises ethical concerns. Even though participants were debriefed, they may be left with implanted false memories which lingered after the study was finished. Therefore the study may have caused psychological harm, an ethical issue.
EXTRA: Real-world application	One strength is that this research has implications for eyewitness testimony (EWT). The results suggest that police questioning could accidentally implant false memories. Therefore this research has been beneficial in explaining why EWT might be unreliable.

Exam booster

Research methods is key

Make sure you know research methods inside out as research methods questions can appear in all sections of the two exam papers in addition to the dedicated section on research methods on Paper 1. **In total there is a requirement that 20% of the total mark across both papers must be on research methods topics.**

You also use your knowledge of research methods to help you evaluate research.

APPLY IT – Research Methods

In a study on false memory, 20 mothers are asked to describe 10 childhood events to their 14-year-old child. Before the study the psychologist tells the mothers to include a false event that never happened. Four weeks later the psychologist asks the children to write down what happened in each of the 10 events.

1. Is the data that is collected primary or secondary data? Explain your answer. **[3 marks]**

2. The study produced qualitative data. What is meant by the term 'qualitative data'? **[2 marks]**

3. Identify and briefly explain **one** ethical issue the psychologist should have considered in this study. **[2 marks]**

KNOWLEDGE CHECK

1. Outline what is meant by a 'false memory'. **[1 mark]**

2. Describe the effect that false memories have on the accuracy of memory. **[2 marks]**

3. Describe and evaluate **one** way in which false memory was investigated. In your answer include the method used, the results obtained and the conclusion drawn. **[9 marks]**

False memory crossword

See how much you know about false memories by completing the crossword.

DOWN

1. The kind of harm the study might have caused. P_____ (13)
2. The stories were about events from C_____. (9)
5. The study raised some of these issues. E_____ (7)
7. Can this implant a false memory? S_____ (10)
9. A R_____ of the participant told the researchers the true story. (8)

ACROSS

3. The kind of memories the study was about. F_____ (5)
4. Number of true stories for each participant. T_____ (5)
6. Jacqueline, one of the researchers. P_____ (8)
8. Lost in here, according to the false story. S_____ M_____ (8,4)
10. Number of participants recalling false story. S_____ (3)
11. The kind of memories recalled in therapy. T_____ (9)
12. Elizabeth, one of the researchers. L_____ (6)

Match them up

Indicate in the table, with a tick or a cross, whether the statements are true or false. You can then rewrite the false statements to make them true.

		True or false?	
1	Loftus and Pickrell wanted to use suggestion to see if false memories could be implanted.		
2	The participants read five stories about recent events.		
3	Three of the stores were true.		
4	Two of the stories were false.		
5	Participants had to explain out loud what they remembered about each story.		
6	25% of the true stories were remembered.		
7	18 participants had no memory of the false story.		
8	The researchers concluded that it is impossible to implant a false memory.		

The difference between sensation and perception

Sensation	Physical stimulation of the sensory receptors is processed by sense receptors.
	Our brain interprets the information from our five senses which leads to perception.
Perception	Organisation and interpretation of sensory information by the brain.
	Information received from sense receptors is combined with the brain's interpretation of what that information means.
Difference between sensation and perception	Sensation is the detection of a stimulus in the environment, such as light or sound waves.
	Perception is the brain interpreting and understanding these sensations.
Theories of perception	Theories of perception differ.
	Gregory's *constructivist theory* sees a difference between sensation and perception.
	Gibson's *direct theory* sees sensation and perception as the same.

Introducing some visual illusions

Ponzo illusion	Misinterpreted depth cue.
	Two separate horizontal lines of the same length, one above the other, surrounded by two lines converging, gives the appearance of depth.
	People perceive the top horizontal line as longer than the one below because it appears to be more distant.
Müller–Lyer	Misinterpreted depth cue.
	Two separate vertical lines of the same length, side by side, one with outgoing fins (a) and the other with ingoing fins (b).
	Vertical line with outgoing fins perceived as longer than the vertical line with ingoing fins.
Rubin's vase	An ambiguous figure.
	Image of two faces and a vase in same picture.
	Both are correct so your brain can't decide which image is shown.
Ames Room	Misinterpreted depth cue.
	Room looks normal but actually trapezoid shape.
	When two people stand on either side on the back wall, one appears to be much bigger than the other even though both are same size.

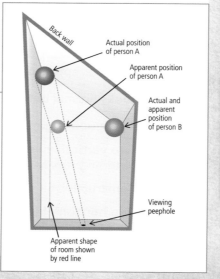

Back wall
Actual position of person A
Apparent position of person A
Actual and apparent position of person B
Viewing peephole
Apparent shape of room shown by red line

The Ames Room.

The specification says...

The difference between sensation and perception.
Examples of visual illusions: the Ponzo, the Müller-Lyer, Rubin's vase, the Ames Room.

Exam booster

Think Link

It is good practice to make links between topic areas to see how the research fits together. Perception is a particularly good section to do this as, for example, the visual illusions on this spread are also used to evaluate Gibson's and Gregory's theories of perception later on in the chapter whilst the information on visual cues and constancies on page 33 can be used to explain how these visual illusions work – something else you need to know for the exam.

APPLY IT – Research Methods

A psychologist was interested in whether people who are creative are more able to flip between the face and the vase in the Rubin's vase illusion within three seconds than those who are not creative. She showed the image to 80 people, 40 who were classed as creative and 40 non-creative. She found that 38 creative people could flip between the face and the vase within three seconds compared to 14 of the non-creative people.

1. Express the **two** findings as percentages of the participants in each condition. Show your workings. **[4 marks]**

2. Draw a bar chart of the data. Label the axes carefully and give it a suitable title. **[4 marks]**

3. Write **one** conclusion you could draw from your graph. **[2 marks]**

KNOWLEDGE CHECK

1. What is meant by the term 'perception'? **[2 marks]**

2. Briefly describe the Ames Room illusion. **[2 marks]**

3. The Ponzo illusion is an example of a visual illusion. Explain the illusion. **[2 marks]**

Sensation and perception wordsearch

Can you find the words related to the topic of sensation and perception?

There are 12 of them. They could be horizontal, vertical or diagonal (but not backwards).

```
X Q P I J P K F T X G M T M B G Z E X N
F J P O G Q A C D X C V Z U T O C A U B
F R C R D U B H C X D N G I B S O N T K
D H P V U F L P W T R Y W R U M V Y F C
R D N P L B I G M B V S D N P X B M V S
E M I B G X I A T U B S C P S E N S E E
C D N E R H X N E K N K S S F I Z S F N
E S T P E A Y C S C R A V V I M H C P S
P Y M F G R I V V V E M E G P O N Z O A
T G E B O Q F N V P A E Z O J M N M W T
O B B K R Y W Z Y K Y S W Z A U K S O I
R D B T Y Q P U I F O R E A M L W I A O
S B E S T I M U L U S O H U C L M Q R N
W R P M R N T A P S Y O N B W E B Y G M
B D P A D N U H T F M M Q K L R D H Y R
S L G V X U W R X I Q B V O S L Q I A K
S Y F P P L C N O M E F F A C Y F P I O
P E R C E P T I O N T B X G G E D H K L
R D V A P Z U O V M Y Q S F Q R Q K F J
Z X A O F C B D G L P K M V C Z A I F F
```

Match them up

Work out which statements in the first column go with the statements in the second column.
Draw in lines to connect them.

1. Sensation	A. The brain organises and interprets sensory information.
2. Perception	B. Direct.
3. Gregory's theory	C. Sense receptors process physical stimulation.
4. Gibson's theory	D. Looks normal but actually trapezoid shape.
5. Ponzo illusion	E. Ambiguous figure.
6. Müller–Lyer	F. Two vertical lines of same length, side by side, one with outgoing fins and the other with ingoing fins.
7. Rubin's vase	G. Constructivist.
8. Ames Room	H. Two horizontal lines of same length, one above the other, with two converging lines on either side.

Description

Visual cues and constancies		Visual cues = features of the environment that give us information about movement, distance, etc.
		Visual constancies = objects look the same despite seeing them from different angles and distances.
Binocular depth cues (two eyes)	Retinal disparity	Each eye sees things differently as they are positioned on the face about 6 cm apart. Retinal disparity is the difference between the left and right eye's view. The brain uses this information to work out depth and distance.
	Convergence	The eyes become closer together (converge) when objects are close to us.
		Muscles in the eye work harder when objects are close. This information is sent to the brain to give information about depth and distance.
Monocular depth cues (one eye)	Height in plane	 Objects that are higher up in the visual field appear further away.
	Relative size	 Smaller objects in the visual field appear further away.
	Occlusion	 Objects that are in front of others appear closer to us whilst objects behind other objects seem further away.
	Linear perspective	 When parallel lines converge in the distance, the point at which they come together is perceived to be further away.

The specification says...

Visual cues and constancies:
Binocular depth cues: retinal disparity, convergence. Monocular depth cues: height in plane, relative size, occlusion and linear perspective.

Monocular.

Exam booster

Identify means just name it

Sometimes you will get 1-mark questions in the exam that require you to identify something. In this case you just need to give a very brief answer and don't need to elaborate any further. For example, if the question was: *Identify a binocular depth cue [1 mark]*, then just writing 'retinal disparity' would be enough to get you the mark – you would not need to go on to explain what retinal disparity is.

APPLY IT

Read the item below and then answer the question that follows.

Dave had a nasty accident that resulted in him losing the vision in one eye. Since this happened he has noticed that he is bumping into things far more than he used to do.

- Use your knowledge of binocular depth cues to explain why this would occur.   **[3 marks]**

KNOWLEDGE CHECK

1. What is meant by the term 'convergence' in the context of perception?   **[1 mark]**

2. Identify **two** monocular depth cues and explain how each helps us to perceive the distance of objects. **[4 marks]**

3. Outline how binocular depth cues can be used to perceive distance and depth.   **[5 marks]**

True or false?

Some of the statements below about visual cues and constancies are true and some are false. Indicate which is which and rewrite the false statements to make them true.

		True or false?	
1.	Visual cues are part of the human visual system.		
2.	Visual constancy refers to objects looking the same despite seeing them from different angles and distances.		
3.	There is just one major binocular depth cue.		
4.	Retinal disparity is a monocular depth cue.		
5.	Convergence refers to objects higher up in the visual field appearing further away.		
6.	You need two eyes to see monocular depth cues.		
7.	There are four main monocular depth cues.		
8.	Relative size refers to how smaller objects appear further away.		
9.	Height in plane means that objects in front of others appear nearer.		
10.	Linear perspective is created when parallel lines appear to converge.		

Boost your description with examples

Giving examples is a great way to add detail to your descriptions. In the boxes below, write down definitions of visual cues and constancies. Add examples to take your definitions further. Try to think of different examples from the ones on the previous page.

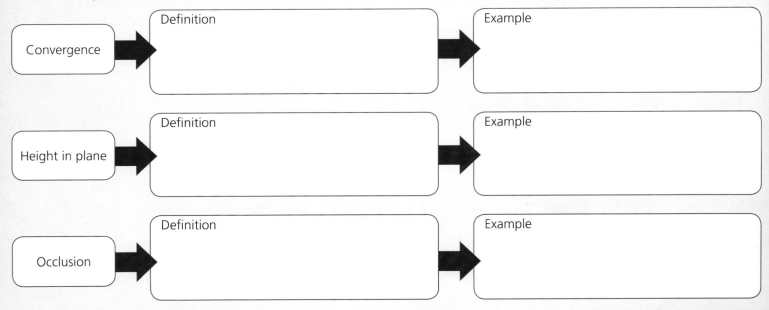

Convergence	Definition	Example
Height in plane	Definition	Example
Occlusion	Definition	Example

Explaining visual illusions

Size constancy	The brain perceives familiar objects as a constant size despite the size of the image they produce on our retina changing with distance.
Misinterpreted depth cues	Objects in the distance that appear smaller are scaled up by our brain so they look normal size.
	Sometimes the brain sees distance when there isn't any which creates a visual illusion as in the following two examples.
Ponzo illusion	Converging lines give the illusion of distance.
	The brain uses size constancy and mentally scales up the more distant line while mentally scaling down the closer line.
Müller-Lyer illusion (a) (b) 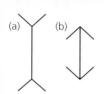	Outgoing fins (a) are shaped like the inside corner of a room which is stretching away from us.
	Ingoing fins (b) are shaped like the outside of a building projecting out.
	This gives the illusion of distance/nearness.
	We mentally scale up the line that appears closer (outgoing fins) so it appears longer.
Ambiguous figures	A type of visual illusion where there are two possible interpretations of the same image, and the brain cannot decide which one to choose.
Necker cube	The same image of a cube can be perceived as either pointing upwards to the right, or downwards to the left.
Fiction	A type of visual illusion that causes the brain to see something that is not there.
Kanizsa triangle 	Illusory contours to create the impression that a second triangle is overlapping the first one.

Exam booster

Don't mess up multiple choice questions

Questions in this area of perception can be asked as multiple choice questions. At first glance this type of question looks easier than ones that require you to write extensively. However, you will be surprised how frequently students can get these questions wrong. Therefore, make sure that you proofread your answers to multiple choice questions so you don't end up losing easy marks in the exam.

APPLY IT – Research Methods

A GCSE Psychology student is interested in visual illusions. He conducts a structured interview with 30 people in his psychology class. One question he asks the participants is to score how much they like the Necker cube illusion out of 10, where 1 means they don't like it and 10 means they love it. He collects the following data: 5, 8, 7, 3, 2, 4, 3, 2, 7, 8, 9, 10, 2, 5, 5, 7, 6, 8, 7, 8. 9, 3, 4, 6, 7, 8, 2, 1, 5, 6, 9

1. Construct a frequency table of the results. Make sure it is accurately labelled and give it an appropriate title. **[4 marks]**

2. The study produced a lot of quantitative data. What is meant by the term 'quantitative data'? **[1 marks]**

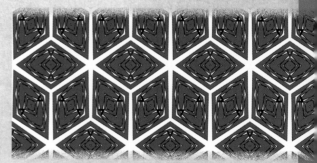

Mary was offended when the neighbours had described her new wallpaper as 'a bit garish', but she was starting to wonder whether they had a point.

KNOWLEDGE CHECK

1. Identify **one** ambiguous figure. **[1 mark]**
2. With reference to the Müller-Lyer illusion, outline what is meant by a 'misinterpreted depth cue'. **[5 marks]**
3. Briefly describe **two** visual illusions and explain how each of them works. **[6 marks]**

Draw your own

Have a go at drawing the four visual illusions for this topic for yourself. Try to complete the table from memory, without looking at the book. Your drawing doesn't have to be a work of art – substance is more important than style. Write the name of the illusion in the top row, and draw it underneath.

Visual illusion match-up

Match up the statements in the four columns by drawing lines to link them.

Ponzo

Fiction

Triangle

Illusory contours create appearance of overlap.

Müller-Lyer

Misinterpreted depth cues

Cube

Appears to point upwards to the right or downwards to the left.

Necker

Misinterpreted depth cues

Converging lines

One line looks like the inside corner of a room and the other looks like the outside corner of a building.

Kanizsa

Ambiguous figure

Fins and arrows

Size constancy scales up the upper line and scales down the lower line.

The specification says...

Gibson's direct theory of perception – the influence of nature: The real world presents sufficient information for direct perception without inference.

Role of motion parallax in everyday perception.

Description

Gibson's direct theory	Gibson's theory suggests that the environment gives us all the information required for perception.
	Gregory's theory suggests that perception is to do with past experiences.
Direct perception	Sensation and perception are the same thing.
	The eyes detect everything we need to judge depth, distance and movement. We don't need past experience.
Optic flow patterns	When moving, the point we are moving towards is stationary, everything else rushes away from it.
	This monocular depth cue is detected by our eyes which tells the brain that we are moving, so we know the speed and direction that we are travelling in.
Motion parallax	This is another monocular depth cue which tells the brain the speed we are moving.
	Objects closer in our visual field move faster than objects further away.
The influence of nature	Gibson's view was that the ability to perceive is inborn – we don't learn it.
	The eyes detect fine changes in light, texture, movement and depth so we can understand distance and depth.

Evaluation

Real-world meaning	One strength of Gibson's theory is that it has real-world meaning.
	Research was based on the experience of pilots from the Second World War.
	This makes it more relevant to explaining how we perceive the world on a daily basis.
The theory struggles to explain illusions	One weakness of Gibson's theory is that it struggles to explain visual illusions.
	Gibson proposed that we will always perceive accurately whereas illusions trick the brain into misperception.
	This suggests there is more to perception than his theory proposed.
EXTRA: Support for the role of nature	Another strength comes from Gibson and Walk's study.
	Very few infants would crawl off a 'visual cliff' (see right).
	This suggests that infants have an innate ability to perceive depth, which shows that some perception is innate.

KNOWLEDGE CHECK

1. Outline what is meant by the term 'motion parallax'. **[2 marks]**
2. Explain the role of nature in Gibson's direct theory of perception. **[3 marks]**
3. Describe and evaluate Gibson's direct theory of perception. **[9 marks]**

Exam booster

Follow the instructions on the paper

All of your questions on the exam paper are scanned and clipped so that they can be marked electronically. An examiner only sees a clip of your answer to one question. If your answer goes beyond the space provided for the question the examiner won't see it. If you need to write more, then use an additional sheet otherwise you may lose vital marks.

APPLY IT

Read the item below and then answer the question that follows.

Mellissa is a curious child, constantly asking her mum questions about the world. As they are driving on the motorway Mellissa can see the hotel that they are going to but it doesn't appear to be getting any closer whereas other objects are. She also notices that bushes at the side of the road are rushing past at a faster rate than the houses behind them.

- Use your knowledge of Gibson's direct theory of perception to explain why the objects in Mellissa's visual field are moving at different speeds. **[4 marks]**

Cliff was the type of guy who liked to live life on the edge.

Fill in the blanks

Complete the passage by filling in the missing words from this description of Gibson's direct theory of perception. Try to complete the activity without referring to your notes or the previous page. The words you need to choose from are on the right if you really get stuck.

Gibson's theory is a _____ theory of perception. It suggests that all of the information we need for perception comes from the _____. According to Gibson, _____ and perception are the same thing.

Gibson explained perception of movement in terms of _____ flow patterns. When we move, the point we are moving towards stays _____ and everything else appears to rush away from it. Our eyes detect this flow pattern, which tells the _____ we are moving. We can perceive the _____ and direction we are travelling in.

Another monocular depth _____ which tells the brain we are moving is motion _____. Objects that are closer in our field of vision appear to move _____ than objects that are further away.

Gibson argues that we do not _____ the ability to perceive – we are born with it. He believed that nature explains perception, not _____. We have an innate visual system that is able to detect fine changes in light, texture, movement and depth.

sensation
environment
parallax
direct
faster
nurture
fixed
optic
cue
learn
brain
speed

Instant messaging evaluation

Two students are having an instant messaging conversation about Gibson's theory of perception (as you do). They are building evaluation points step by step. Some of the conversation has gone missing for some reason, so you need to fill in the gaps.

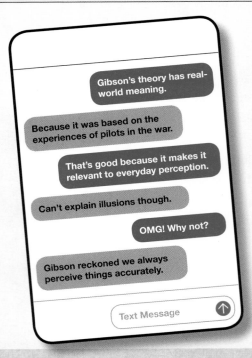

Gibson's theory has real-world meaning.

Because it was based on the experiences of pilots in the war.

That's good because it makes it relevant to everyday perception.

Can't explain illusions though.

OMG! Why not?

Gibson reckoned we always perceive things accurately.

Text Message

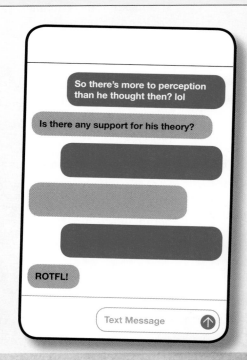

So there's more to perception than he thought then? lol

Is there any support for his theory?

ROTFL!

Text Message

Description

Gregory's constructivist theory of perception	This contrasts with Gibson's theory that sensation and perception are the same thing. Gregory's theory proposes that we use past experience to make sense of the world around us.
Perception is a construction	The brain uses incoming sensory information plus information that we already know about the world. Perception is therefore a construction.
Inference	The brain uses sensory information that is available and then fills in the gaps. Past experience means we infer what should be there and draw a conclusion.
Visual cues	When making inferences, features of the environment (visual cues) give the brain information about depth, distance, etc. Visual illusions occur because the brain has drawn the wrong conclusion from these cues.
Past experience – the role of nurture	Gregory proposes that perception depends on experience, i.e. learning. For example, learning to see a chair as a chair. The more we interact with the world, the more sophisticated our perception becomes.

Evaluation

Support from research in different cultures	One strength is that Gregory's theory has support from studies of cultural differences in perception. For example, Hudson's study showed that experience affects how visual cues are interpreted. This means that their different experiences have affected their perception.
Visual illusions	One weakness relates to Gregory's use of visual illusions to support his theory. They are artificial two-dimensional (2D) images that are deliberately designed to fool us. As a consequence, his theory may not tell us much about how perception works in the real world.
EXTRA: How does perception get going?	Another weakness is that Gregory's theory cannot explain how perception gets started. Research has shown that babies have some perceptual abilities at birth, such as they prefer human faces to random patterns (Fantz). Therefore not all perception is the result of experience.

The specification says...

Gregory's constructivist theory of perception – the influence of nurture: Perception uses inferences from visual cues and past experience to construct a model of reality.

APPLY IT

Look at the picture below and answer the questions that follow.

1. Use your knowledge of Gregory's theory to explain why people see a face in this tree. **[2 marks]**

2. Gregory's theory has been criticised. Use your knowledge of psychology to explain how the example of perceiving faces can be used to evaluate Gregory's theory.

[2 marks]

Too much detail is a bad thing

You may get a 4-mark question in the exam asking, for example: *Describe Gregory's constructivist theory of perception [4 marks].* It is tempting to write everything that you know about the theory and go into too much detail as a result. Writing 100 words of description (AO1) is sufficient. A good way to guide your writing is to write four key points for a 4-mark question. You can use the headings on the left (e.g. perception is a construction, inference, visual cues and past experience). Four clear points makes it easier for the examiner to award you four marks.

Exam booster

In Fantz's study babies 'preferred' the face pattern on the left to the other two patterns.

KNOWLEDGE CHECK

1. What is meant by a 'constructivist theory of perception'? **[2 marks]**

2. Explain the role of nurture in relation to Gregory's constructivist theory of perception. **[3 marks]**

3. Outline and evaluate how, according to Gregory, perception uses inferences from visual cues and past experiences to construct a model of reality. **[9 marks]**

Writing well-organised answers

Here's a typical 9-mark question: Describe and evaluate Gregory's constructivist theory of perception.

An excellent way to boost your marks to such a question is to organise your answer clearly. The table below offers a way to visualise your answer.

For the describe part, identify 4 key points (each in a different colour):	For the evaluate part, identify 3 points:
1.	1.
2.	2.
3.	3.
4.	

Now use this framework to write out your essay in full on a separate piece of paper. Use the same colours to write out each description point.

For the description you should write about 25 words for each point.	For the evaluation you need to provide an explanation and a conclusion for each point.

Constructivist theory crossword

It's a crossword. What more do you need to know?

ACROSS

4. Visual illusions are A_____ images. (10)

5. Gregory's is this type of theory. C_____. (14)

7. Children are born with the ability to perceive these. F_____ (5)

8. He investigated the effects of culture. H_____. (6)

9. Perception is different in different C_____. (8)

11. Perception develops through L_____. (8)

13. Gregory's theory can explain visual I_____. (9)

14. An important visual cue. D_____. (5)

DOWN

1. Features of the environment telling us about distance, etc. V_____ C_____. (6,4)

2. We use past E_____ to perceive the world. (10)

3. He investigated 7 across. F_____. (5)

6. We fill in the gaps by making I_____. (10)

10. The brain uses S_____ information. (7)

12. Perception is due to N_____ not nature. (7)

The specification says...

Factors affecting perception: Perceptual set and the effects of culture.

Description

Perceptual set and culture	Perceptual set = tendency for our brain to notice some aspects of the environment more than others. Culture = the social world that surrounds you.
Aim	Hudson aimed to find out whether people from different cultural/educational backgrounds perceived depth cues in 2D images differently.
Method	South Africans were shown 2D drawings – native black people (schooled or unschooled) and white Europeans (schooled or unschooled). Participants had to say which animal the man was trying to spear. Depth cues (height in the visual field and relative size) suggest the spear was actually being aimed at the antelope not the elephant.
Results	Many believed the spear was aimed at the elephant. Schooled participants were more likely to perceive depth than unschooled participants. White schooled participants were more likely to perceive depth than black schooled participants.
Conclusion	People from different cultural/educational backgrounds use depth cues differently and have a different perceptual set. This supports Gregory's theory as it shows that depth cues are learned.

Evaluation

Cross-cultural research	One weakness is the instructions may lack sense. The language barrier means translations of the method may have been unclear. This will therefore affect the validity of the results.
Problems with the method	Another weakness is that some of the participants may have been confused by seeing drawings on paper. When more familiar materials such as cloth were used they gave different answers. This shows representation affects results.
EXTRA: Poor design	A further weakness is that Hudson's study is from a long time ago and had some design issues. For example, the tester asked the questions out loud and may have unconsciously indicated which answer to give. This means that the conclusions may lack validity.

Exam booster

Extraneous variables

There are four factors that affect perception, so you can use them to evaluate each other. If you are evaluating research into culture, you could say that the participants' perception in the study could have been affected by their motivation levels and this acts as an extraneous variable. This would mean that the results of the study may lack validity in terms of illustrating the precise role that culture plays on perception.

Hudson used pictures like the one above to test how people interpreted depth cues in a two-dimensional (2D) image. Which animal is the man trying to spear in this picture?

APPLY IT – Research Methods

In his study Hudson compared different cultures who were schooled and unschooled.

1. Explain why it was important for Hudson to use standardised procedures with each participant in this research. **[3 marks]**

2. Name and explain **two** ethical issues that could be a problem in this research. **[4 marks]**

3. Explain how **one** of these ethical issues could be dealt with in this study. **[3 marks]**

KNOWLEDGE CHECK

1. What is meant by the term 'perceptual set'? **[1 mark]**

2. Briefly outline what the participants were asked to do in a study into culture and perceptual set. **[2 marks]**

3. Describe and evaluate the influence of culture on perception. **[9 marks]**

Storyboard Hudson's study

They say a picture is worth a thousand words. If that's true, then this book would be a lot shorter. But visual images can be useful, so why not outline Hudson's study in pictures? Take the main elements of the study and try to represent them with drawings, like a film director might do with a 'storyboard', a series of images that tell the story of the film (or study) from start to finish. Here's a template to help you along.

Key phrase evaluation

Below are some evaluative phrases for this topic. Decide which ones go together in pairs. For each pair, write a sentence for each of the statements and write a further sentence to explain why each point is a weakness (they are all weaknesses). The first one has been done as an example

Drawings on paper

No control group

Cross-cultural research

Old study

Language barrier

Familiar materials

Pair	Descriptions	Explanation
Cross-cultural research + Language barrier	*Cross-cultural research:* The study was conducted in a different culture.	This means the results would lack validity so it is unclear what it tells us about cultural influences on perception.
	Language barrier: The method had to be translated so the language barrier may have meant some things were unclear.	

The specification says...

Factors affecting perception:
Perceptual set and the effects
of emotion.

Description

Perceptual set and emotion	The tendency for our brain to notice things that are exciting, interesting or unusual. But also block things that make us anxious or we find threatening.
Aim	McGinnies wanted to see whether things that cause anxiety are less likely to be noticed than things that are emotionally neutral.
Method	Eight male and eight female students were shown neutral and offensive 'taboo' words flashed on a screen. Participants had to say each word out loud. The amount of emotional arousal was measured through their *galvanic skin response* (GSR).
Results	Participants took longer to say offensive words (e.g. 'bitch') than neutral ones (e.g. 'apple'). Taboo words produced bigger changes in the GSR than neutral words.
Conclusion	This shows that emotion affects perceptual set. Perceptual defence is used by the brain when dealing with words that cause offense or anxiety.

Evaluation

Objective measurement	One strength of this study is that it used an objective measurement of emotion. A scientific method was used – the galvanic skin response – to test biological anxiety responses. This produces results that are less open to bias than, for example, rating scales.
Embarrassment not defence	One weakness is that delayed recognition may be more to do with embarrassment. Participants may have hesitated in giving their response as they were uncomfortable repeating rude words in a study. This suggests that awkwardness may have been an extraneous variable.
EXTRA: Results are contradictory	Another weakness of studies in this area is that the results are contradictory. Sometimes perceptual defence occurs and sometimes perceptual sensitisation. But we don't know why this happens. This makes it difficult to draw firm conclusions.

APPLY IT

Read the item below and then answer the question that follows.

Oli has been dating Aimee for two months now and he couldn't be happier. He has always listened to the radio on the way to school but recently he has noticed that so many of the songs that he hears are about love.

- Use your knowledge of the role of emotion on perception to explain Oli's experience. **[3 marks]**

GSR measures electrical changes in the skin – when a person is anxious or embarrassed (or lying) the autonomic nervous system responds by activating the 'fight or flight response'. The result is increased breathing rate, rapid heartbeat and the person sweats. The sweating increases the electrical conductivity of the skin. Jeremy Kyle swears by it.

Evaluation – less is more

Exam booster

Students sometimes get frustrated at the amount of evaluation there is to know. A way round this is to write fewer points in more detail. For example, in a 9-mark describe and evaluate question, you do not need to write all three evaluations on the left. You could write just two and give yourself more time to elaborate. The elaboration shows you really understand the point you are making and gains more marks than three superficial points.

KNOWLEDGE CHECK

1. Outline what is meant by 'emotion' in relation to perceptual set. **[2 marks]**
2. Explain **one** criticism of research on the effect of emotion on perceptual set. **[4 marks]**
3. Describe and evaluate how research has increased our understanding of the effect of emotion on perceptual set. **[9 marks]**

AO1 – True or false

How much do you know about the study by McGinnies? Find out by identifying which of the statements below are true and which are false. Rewrite the false statements to make them true.

		True or false?	
1.	McGinnies aimed to find out if culture influences perception.		
2.	There were 16 participants in total.		
3.	The participants were male office workers.		
4.	Neutral and offensive words were both used.		
5.	An example of an offensive word was 'apple'.		
6.	Participants listened to the words read out by the experimenter.		
7.	McGinnies used a questionnaire to measure the amount of emotional arousal.		
8.	It took longer for the participants to say the offensive words than the neutral ones.		
9.	GSRs increased more for neutral words than offensive ones.		
10.	McGinnies concluded that emotional arousal affects perceptual set.		
11.	The brain uses perceptual attack to cope with words that cause anxiety.		

AO3 – McGinnies match-up

Fill in the missing information. Then decide which sentences go together.

A This means that the participants' discomfort might have been an _____ variable, reducing the _____ of the results.

B This is a strength because it means the results are relatively un_____ compared with _____-report methods (e.g. rating scales and questionnaires).

C A weakness is that results from different studies are mixed and _____ each other.

D A weakness is that the findings may have been due to embarrassment.

E A strength is that _____ was measured objectively.

F For example, the participants may have been reluctant to repeat _____ words and so took longer.

G Galvanic _____ response is a scientific way of assessing people's anxiety responses.

H This means it is hard to draw firm _____ because we do not know why this happens.

I Some studies find that perceptual _____ occurs and other studies find perceptual sensitisation occurs.

The specification says...

Factors affecting perception: perceptual set and the effects of motivation. The Gilchrist and Nesberg study of motivation.

Description

Perceptual set and motivation	The force that drives your behaviour (motivation) can affect how you perceive things. Wanting something can increase its attractiveness.
Aim	Gilchrist and Nesberg aimed to find out if food deprivation affects the perception of food pictures.
Method	Two groups of students: one group deprived of food for 20 hours and a control group (not hungry). Students were shown four slides of meals. The slide was displayed for 15 seconds. The picture was shown again, but dimmer, and participants had to adjust the lighting to make it look the same as it did before.
Results	Participants perceived the food as brighter if they were deprived of food. The control group (who were not deprived of food) didn't perceive the food as brighter.
Conclusion	Being deprived of food increased perceptual sensitivity. This shows that hunger is a motivating factor affecting the way food is perceived.

The new McLizard Nugget range was not exactly flying off the shelves.

Evaluation

Support from similar studies	One strength is that similar studies have found similar results. Sanford deprived participants of food and showed them ambiguous pictures. The longer the food deprivation the more likely they were to see food. This increases the validity of the Gilchrist and Nesberg results.
Ethical issues	One weakness with studies in this area is that they are unethical. This is because depriving participants of food and water could cause them to feel uncomfortable. This is an issue as you should not do this in psychological research.
EXTRA: Not like everyday life	Another weakness with the study is that it was not like everyday life. Participants were asked to judge pictures of food rather than real food. This makes it harder to apply the results to situations in the real world.

Exam booster

This suggests that ...

This is a named study on the specification, so you need to know its methods, results and conclusions. In a 9-mark essay you need to include all three to get in the top mark band. One note of caution – students sometimes lose marks because they don't distinguish between results and conclusions. An easy way to draw a conclusion is to start it off with the phrase 'the results suggest that ...'. This forces you to interpret the results and so you are more likely to write a valid conclusion rather than just repeat the results again.

APPLY IT – Research Methods

Gilchrist and Nesberg's study into motivation and perceptual set was an experiment using an independent groups design. Participants were randomly allocated to the two conditions in the study.

1. Identify the independent variable in Gilchrist and Nesberg's study. **[1 mark]**

2. Explain **one** strength of using an independent groups design for this study. **[2 marks]**

3. Explain why the researchers used randomisation to allocate participants to the two conditions. **[2 marks]**

KNOWLEDGE CHECK

1. What is meant by the term 'motivation' in relation to perceptual set? **[2 marks]**

2. Outline **one** way that research by Gilchrist and Nesburg has increased our understanding of how motivation affects perceptual set. **[2 marks]**

3. Describe and evaluate **one** study into how motivation affects perceptual set. **[9 marks]**

Broken sentences match-up

Below are some sentences that describe Gilchrist and Nesberg's study. They have become broken and muddled up, so put them back together again by matching the first half of each sentence in the left-hand column with the second half in the right-hand column.

1. Gilchrist and Nesberg's aim was to …	**A.** … students.
2. The experimental design of the study was …	**B.** … was displayed for 15 seconds.
3. The participants were …	**C.** … increased perceptual sensitivity.
4. The participants in the experimental group …	**D.** … adjust the brightness.
5. The participants were shown …	**E.** … hunger is a motivating factor that affects how food is perceived.
6. Each slide …	**F.** … find out if food deprivation affects how people perceive images of food.
7. Each picture was shown twice and the second time the participants had to …	**G.** … the food-deprived participants perceived the images as brighter.
8. Gilchrist and Nesberg found that …	**H.** … were deprived of food for 20 hours.
9. Being deprived of food …	**I.** … independent groups.
10. Gilchrist and Nesberg concluded that …	**J.** … four slides of meals.

Motivation anagrams

Time to unjumble these words relating to Gilchrist and Nesberg's study. Can you do it without looking at the clues?

1. VITAMINTOO		The behaviour that this is all about.
2. OVERPAIDNIT		Gilchrist and Nesberg used food _____ in this study.
3. DUSTNETS		The participants were all _____.
4. CORNLOT		One type of group in the study.
5. NIGHGILT		This is what the participants had to adjust.
6. YETISINSITV		The deprived participants had more perceptual _____.
7. FANSROD		He carried out a similar study.
8. ACHEUNTIL		Some have criticised the study for being _____.
9. EPICRUST		The researchers used _____ rather than real food.
10. VARYEYED		The study wasn't really like _____ life.

Description

Perceptual set and expectation	The belief about what is likely to happen based on past experiences can affect how much we attend to or notice things in the environment.
Aim	Bruner and Minturn aimed to find out whether an ambiguous figure was seen differently if the context of the figure was changed.
Method 12 A B C 14	An independent groups design was used where participants were either presented with a sequence of letters or a sequence of numbers with the same ambiguous figure in the middle. The ambiguous figure could be seen as either the letter B or as the number 13.
Results	Those who saw a sequence of letters were more likely to report the figure as being the letter B. If shown numbers they were more likely to say it was the number 13.
Conclusion	This shows that expectation of what the figure represented was affected by the context that the figure was presented in.

Evaluation

Artificial task	One weakness of the study is that it used an artificial task. An ambiguous figure is designed to trick perception. This makes the results lack validity.
Independent groups design	Another weakness relates to the fact that there may be individual differences between groups. This is because an independent groups design was used. This is an issue as differences in perception between the groups may have been due to participant variables rather than their expectations.
EXTRA: Real-life application	One strength of this study is that it has real-life application. It can explain errors such as misidentifying an aircraft as an enemy plane because of expectations. This therefore helps to explain why people sometimes make serious mistakes on tasks in the real world.

KNOWLEDGE CHECK

1. Outline the effect of expectation on perceptual set. **[3 marks]**
2. Outline what the participants were asked to do in the study by Bruner and Minturn into expectation and perceptual set. **[2 marks]**
3. Describe and evaluate Bruner and Minturn's study into the effect of expectation on perceptual set. In your answer include details of the method used, the results obtained and the conclusion drawn. **[9 marks]**

The specification says...

Factors affecting perception: Perceptual set and the effects of expectation. The Bruner and Minturn study of perceptual set.

Travis the Rabbit was having what his friends referred to as one of his 'duck moments'.

Exam booster

Design a study

You could be asked to design a study on expectation. If you know the method of a study such as Bruner and Minturn in detail (design, sample, task used) that can help you get more marks on such 'design a study' questions.

APPLY IT

Read the item below and then answer the question that follows.

A psychology teacher carries out a study with two classes of GCSE students. With one class he tells them a story about a young lady who goes to a fancy ball with her husband whilst the other class are told a story about an old witch-like lady who scares young children. Both classes are then told to look at the picture on the left and describe what they see.

• Use your knowledge of the role of expectation on perception to speculate what the researcher would find. Explain your answer **[3 marks]**

Put it right

The passage below is a description of Bruner and Minturn's study. Unfortunately several mistakes have crept into it. Your task is to identify the errors and correct them.

Bruner and Minturn wanted to find out if we perceive an ambiguous figure differently if we are hungry. They used a matched pairs experimental design.

They showed their participants an ambiguous figure, which could be perceived as either the letter B or the number 23. One group saw the figure at the end of a sequence of letters. Another group saw the figure at the start of a sequence of numbers. A third group just saw the ambiguous figure on its own.

The researchers found that the participants who saw the sequence of letters were more likely to report the ambiguous figure as '13'. The participants who saw the sequence of numbers were more likely to interpret the figure as 'B'.

Gilchrist and Nesberg concluded that the participants' culture affected their perception of the figure.

Elaborate to evaluate

Complete each sentence below to practise elaboration for an evaluation point.

Point 1: An artificial task …	An ambiguous figure …	This is a weakness because …
Point 2: An independent groups design …	Individual differences …	This is a weakness because …
Point 3: A real-life application …	For example, …	This is a strength because …

Basic outline of early brain development

Brain stem	Highly developed at birth.
	Connects brain to the spinal cord. Carries motor and sensory nerves to the brain from the body.
	Controls autonomic functions, e.g. heartbeat, breathing, etc.
Cerebellum	One of the last parts of the brain to develop.
	Located near the top of the spinal cord.
	Main role is the coordination of movement and sensory information (sensorimotor).
Thalamus	Located deep inside the brain in each hemisphere.
	Acts as a hub of information, receiving signals from other areas of the brain and sending these signals on.
Cortex/ cerebral cortex	Cortex is thin, highly folded and covers the brain.
	Divided in two hemispheres and several regions: frontal cortex (thinking), visual and auditory cortex (sight and hearing), motor cortex (movement).
	The cortex functions in the womb, e.g. sensory and motor functions. At birth the cortex is basic and develops through life.

The roles of nature and nurture

Roles of nature and nurture	Nature is the influence of things you have inherited.
	Nurture is the influence of your environment on your development.
Smoking	Mothers who smoke during pregnancy may have smaller babies with smaller brains as nicotine slows brain growth.
Infection	Mothers who get German measles (rubella) during pregnancy may have babies with brain damage and/or hearing loss.
Voices	Babies learn to recognise their mother's voice and even respond to book passages that have been read to them in the womb (DeCasper and Spence).
The interaction between nature and nurture	Your brain is formed due to nature but even in the womb your environment influences the development of the brain.
	It is nature *and* nurture rather than just one or the other.

KNOWLEDGE CHECK

1. Distinguish between nature and nurture. **[3 marks]**
2. Outline the role of the thalamus and cerebellum. **[4 marks]**
3. Briefly explain the development of the brain. **[5 marks]**

The specification says…

Early brain development: A basic knowledge of brain development, from simple neural structures in the womb, of brain stem, thalamus, cerebellum and cortex, reflecting the development of autonomic functions, sensory processing, movement and cognition.

The roles of nature and nurture.

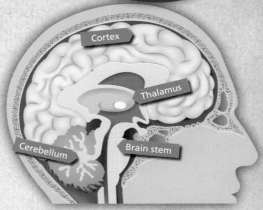

The outer thin layer of the brain is the cerebral cortex, sometimes just called the 'cortex'. It is only about 3 millimetres thick!

Exam booster

Function and location

Make sure you can explain what each of the brain structures do and also where they are located in the brain. Exam questions on this topic could ask you to describe the function of these components or label a diagram of the brain with the terms for each part.

APPLY IT

Read the item below and then answer the question that follows.

Issy is a 23-year-old woman who has severe depression. Issy has always wondered why she has the disease but her mum, dad and older brother have never had depression. Her grandmother, who also experienced the same mental illness, thinks it has something to do with Issy's mother having a virus during her pregnancy. In addition to this Issy's parents split up when she was two and this may also have had an effect.

• Use your knowledge of psychology to explain the role that nature and nurture might play in Issy's behaviour. **[4 marks]**

AO1 – Anagrams

Time to unjumble these words relating to early brain development. Can you do it without looking at the clues?

1. RANBI METS		Attached to the spinal cord.
2. CRUMBLELEE		Co-ordinates movement and sensory information.
3. HAULMAST		The brain's hub.
4. REXCOT		Thin layer covering the brain.
5. CAUTIONOM		Functions such as heartbeat, breathing, etc.
6. PLAINS DORC		Attached to the back of the brain.
7. HEMEPERISH		The brain has two of these.
8. RESNOSY		Information relating to the senses.
9. EVENTMOM		Co-ordinated by the cerebellum.
10. MRTOO		The cortex that controls item 9 above.

Nature/nurture – True or false?

What do you know about nature and nurture in development? Find out by identifying which of the following statements are true and which are false. For the false ones, write them so that they are true.

		True or false?	
1.	Nature is to do with how the environment affects your development.		
2.	Nurture includes influences such as learning.		
3.	Smoking affects the development of babies in pregnancy.		
4.	German measles does not really affect babies developing in the womb.		
5.	DeCaspar and Spence did a study into the effects of German measles.		
6.	Another name for German measles is rubella.		
7.	A baby can learn to recognise his or her mother's voice in the womb.		
8.	The initial formation of the brain is due to nature.		
9.	The environment has no effect on brain development.		
	The influence of nature on development is always greater than the influence of nurture.		

The specification says...

Piaget's Theory
of Cognitive Development
including concepts of assimilation
and accommodation.

Description

The theory	'Cognitive' refers to mental processes, such as thinking. 'Cognitive development' is about the changes in the way we think across time. Piaget believed that children think differently from adults.
Stages	Piaget believed that children's brains are not mature enough to think in a logical way at the beginning. Their brains develop in stages and at each stage different kinds of thinking occur.
Schema	As children develop they create mental representations of the world which are stored in the form of schemas. A schema is a mental structure containing knowledge. They become more complex through assimilation and accommodation.
Assimilation	Assimilation occurs when we understand a new experience through adding new information to an existing schema. For example, a car schema is changed when a two-seated sports car is seen for the first time.
Accommodation	Accommodation occurs when we acquire new information that changes our understanding so we need to form new schema(s). For example, when a child sees a tractor they change their car schema or form a new tractor schema.

Evaluation

Research evidence	One strength of Piaget's theory is that it has led many studies to be carried out. These have helped test the claims of his theory. This is an important part of any theory – if we can't test it we don't know if it is right or wrong.
Real-world application	Another strength of Piaget's theory is that it has helped change classroom teaching for the better. It has led to teachers doing more activity-based learning. This has helped children learn in a more effective way.
The sample	One weakness of Piaget's theory is that much of the research was carried out on middle-class Swiss children. These children were from families where academic studies were more important than making things. Therefore his theory may not be universal.

KNOWLEDGE CHECK

1. What is meant by the term 'accommodation' in Piaget's theory? **[1 mark]**
2. Explain the role of assimilation in the development of intelligence. **[3 marks]**
3. Describe and evaluate Piaget's theory of cognitive development. **[9 marks]**

APPLY IT – Research Methods

A psychologist uses opportunity sampling to select 23 children from St Mary's Primary School. She asks them to write down the first three words that they think of when asked to visualise a bank robbery. The psychologist thinks most children have similar schemas. She finds that 19/23 write down the word 'gun', 13/23 write down the word 'mask' and 6/23 write down 'scared'.

1. Convert the data into percentages for the number of children who wrote down the words gun, mask and scared. Give your answer to **one** decimal place. **[6 marks]**
2. Explain **one** strength and **one** weakness of using an opportunity sample. **[4 marks]**
3. Explain how the psychologist could have used a random sample to gather the participants for her study. **[3 marks]**

assimilation   **accommodation**

Evaluation is more than just criticising

When evaluating Piaget's theory or any other piece of research in psychology, remember that you can talk about the positive as well as the negative. His theory had a big impact on the real world, particularly in education, so it is important to comment on this as well as pointing out the flaws in the theory.

Exam booster

The Piaget cube

Make a small cardboard cube using this template. Roll the cube and whichever term/phrase comes up, provide a detailed explanation of it. You can do this on your own, but if you're with other students you can take turns to explain to each other. Keep the explanation going until everyone understands it.

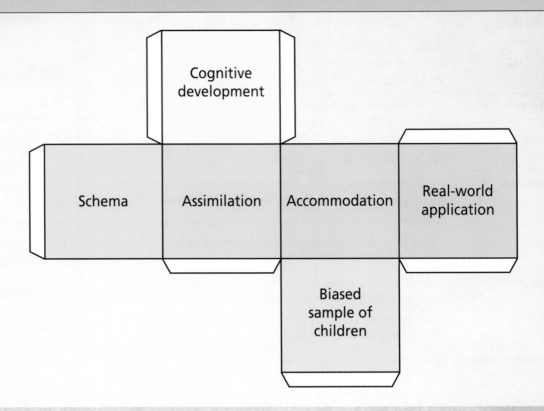

Explaining examples

Examples are great things – they can add detail to descriptions, especially when you explain how the example relates to a concept. Here's an activity to help you get thinking about examples and what they mean. The first column of the table has examples relating to some of Piaget's concepts. In the second column are sentence starters – you have to explain the example in more detail and then try and come up with another example of your own.

A young child believes all furry animals with four legs are 'doggies'.	This is an example of a schema because …
The child sees a breed of dog for the first time. She says, 'Look, a doggie.'	This is an example of assimilation because …
The child sees a cat and says, 'Look, a doggie.' Mum says, 'No that's a cat.' The next time the child sees a cat, she says 'Look, a cat.'	This is an example of accommodation because …

The specification says...

Piaget's stage theory and the development of intelligence: Development of conservation.
McGarrigle and Donaldson's 'naughty teddy study'.

McGarrigle and Donaldson's 'naughty teddy study'

Conservation	The ability to realise that quantity remains the same even when the appearance changes. Piaget's research showed that younger children can't conserve with number or volume.
Aim	McGarrigle and Donaldson wanted to see if younger children could conserve if there wasn't a deliberate change in a row of counters.
Method	4–6-year-olds were shown a naughty teddy and two rows of four counters. Teddy messed up one of the rows. Each child was asked before and after the teddy appeared 'Is there more here or more here or are they both the same number?'
Results	41% of the children conserved if the change was intentional (i.e. as Piaget did it). 68% conserved if the change was accidental. Older children gave more correct answers than younger children.
Conclusion	This shows that Piaget's method of testing conservation doesn't actually demonstrate what children are capable of. Children aged 4–6 conserved when the change was accidental, performing better than Piaget predicted. This supports Piaget's idea of age-related changes but not the age that conservation develops.

Messing up counters was not the only naughty thing that Teddy did.

Exam booster

So much Piaget

Piaget's theory takes up over half of this chapter, so it is important to read any exam question carefully so that you work out which 'bit' of Piaget it is referring to.

Evaluation

The sample	One weakness is that the sample only came from one UK city and a narrow age range. Their performance on Piaget's tasks may not reflect how all children would respond in these situations. Age changes were unclear given the narrow age range.
The change was not noticed	Another weakness is that children may not have noticed the change in the accidental condition. If the teddy actually took a counter away, children still said the rows were the same (Moore and Frye). This means it wasn't that the children weren't conserving, they were just distracted.
Challenges Piaget	One strength of the study is it challenges Piaget's view. McGarrigle and Donaldson's study implies that Piaget's original study confused young children. Therefore this study helped refine this type of child development research.

APPLY IT

Read the item below and then answer the questions that follow.

Mark and Nick are both very excited as their Dad has some lemonade for them as a special treat. Dad pours an equal amount of lemonade into two different shaped glasses – one glass is tall and thin and the other short and wide. Nick, aged four, gets upset when he is given the shorter glass. Mark, who is seven, tells his brother not to be so silly as they have the same amount of lemonade in their glasses.

1. Use your knowledge of the development of conservation to explain why Nick is upset but Mark isn't.   **[2 marks]**

2. Explain why Nick's reaction is not typical of all children of his age. Refer to McGarrigle and Donaldson's 'naughty teddy study' in your answer.   **[2 marks]**

KNOWLEDGE CHECK

1. Explain what is meant by the term 'conservation' in Piaget's stage theory.   **[2 marks]**

2. Outline the results of McGarrigle and Donaldson's 'naughty teddy study'.   **[2 marks]**

3. Describe and evaluate McGarrigle and Donaldson's 'naughty teddy study'.   **[9 marks]**

Classic study mix-up

Here is a typical 9-mark question.

Describe a study that investigated Piaget's theory of conservation.

Below are some sentences about the study by McGarrigle and Donaldson. You can use them to help you answer the exam-type question above, but they have become mixed up.

Put the numbers of the sentences in the right boxes below so that the answer makes sense.

Aim	Method	Results	Conclusion

1. When the researchers deliberately changed one of the rows, 41% of the children were able to conserve.

2. While the naughty teddy was playing, he 'messed up' one of the rows.

3. Piaget was right on the issue of age-related changes in conservation, but he was wrong about the age that conservation develops.

4. McGarrigle and Donaldson intended to find out if children's ability to conserve depended on whether or not a row of counters was deliberately changed.

5. This showed that Piaget's method of testing children limited what they could do.

6. Each child had to answer the following question before and after the teddy appeared: 'Is there more here or more here or are they both the same number?'.

7. Piaget also underestimated young children's thinking abilities.

8. The participants were children aged between four and six years.

9. When the row was changed accidentally (by naughty teddy), 68% of the children could conserve.

10. The researchers showed the children a 'naughty' teddy bear along with eight counters split into two rows of four.

11. The researchers also found that older children gave more correct answers than younger children.

Unjumble the AO3

There is an evaluation of Piaget's conservation theory lurking somewhere in the following sentences.

First, put the sentences together correctly (the first half is in the first column, the second half is in the second column).

Then, take the completed sentences and put them together into three elaborated evaluation points of three sentences each.

1. This means that how the children performed on the conservation task …

2. For example, Moore and Frye showed that if naughty teddy took a counter away …

3. This is a strength because the study helped to …

4. One weakness is that the children in the sample …

5. A strength of the study is that it challenges …

6. Another weakness is that the children might not have noticed …

7. The procedure that McGarrigle and Donaldson used suggests that …

8. This is a weakness because the age-related changes …

9. This is a weakness because it means the children were not actually conserving but instead …

A. … Piaget's original study confused young children.

B. … refine and progress research into children's conservation abilities.

C. … might not be how all children would perform in this situation.

D. … naughty teddy 'accidentally' changing one of the rows.

E. … they were just distracted.

F. … Piaget's theory of conservation.

G. … were from a narrow range of ages and just one city in the UK.

H. … the children still said that the rows were the same.

I. … were unclear given the narrow range.

The specification says...

Piaget's stage theory and the development of intelligence: Reduction of egocentricity. Hughes' 'policeman doll study'.

Hughes' 'policeman doll study'

Egocentrism	Egocentrism means to see the world only from one's own point of view.
	Piaget tested children with his three mountains task and concluded that they are egocentric until age 7.
Aim	Hughes aimed to create a test of egocentrism that would be more understandable to children younger than 7 years.
Method	Children aged 3½ to 5 years old were shown a model with two intersecting walls.
	The child was asked to hide one boy doll from one policeman doll to ensure they understood the task.
	The child's egocentrism was then tested by asking the child to hide the boy doll from two policemen.
Results	90% of the children aged 3 to 5 could hide the boy doll from two policemen.
	When a complex model was used with five or six walls, 60% of 3-year-olds and 90% of 4-year-olds hid the boy doll correctly.
Conclusion	The study shows that children aged 4 years are mostly not egocentric.
	Piaget underestimated younger children's abilities because his three mountains task didn't make sense to the children.

Egocentric? Moi??

Evaluation

More realistic	One strength of the study is that the task made better sense to children.
	Hiding from a policeman is easier to think about than selecting a view of a mountain top (Piaget's method).
	Thus it is a more realistic test of children's abilities.
Effects of expectations	One weakness is that the researchers' expectations may have influenced the children's behaviour.
	They may unconsciously have given the children cues how to behave in the policeman task.
	This could have caused the results to lack validity.
Challenges Piaget	Another strength of this study is it challenges Piaget's view.
	The results imply that Piaget's original study confused young children because the task didn't make sense to them.
	Therefore this study helped refine this type of child development research.

KNOWLEDGE CHECK

1. What is meant by the term 'egocentrism' in relation to Piaget's stage theory? **[2 marks}**
2. Outline what the participants were asked to do in Hughes' 'policeman doll study'. **[4 marks]**
3. Describe and evaluate **one** study that investigated egocentrism. **[9 marks]**

Exam booster

Don't forget the variables

An exam question might ask you to describe the method of Hughes' policeman study. Remember to comment on the independent and dependent variables by talking about the different conditions in the study and what is being measured across the two conditions.

APPLY IT – Research Methods

A psychologist decided to repeat Hughes' (1975) policeman doll study. She obtained a sample of 200 children aged between 3½ and 5 years. She found that 150 of the children were able to hide the boy doll from two policemen.

1. Calculate the fraction of children who could and could **not** hide the boy doll from two policemen. Show your workings. **[2 marks]**
2. The psychologist gathered quantitative data. Outline **one** weakness of using quantitative data in this study. **[3 marks]**
3. The psychologist wanted to ensure that the study was high in validity. Outline what is meant by 'validity' and what she could do to ensure high validity. **[4 marks]**

AO1 – Fill in the blanks

Fill in the blanks in the following description of egocentrism and Hughes' study. The words are given below if you get stuck, but try and do the activity without them first.

The term egocentrism refers to seeing the world only from your own _____.

Piaget used the three _____ task to show that children are egocentric in their thinking up to the age of _____ years. However, Hughes thought that Piaget's task was hard for young children to _____.

The children in his study were aged between 3½ and _____ years. They saw a simple model with two intersecting _____ and had to hide a boy doll from two _____ dolls. Hughes found that _____ of the children could successfully complete this task.

Hughes then used more complex models with 5 or 6 walls. _____ of three-year-old children and 90% of four-year-olds were able to hide the boy doll.

Hughes concluded that children as young as _____ years are mostly not egocentric in their thinking. This meant that Piaget _____ younger children's thinking abilities.

90%   5   viewpoint   policeman   4   understand

7   underestimated   walls   maintains   60%

Evaluate with trigger phrases

Here are some 'trigger' phrases related to Piaget's theory of egocentrism. The first thing to do is decide which phrases go together by putting them into pairs in the first two columns of the table.
Then write a sentence in column 3 for each pair without looking at your notes or elsewhere on the previous page.
Finally, write a further sentence in column 4, to explain why your first sentence is a strength/weakness.

What researchers' thought might happen affected children's behaviour

The findings were different from Piaget's original results

Challenges Piaget

Children were able to understand the task

More realistic

Effects of expectations

The specification says…

Piaget's stage theory and the development of intelligence: The four stages of development: sensorimotor, pre-operational, concrete operational and formal operational.

Stages of cognitive development

Stages of cognitive development	There are four stages of cognitive development.
	As the brain matures you can think in a different way and this happens in the same order in all children all over the world.
Sensorimotor stage **0–2 years approximately.**	Focus of development is on relating what is seen/heard (sensory) with movement (motor).
	Object permanence: children over 8 months believe that an object that is not visible still exists.
Pre-operational stage **2–7 years approximately.**	By 2 years, a toddler can walk but language is not fully developed.
	Children under age 7 can't think with consistent logic so are egocentric and lack conservation.
Concrete operational stage **7–11 years approximately.**	At 7 years, most children can conserve and show less egocentrism.
	Logical thinking is the key characteristic but can only be applied to physical items not objects or situations that cannot be seen.
Formal operational stage **11+ years.**	Children can come to conclusions about problems presented in an abstract form.
	They can focus on the form of an argument and not be distracted by its content.

Evaluation

Underestimated children's abilities	One weakness with Piaget's theory is that he underestimated children's abilities.
	Other research has found that younger children can show conservation and a reduction in egocentrism.
	This suggests that certain types of thinking develop earlier than he proposed.
Overestimated children's abilities	Another weakness is that Piaget also overestimated what children could do.
	He argued that 11-year-old children should be capable of abstract reasoning when other research (e.g. Wason's card task, see right) has found this is not true.
	This shows that not all children's thinking is as advanced as he suggested.
Basic idea is correct	One strength of Piaget's theory is that it does show that children's thinking changes with age.
	Although research shows that changes in thinking occur earlier, the fact remains that they still occur.
	Therefore the basic principle of the theory is valid.

Exam booster

Write in continuous prose

It is probably best not to bullet point your answers because it tends to restrict elaboration, and you need elaboration to pick up the top marks. If you are describing Piaget's theory for 4 marks, you should be aiming to write about 100 words of detail.

APPLY IT

Read the item below and then answer the question that follows.

Adam is teaching in a summer school and has children from the ages of 9 to 14 in his class. They all have to write a story about what they would do if they won the lottery. He finds that the children aged 12 to 14 tend to think of far more ideas than those aged 9 to 11.

- Use your knowledge of Piaget's stage theory to explain why the older children found this task less challenging. Refer to the formal operational stage in your answer. **[4 marks]**

KNOWLEDGE CHECK

1. Outline Piaget's sensorimotor stage of cognitive development. **[3 marks]**
2. Explain the difference in children's thinking in the pre-operational and the concrete operational stage of development. **[4 marks]**
3. Describe and evaluate Piaget's stage theory. **[9 marks]**

Wason's card task

Here are four cards, each with a letter or digit on each side of the card.

There is a rule: *If a card has a vowel on one face, then that card has an even number on the opposite face.*

What card or cards would you turn over to test this rule?

Answer at bottom right of next page.

True or false?

Here are some sentences about Piaget's theory of cognitive development. Indicate whether you think each one is true or false. For the false statements, write down the true versions in the spaces provided.

		True or false?	
1.	Piaget believed there are five stages of cognitive development.		
2.	Children all over the world pass through the stages in the same order.		
3.	The first stage of cognitive development is the concrete operational stage.		
4.	In the sensorimotor stage, children relate what they see and hear to movement.		
5.	Object permanence develops in the formal operational stage.		
6.	The pre-operational stage takes place between about two and seven years.		
7.	Children develop the ability to conserve during the sensorimotor stage.		
8.	Egocentric thinking is closely associated with the formal operational stage.		
9.	Formal operational thinking develops before concrete operational thinking.		
10.	In the concrete operational stage, children can think logically about objects that are not present.		
11.	Children in the formal operational stage can think in abstract terms.		
12.	Children in the formal operational stage focus more on the content of an argument than its form.		

Match the evaluation sentences

Match up the sentences to make three full evaluation points of three sentences each. Fill in the missing information.

1. For example, other studies (such as McGarrigle and _____) have found that younger children are able to _____ number and have less egocentric thinking.	**2.** This is a strength because it means the underlying _____ of the theory are valid.	**3.** This is a weakness because it suggests that some thinking develops _____ than Piaget believed.
4. This is a _____ because not all children's thinking is as developed as Piaget suggested.	**5.** A weakness of Piaget's theory is that he _____ children's real cognitive abilities.	**6.** One strength is that Piaget was able to show that children's thinking changes with _____.
7. Piaget was _____ about exactly when changes occur, because research shows he over- and underestimated children's abilities – but the differences are real.	**8.** Another _____ is that Piaget also sometimes overestimated what children can do.	**9.** For example, he believed that _____ reasoning is possible at age 11, but other studies (e.g. Wason's card task) have shown this is not true.

Answer for Wason's card task on page 57 is A and 7.

The specification says...

The role of Piaget's theory in education: Application of the four stages in education.

Description

Readiness	Piaget suggested that age-related changes mean you cannot teach a child something before they are biologically 'ready'. Activities should be at appropriate level for age.
Learning by discovery and the teacher's role	Children must discover concepts for themselves rather than rote-learn. Teachers plan lessons that challenge schemas so assimilation and accommodation occur, and thinking will develop.
Individual learning	Children go through the same developmental stages in the same order but at different rates, so classroom activities should be for individuals and groups of children rather than for the whole class.
Application to stages	Sensorimotor stage – Rich stimulating environment, sensory experiments to learn motor coordination. Pre-operational stage – Games that involve role play to reduce egocentricity. Discovery learning rather than written work. Concrete operational stage – Should be given concrete materials to manipulate. Cooking is good as it involves a logical sequence of instructions. Formal operational stage – Scientific experiments to develop logical thinking. Group discussions.

Marvin was self-discovering that his idea of cooking his wife a surprise birthday meal was not quite working out as he'd hoped.

Evaluation

Very influential	One strength is that Piaget's theory has had a positive impact on education in the UK. It led to schools taking on a more child-centred, activity-based approach. This has helped students learn more effectively.
Possible to improve with practice	One weakness of Piaget's theory is that it suggests that practice should not improve performance. In fact children's thinking can develop at an earlier age than expected if they are given enough practice on a task (Bryant and Trabasso). This suggests that children don't have to be 'ready'.
Traditional methods may be good	Another weakness is that discovery learning may not always be best. Bennett showed that formal teaching methods work best for maths, reading and English. This suggests that some parts of the curriculum are best delivered through direct instruction.

Exam booster

Extended writing questions

You will get two 9-mark questions on each exam paper. It is important to answer them well as they together are worth almost 20% of your mark on the paper, equivalent to two grade boundaries! One tactic is to answer them before you answer the other questions so that you make sure that you have enough time to complete them.

APPLY IT - Research Methods

Jack is interested in how experienced teachers apply Piaget's theory in the classroom. He decides to interview 20 teachers who had each taught for more than 10 years and ask them how they apply Piaget's stages in their teaching.

1. Explain **one** strength and **one** weakness of using an interview to collect his data.   [4 marks]

2. Write **one** question Jack could ask the teachers that would gather quantitative data and **one** question that would produce qualitative data.   [4 marks]

3. Explain whether Jack's research produces primary or secondary data in his study.   [2 marks]

KNOWLEDGE CHECK

1. Outline **two** ways in which a teacher could apply Piaget's theory in education.   [4 marks]

2. Explain **one** criticism of Piaget's application in education.   [4 marks]

3. Describe and evaluate how Piaget's theory has been applied to education.   [9 marks]

Be thorough

Here is typical 9-mark question: Describe and evaluate the role of Piaget's theory in education. *[9 marks].*

Plan a THOROUGH answer in the table below by responding to the statements in each box.

In your own words, summarise the theory in eight sentences, each sentence should have some detail and be about 10 words long.	*Explain a strength of the theory in three sentences – Point / Example / Conclusion*
•	
•	*Explain a weakness of the theory in three sentences – Point / Example / Conclusion*
•	
•	
•	*Explain a weakness of the theory in three sentences – Point / Example / Conclusion*
•	
•	
•	

Crossword

Complete the crossword to see how familiar you are with terms relating to the educational applications of Piaget's theories.

DOWN

1. Learning should be tailored to the I_____. (10)
2. Sometimes, direct I_____ is better than discovery learning. (11)
3. One of the ways thinking develops: A_____. (13)
4. The type of learning Piaget was keen on: D_____. (9)
7. The other way thinking develops: A_____. (12)
8. Mental structures are called S_____. (7)

ACROSS

5. Children can't learn until this happens R_____. (9)
6. L_____ thinking develops in the formal operational stage. (7)
9. Teachers could use R_____ P_____ to reduce egocentric thinking in the pre-operational stage. (4,4)
10. M_____ co-ordination develops in the sensorimotor stage. (5)
11. Children don't have to be ready to learn, they can improve through P_____. (8)
12. Good activity for concrete operational stage, C_____. (7)
13. Education became much more C_____ C_____ thanks to Piaget. (5,7)

The specification says...

The effects of learning on development: Dweck's Mindset Theory of learning: fixed mindset and growth mindset.

Description

Dweck's theory	The difference between people who are successful and not successful is their mindset.
Fixed mindset	People with a fixed mindset believe that abilities are fixed in the genes.
	They think that putting in extra effort won't help if someone is failing because success is talent-based.
	They are focused on performance goals and feel good when performing well.
Growth mindset	People with a growth mindset think you can always improve yourself with effort.
	They enjoy a challenge and don't focus on success.
	They focus on learning goals and feel good when working hard.
Dealing with failure	Fixed mindset – failure is due to lack of talent so no point trying harder.
	Growth mindset – failure is an opportunity to learn more and put in more effort.
A continuum	People are not simply one or the other but a mixture, on a continuum from fixed- to growth-oriented.
	Where you are on the continuum depends on the situation.

Evaluation

Research support	One strength is evidence that a growth mindset leads to better grades.
	Dweck found that seventh graders taught a growth mindset had better grades and motivation than a group who were just taught about memory.
	This suggests that the approach can improve performance.
Both mindsets involve praise	One weakness is just any sort of praise may be bad.
	Praising effort still leads people to do things for approval rather than doing it for themselves.
	Growth mindset can therefore discourage the type of independent behaviour it is trying to promote.
Real-world application	Another strength is good real-world application.
	Mindset is used to improve performance in schools, businesses, sports and relationships.
	Teaching people to see failure as a lack of effort rather than lack of talent motivates future effort.

Vernon had always had a growth mindset.

Exam booster

How much elaboration?

Not all evaluation needs to be well elaborated to gain top marks. If you are asked to briefly evaluate Dweck's mindset theory of learning for 5 marks, you could write one very detailed criticism and two others that are just reasonably detailed.

APPLY IT

Read the item below and then answer the question that follows.

Cristiano Ronaldo and David Bentley are both professional footballers. When they started their careers, both were deemed to have a lot of talent but it is only Ronaldo who has fulfilled his potential. Ronaldo worked tirelessly on his weaker areas, continuously set new goals for himself and was never afraid to try out new things on the pitch even if they did not come off. Bentley on the other hand thought he would never get any better than he was at 21 and so didn't train as hard, fell out of love with the game and ended up taking early retirement.

- Use your knowledge of Dweck's mindset theory to explain the differences between the two footballers' careers. **[4 marks]**

KNOWLEDGE CHECK

1. What is meant by the term 'fixed mindset'? **[2 marks]**
2. Outline the difference in the way a person with a growth mindset approaches learning compared to a person with a fixed mindset. **[3 marks]**
3. Describe and evaluate Dweck's mindset theory of learning. **[9 marks]**

Using examples to boost your AO1

Giving examples is a great way to add detail to your descriptions. In the boxes below, write down definitions of fixed and growth mindsets. Add examples to take your definitions further, including examples of how people with each kind of mindset deal with failure. Try to think of different examples from the ones on the previous page.

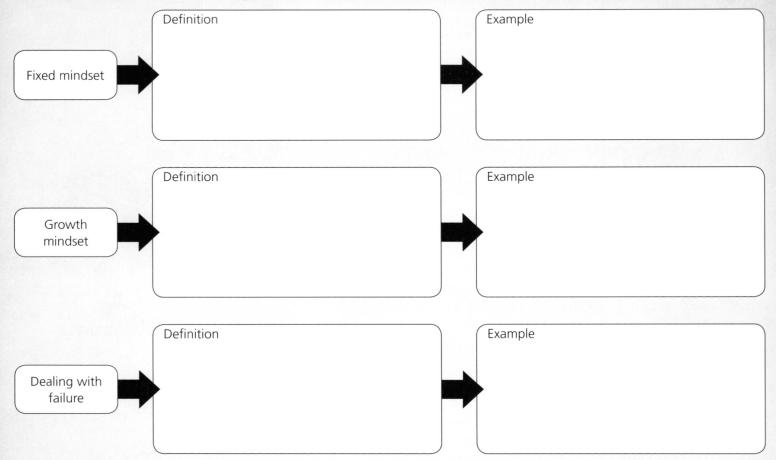

AO3 Match up

Work out which statements in the first column go with the statements in the second column.

1. Dweck's theory encourages us to praise effort but this can backfire.	**A.** Unfortunately this can have the opposite effect of discouraging the behaviour the theory is trying to promote.
2. Dweck's theory has applications in the real world.	**B.** These children achieved more than children who were just taught how to improve their memories.
3. There is some research evidence that supports Dweck's theory.	**C.** Taking this approach can help motivate people to make greater efforts in the future.
4. It is better to teach people to view failure as a lack of effort and not a lack of talent.	**D.** The concept of mindsets has been used in schools and organisations to improve performance.
5. A growth mindset is supposed to develop independent behaviour.	**E.** Doing this means that people are still working for the approval of others.
6. Dweck carried out a study to develop a growth mindset in seventh-graders.	**F.** Studies show that a growth mindset can lead to better grades.

The specification says…

The effects of learning on development: The role of praise and self-efficacy beliefs in learning.

Description

Positive effect of praise	Praise is a reward and makes someone feel good, so they repeat behaviours. Praise must fit performance and not be used for everything.
Praise effort rather than performance	Praising effort is motivating – it gives a sense of control as people can always put in more effort. Praising others for their performance is demotivating especially when you can't compete.
Self-efficacy	A person's belief in their own capabilities – related to the expectations that they have about future performance. Parents and teachers should create opportunities to experience success and therefore increase self-efficacy.
Effect of self-efficacy on motivation	Self-efficacy affects motivation because if it is high you will put in greater effort, persist longer, have greater task performance and more resilience than if you think you can't do it.

Well done! You've made it to page 63. You deserve a short break.
Did you enjoy it? Now turn to page 64.

Evaluation

Praise destroys internal motivation	One weakness with using praise to encourage learning is that it can have the opposite effect. Research by Lepper *et al.* found that children were less interested in doing a task if they had previously been rewarded for it. This suggests that praise can be demotivating.
Low self-efficacy can lower performance	One strength is that support for self-efficacy comes from research into the stereotype effect. Steele and Aronson found that African-American students scored lower on an IQ test if they had to indicate their race beforehand. This suggests that their performance was affected by how they expected to do, supporting the theory of self-efficacy.
Criticise effort instead of praising performance	Another strength is the value of understanding rewards. Dweck found that students who were criticised for their effort performed better on a test than those who had been previously praised. This shows that the kind of praise that is given is important.

Exam booster

Be synoptic when you can

Examiners are always very impressed when you can make links between areas of the specification. Some exam questions may ask you to do this anyway but even if they don't, it still looks good if you can elaborate on a point by making reference to a similar concept in another area. For example, praise plays a key part in Dweck's theory on the previous page as it suggests you need to praise the effort someone puts in rather than their performance. Mentioning this shows you understand the concept well which will boost your AO1 marks.

APPLY IT – Research Methods

A psychologist is interested in the effect of praise and levels of self-efficacy on success at school. He conducts a case study with a sample of 10 students and studies them across a year collecting mainly qualitative data.

1. Explain why the case study method is likely to be the most suitable research method to use in this study. **[3 marks]**

2. The psychologist gathers mostly qualitative data. Explain why qualitative data may be less reliable than quantitative data. **[3 marks]**

KNOWLEDGE CHECK

1. What is meant by the term 'self-efficacy'? **[2 marks]**
2. Outline the role of praise in learning. **[3 marks]**
3. Describe and evaluate the role of self-efficacy beliefs in learning. **[9 marks]**

AO1 – Step-by-step

Let's try and develop your AO1 for this topic step-by-step. Start by writing the basic descriptive point you want to make (in the first step). Then try adding a little bit more detail in the next step – explain what you mean, or use an example to illustrate the point you have made. If there is something else you can add to the point, then do so. Otherwise go on to the next point (the next step) and develop it in the same way.

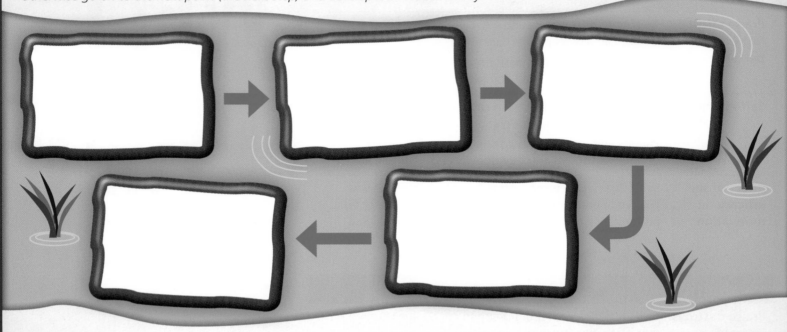

Elaborate your evaluation

Don't waste your AO3 points. Make the most of them by elaborating – develop and explain them fully, just like we do in this book. You can do this in this activity by using the trigger phrases to help you construct an evaluation. Try to do this without just copying from the book. The first one has been done for you.

1. A weakness Praise destroys internal motivation	*Using praise …* … is not always a good thing because sometimes it can backfire.	*Lepper …* … showed this when he found that children who were praised for their performance on a task showed less interest in it.	*This suggests that …* … praise can have the opposite effect to the one intended and be demotivating.
2. A strength	*Support comes from …*	*For example, Steele and Aronson …*	*This suggests that …*
3. Another strength	*Understanding rewards …*	*For example, Dweck …*	*This shows that …*

Description

What is a learning style?	People differ in how they learn. Matching teaching to a student's preferred learning style should improve learning.
Verbaliser	Someone who prefers to process information verbally, by hearing it or reading it. They remember best by repeating sounds, talking or writing in words.
Visualiser	Someone who prefers to process information visually, by seeing it – especially the spatial relationships. They remember best using diagrams, mind maps, graphs and charts. They find it more difficult to process written information.
Kinaesthetic learners	Someone who is a 'hands-on' learner, preferring active exploration, making things and experimenting. They prefer physical activities rather than watching others or reading.

Evaluation

A change from traditional methods	One strength of learning styles is that they have encouraged teachers to focus on other teaching methods rather than just traditional verbal ones. Teachers have thus been encouraged to adopt a more varied approach. This has benefited their students' learning.
No supporting evidence	One weakness is that there is little evidence to suggest that learning styles work. Pashler *et al.* reviewed many good quality research studies and found no support. This challenges the claim that learning styles improve performance.
Too many different styles	Another weakness is that there are too many learning styles. Coffield *et al.* identified 71 different types. This is a problem as it makes it difficult for people to work out their preferred learning style.

Mrs Jennings was regretting agreeing to cover the weekly anger management class.

Exam booster

Apply it
When you have an application question in the exam (such as the one below about Annie and Levi), remember to make reference to the stem of the question in your answer otherwise you will lose marks. Underline key words or phrases in the stem and then quote them in your answer, which will show the examiner that you are showcasing this application (AO2) skill.

APPLY IT

Read the item below and then answer the question that follows.

Annie and Levi have ordered a new bed online and are disappointed to find out that they have to assemble it when it arrives. Levi is dismayed at the quality of the instructions they have been given, which consist of a series of diagrams rather than a list of written instructions. Annie finds the diagrams easy to follow but Levi eventually gives up and lets her complete the job herself.

- Identify which learning style Annie and Levi seem to have. Give reasons for your answers in both cases. **[4 marks]**

KNOWLEDGE CHECK

1. Explain what is meant by the term 'learning style'. **[2 marks]**
2. Explain how visualisers would prefer to learn information. **[3 marks]**
3. Describe and evaluate learning styles. Refer to verbalisers and visualisers in your answer. **[9 marks]**

Fake learning styles news

Here are some fake news headlines for you. You need to rewrite them so they are true statements about learning styles. Once you've done that, explain the headline by writing the first sentence of the imaginary article that would appear underneath it.

Fake news title	Revised 'true' version	The first sentence of the imaginary article
1. Everyone learns in the same way, claim psychologists.		
2. Verbalisers like visual images, argue teachers.		
3. Verbalisers 'hands on', suggest scientists.		
4. Good evidence for learning styles, say learning styles fans.		

You are the teacher

Imagine you are a teacher for a minute. In each of your classes you have students with different learning styles. You have to plan your lessons so that each learning style is catered for. In this activity you will be delivering a lesson on the contents on this topic. Complete the table by explaining how you would do this for each learning style – what tasks could you set to match the content to the learning styles? Be as specific and detailed as possible.

In the third column, explain why this would help the students with each learning style.

At the end of this activity, evaluate by explaining two reasons why there is probably no need for you to go to all this trouble after all.

Verbaliser		
Visualiser		
Kinaesthetic learner		
Evaluation		

Description

Willingham's learning theory	Willingham criticises the theory of learning styles because of a lack of scientific evidence.
	He argues that we can improve learning by applying the results of scientific research in cognitive psychology and neuroscience.
Praise	Praising effort should be unexpected.
	Lepper *et al.* found that, if performance depends on praise, a person works to get the praise rather than to feel good.
Memory and forgetting	Memory research has found that forgetting often occurs because of a lack of the right cues (Tulving and Psotka).
	People should practise retrieving information from memory (Roediger and Karpicke).
Self-regulation	Self-control or self-regulation is being able to control your behaviour: your emotions, attention and cognitive processes. This has been assessed with the marshmallow test.
	Linked to better school progress (Shoda *et al.*).
Neuroscience	Brain waves in children and adults with dyslexia are different from those in people without dyslexia.
	If a specific pattern is associated with dyslexia they could receive help earlier, which will benefit progress (Willingham and Lloyd).

Evaluation

Evidence-based theory	One strength is the theory uses scientific evidence.
	The studies on which it was based were well-designed, objective investigations.
	This gives the claims of his theory greater validity.
Real-world application	Another strength of the theory is real-world applicability.
	Willingham has selected research that has clear relevance to education and has a better foundation than learning styles.
	His approach offers an explanation of what you learn (rather than how you learn).
Application of neuroscience	One weakness with Willingham's research is that dyslexia cannot just be diagnosed by observing people's brain waves.
	There would be a number of other causes that would need to be investigated.
	This makes it unlikely that brain waves would be used for diagnosis in this way.

KNOWLEDGE CHECK

1. Identify **two** features of Willingham's learning theory. **[2 marks]**
2. Explain **one** criticism of Willingham's learning theory. **[3 marks]**
3. Describe and evaluate Willingham's learning theory. Refer to Willingham's criticism of learning styles in your answer. **[9 marks]**

APPLY IT – Research Methods

A psychologist wants to investigate if people show more motivation if praise is given before or after completing a word search. Twenty participants are asked to do a word search. Ten of the participants will be praised before they start the word search and the other ten will be given praise afterwards. Motivation will be measured by the time taken to complete the word search.

1. Identify the independent and dependent variables. **[2 marks]**
2. Explain how the mean would be calculated for each group and how the two means might be used so that a conclusion could be drawn. **[4 marks]**
3. Identify and explain **one** extraneous variable that could have affected the psychologist's results. Explain how this variable could have been controlled. **[4 marks]**

Brain waves: smaller than tidal waves but bigger than microwaves.

Exam booster

Answer the question!

You could be asked to outline two criticisms of Willingham's learning theory for 4 marks. In order to gain full marks for this question you would need to make sure that you have identified and explained two relevant criticisms in the same amount of detail (e.g. approximately 40 words each). Any description of theory would gain no credit.

Willingham word search

There are ten words related to Willingham's learning theory for you to find in the grid below. They could be vertical, horizontal or diagonal (but not backwards).

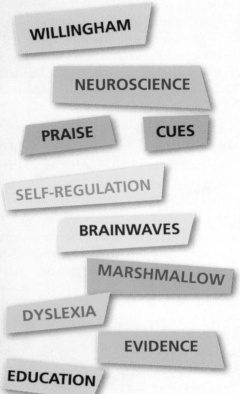

WILLINGHAM

NEUROSCIENCE

PRAISE   CUES

SELF-REGULATION

BRAINWAVES

MARSHMALLOW

DYSLEXIA

EVIDENCE

EDUCATION

D	S	W	J	P	C	I	J	J	P	O	D	R	Z	Q
H	Y	E	N	I	Z	S	W	D	Y	Q	V	G	I	M
W	E	B	L	E	O	U	A	X	M	L	G	V	E	G
W	I	D	R	F	U	A	E	R	R	S	Q	U	V	Z
K	A	L	U	A	R	R	S	F	A	V	A	D	I	S
D	H	Y	L	C	I	E	O	L	X	N	P	W	D	N
Y	M	J	P	I	A	N	G	S	F	Q	Y	T	E	I
S	H	B	S	R	N	T	W	U	C	H	V	M	N	S
L	Q	U	N	L	A	G	I	A	L	I	T	L	C	J
E	G	I	T	L	C	I	H	O	V	A	E	Y	E	K
X	W	B	Z	Z	V	C	S	A	N	E	T	N	J	Q
I	X	J	S	Y	H	U	O	E	M	D	S	I	C	P
A	T	C	T	Q	Z	E	C	Y	H	S	S	F	O	E
N	W	R	M	H	Y	S	T	U	O	U	Z	X	Z	N
B	G	A	Z	M	A	R	S	H	M	A	L	L	O	W

Visualising Willingham

Even if there is no evidence for learning styles, there's no doubt visual images can help you to learn. So for this activity, take each element of Willingham's theory and turn it into an image (preferably a memorable one), using these frames.

PRAISE   MEMORY   SELF-REGULATION   NEUROSCIENCE

Formulation of testable hypotheses: Null hypothesis and alternative hypothesis.

Types of variable: Independent variable and dependent variable.

Types of variable: Extraneous variable.

Research procedures: The use of standardised procedures, instructions to participants, randomisation and extraneous variables (including explaining the effect of extraneous variables and how to control for them).

Description

We have a theory …	A theory is a suggested explanation for behaviour. Psychologists test theories using objective research methods.	
Formulating an aim	A general statement that explains the purpose of a study.	
Variables	Anything that can change or vary within a study.	
	Independent variable (IV)	The variable that the experimenter is deliberately changing. There are usually two levels of the IV to enable comparisons.
	Dependent variable (DV)	What is measured by the researcher. The only thing that should affect the DV is the change in the IV.
	Operationalisation	It is important that variables are measurable, so we identify some clear operational instructions.
	Extraneous variables (EVs)	Unwanted variables that could affect the DV if not controlled. For example noise, temperature, lighting. Controlled best in a laboratory.
Formulating a testable hypothesis	A clear and precise testable statement. Relationship + DV + two levels of the IV.	
	Alternative hypothesis	A statement of the relationship or difference between variables.
	Null hypothesis	A statement of no relationship or no difference between variables.
Research procedures	Instructions to participants	Standardised instructions = giving each participant exactly the same information about the study to ensure what is said to them does not act as an EV.
	Standardised procedures	Researcher uses exactly the same methods and instructions for all participants.
	Randomisation	Using chance (e.g. tossing a coin) to control for bias.

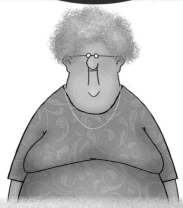

Ms Ivy Devy – a way to remember that the IV comes first and then you measure the DV.

Exam booster

Operationalise

Remember to operationalise the IV and DV when writing a hypothesis in an exam answer. Students who clearly state how both of these variables are measured give themselves a greater chance of getting full marks for this type of question.

APPLY IT – Research Methods

Researchers wanted to see how room temperature affects student performance. To test this, one group of students took a psychology test in a room where the temperature was 30 degrees whilst a different group of students sat the same test in a room with a normal room temperature (20 degrees).

1. Identify the independent and dependent variables in this study. Each variable must be operationalised. **[2 marks + 2 marks]**

2. Identify an extraneous variable in this study and explain how it could have been controlled by the researchers. **[3 marks]**

3. Write a suitable alternative hypothesis for this study. **[2 marks]**

KNOWLEDGE CHECK

1. What is a null hypothesis? **[1 mark]**
2. Explain why extraneous variables are controlled in experiments. **[2 marks]**
3. Outline how randomisation is achieved. **[2 marks]**

Give the IV and DV

Here are some hypotheses for potential psychology studies. Write down the levels of the IV and DV as precisely as possible (don't just repeat the wording in the hypothesis where you can avoid it). We have done the first two for you.

	IV	DV
1. Drug A affects memory.	Presence or absence of Drug A.	Amount remembered.
2. Bulls charge more often when presented with a red rag than when presented with a blue rag.	Whether a red rag or a blue rag is shown.	Number of charges.
3. First children learn to speak earlier than second children.		
4. Men drive faster than women.		
5. Lack of sleep affects learning in ten-year-old boys.		
6. A baby under eight months of age will not search for a hidden object.		
7. Social class affects IQ scores.		
8. Time of day affects alertness.		
9. People learn fewer words in silent conditions than in noisy ones.		
10. Handled rats learn a maze faster than do non-handled rats.		

Directional or non-directional?

Here are some hypotheses – some are directional and some non-directional. Identify which is which. To extend this activity, rewrite the directional hypotheses to make them non-directional (and the non-directional ones to make them directional).

Hypothesis	D or ND?	Rewrite
1. Alcohol affects reaction time.		
2. Men who have beards are perceived as older than clean-shaven men.		
3. Boys are more aggressive than girls.		
4. Watching tropical fish helps you relax.		
5. The faster you type, the more mistakes you make.		
6. Individuals are more likely to conform when in groups of five than when in pairs.		
7. Anxiety affects the level of adrenaline in the blood.		
8. People's running speed will be affected by whether or not they have an audience.		
9. Wearing make-up has an effect on how attractive a person is rated to be.		

Description and evaluation

Quantitative and qualitative methods	Quantitative methods use data that can be counted. Qualitative methods use data that can be expressed in words and are non-numerical, such as a description.
Experiments	Experiments use quantitative data. They look at a measurable change in the DV which has been caused by different levels of the IV. All experiments have an IV and a DV.
Laboratory experiments An experiment conducted in a controlled environment. Experimenter manipulates the IV.	+ EVs can be controlled. Therefore researcher can be sure the IV caused the DV. Cause and effect can be established. + Standardised procedures can be used. So study can be replicated. Can test validity of results. − Environment is not like everyday life. So participants' behaviour is less 'typical'. So can't generalise results to wider world. − Participants may know they are being tested and change behaviour to help experimenter. This means data may not be valid.
Field experiments An experiment conducted in a natural setting. Experimenter manipulates the IV.	+ Often more realistic than laboratory experiments, because participants not aware they are being studied. Enhances validity of the results. + Some control over EVs, because it is possible to use standardised procedures. This means cause-and-effect conclusions are more valid. − Researcher may lose control of some EVs because of real-life setting. This makes it more difficult to show cause and effect. − There may be ethical issues. People may not know they are involved in an experiment. This means they cannot give their informed consent.
Natural experiment An experiment conducted in a natural or laboratory setting. Experimenter does not manipulate the IV. It would have changed anyway.	+ Usually high validity, because variables are naturally occurring and relate to everyday life. However, this is not always the case, e.g. when IV is male versus female behaviour DV tested in controlled conditions (lab). + DV is often tested in a lab. Therefore, EVs can be well controlled because standardised procedures can be followed. − Few opportunities for this kind of research, because it sometimes relies on natural events that occur infrequently (e.g. children who have no TV at home versus those who do). This reduces usefulness of the method. − There may be EVs that could affect the results. For example, unique characteristics of the participants cannot be controlled because they cannot be randomly allocated to groups.

KNOWLEDGE CHECK

1. Distinguish between a natural and field experiment. **[3 marks]**

2. Using an example, explain what is meant by a 'natural experiment'. **[3 marks]**

3. Explain **one** strength and **one** weakness of a laboratory experiment. **[4 marks]**

The specification says...

Designing research: Quantitative and qualitative methods.
Laboratory experiments, field and natural experiments.
Strengths and weaknesses of each research method and types of research for which they are suitable.

A field experiment. Literally.

Exam booster

Understanding the difference

Many people believe that lab experiments have low relevance to the real world but field and natural experiments are more like everyday life. **But this is not always true.** For example, in Milgram's study, obedience was being tested and a realistic authority relationship could be set up quite well in the lab. In some field experiments participants are aware their behaviour is being measured and this may mean they do not behave 'normally'. In a natural experiment the DV may be measured in the lab, reducing the naturalness of the study.

APPLY IT – Research Methods

Identify which type of experiment is used in each of these studies. Explain your answer in each case.

1. A study investigating whether students in a library like a librarian more depending on whether she touches their hands or not when she returns their books. **[2 marks]**

2. Participants were asked to give attractiveness ratings to a picture of a woman when her pupils were either dilated or not. **[2 marks]**

3. Some researchers investigated the impact of a televised boxing match on murder rates in America. The found that murder rates were higher in the week after the match in comparison to the week before. **[2 marks]**

True or false?

What do you know about experiments? Find out by identifying which of the following statements are true and which are false. For the false ones, write them so that they are true (and briefly explain why).

		True or false?	
1.	Experiments usually produce qualitative data.		
2.	All experiments have an IV and DV.		
3.	Laboratory experiments are not very good at controlling extraneous variables.		
4.	It is easier to replicate a field experiment than a laboratory experiment.		
5.	It is easier to generalise results from a laboratory experiment than a field experiment.		
6.	The experimenter manipulates the IV in a field experiment.		
7.	It is harder to show cause-and-effect in a laboratory experiment than a field experiment.		
8.	Participants always give their informed consent in field experiments.		
9.	Natural experiments always take place in real-life situations.		
10.	The most commonly used type of experiment in psychology is the natural experiment.		

What's the difference?

There are three types of experiment and they have some important differences. But what are they? There are four features identified in the table. Briefly explain how each one applies to the types of experiment indicated.

Then finally explain what the difference is between the two (that's the hard bit).

1. Allocation to conditions	In a lab experiment …	In a natural experiment …	So the difference is …
2. Control of EVs	In a lab experiment …	In a field experiment …	So the difference is …
3. Standardised procedures	In a field experiment …	In a natural experiment …	So the difference is …
4. Replication	In a lab experiment …	In a field experiment …	So the difference is …

Description and evaluation

Independent groups	Separate groups of people for each level of the IV.
	There is usually a control and experimental group.
	+ Order effects are not a problem. The participants only do the task once. This means they won't benefit from practice.
	− There are different participants in each group. This means that participant variables may affect the results and act as an EV. This reduces the validity of the results.
	Dealing with participant variables: Allocation to conditions.
	Use a random way of allocating the participants to the conditions (e.g. flipping a coin) or using a systematic method (e.g. placing every other person in the control group).
Repeated measures	All participants take part in all the conditions.
	There is usually an experimental and a control condition.
	+ There are no participant variables. Each participant is compared against themselves rather than other people. This enhances the validity of the results.
	+ Fewer participants are needed. In an independent groups design you need twice as many participants to get the same number of data items. This makes repeated measures less expensive.
	− Order effects occur when participants are tested twice. The order in which they do the tasks may make a difference, e.g. a practice effect. This affects the validity of the results.
	Dealing with order effects: Counterbalancing.
	Half the participants complete the conditions in one order, and the other half in the opposite order.
Matched pairs	Participants paired on relevant variables.
	Participants are then matched and one member of each pair goes in each group.
	+ There are no order effects as participants are tested only once.
	+ There are fewer participant variables. This is because those taking part are matched on a variable that is important for the experiment. This enhances the validity of the results.
	− Matching participants takes time and effort. It doesn't control all participant variables. This means it may not be worthwhile.

Exam booster

RIM

Use this acronym to help you remember the three experimental designs: **R**epeated measures, **I**ndependent groups, **M**atched pairs.

APPLY IT – Research Methods

To test the effect of drinking coffee with caffeine on the alertness of drivers a group of 20 participants were recruited who had all been driving for at least ten years. They took a computer-based driving awareness test where they were assessed on how many hazards they identified in a five-minute period. All participants were then given one cup of caffeinated coffee and had to re-sit the test again to see if there was any difference in their performance.

1. Identify the type of experimental design used in this study. Explain your answer **[2 marks]**

2. Explain **one** weakness of the experimental design that you have identified in question 1. **[2 marks]**

3. Explain how the researcher could have reduced the impact of the problem you identified in question 2. **[2 marks]**

4. Explain how this study could have been carried out using a matched pairs design. **[3 marks]**

ABBA, named after a method of counterbalancing order effects. ... Not really.

KNOWLEDGE CHECK

1. Explain why counterbalancing is needed in a repeated measures design. **[2 marks]**
2. What is a matched pairs design? **[2 marks]**
3. Evaluate independent measures design. **[4 marks]**

Four-column match-up

Match up the statements across the four columns.

Independent groups	(1) All participants carry out both conditions of the IV.	(5) An example of this problem is a practice effect.	(9) This design involves the most time and effort.
Repeated measures	(2) A problem with repeated measures.	(6) Each participant is 'linked' to another across both conditions.	(10) Solved by counterbalancing.
Matched pairs	(3) Different groups of participants for each level of the IV.	(7) This design uses the fewest participants.	(11) A solution to this problem is random allocation to conditions.
Order effects	(4) Researcher identifies relevant variables that could affect the DV.	(8) Participant variables are a problem.	(12) Each participant acts as their own 'control'.

Which would you choose?

For each of the studies in the table, decide which experimental design would be used – independent groups, repeated measures or matched pairs. Then briefly explain why. Sometimes more than one design might be appropriate – it all depends on your explanation.

A study to …	Which would you choose?	Why?
1. … see if there is a difference in the ability of grey and white rats in learning to run a maze.		
2. … investigate whether a twin born first is more confident than a second-born twin.		
3. … see if watching violent television programmes is likely to make children aggressive.		
4. … investigate whether people are more likely to make a risky decision when they are in a group than when they are alone.		
5. … assess the effectiveness of a treatment for fear of spiders, comparing a treatment group with a non-treatment group.		
6. … see if the sex of a child affects how much rough and tumble play they engage in.		
7. … assess whether CBT or antidepressant medication is a more effective treatment for depression.		
8. … see if a list of words organised into categories is better recalled than a list of randomly arranged words.		
9. … investigate whether students are more alert in the morning or the afternoon.		

Topic 4 Sampling methods

The specification says...

Sampling methods:
Target populations, samples and sampling methods and how to select samples using these methods: random, opportunity, systematic and stratified.
Strengths and weaknesses of each sampling method.
Understanding principles of sampling as applied to scientific data.

Description and evaluation

Target populations and samples	The group of people the researcher is studying. Sample of participants from target population.
Generalisation	The sample should be representative so we can generalise to the target population.
Bias	It is difficult to select a group of participants that perfectly reflects the target population.
Random sampling	Putting names of all members of the target population into a hat/computer program so that every member of the target population has an equal chance of being selected.
	+ There is no bias. Every person in target population has equal chance of being selected. So sample more representative.
	− Takes more time and effort than other methods. This is because you need to obtain a list of all the members of your target population and then randomly select them. The effort may not be worth it.
Opportunity sampling	Selecting most readily available group of people.
	+ Easy, quick and cheap to carry out because you simply choose people who are nearby. This makes the method less expensive.
	− Sample likely to be unrepresentative of the population. This is because the sample is drawn from one place. This reduces the generalisability of the results.
Systematic sampling	Selecting every nth person from a list of all the people in the target population.
	+ Avoids researcher bias. The researcher has no say over who is selected. This makes it more representative.
	− May still be biased. Sample may consist of one particular group of people. This decreases the representativeness.
Stratified sampling	Selecting participants in proportion to their frequency in the target population.
	+ Most representative method. All subgroups are represented in proportion to the numbers in the target population. This enhances representativeness.
	− Very time-consuming. It may take a while to identify proportions of subgroups and then recruit participants. This discourages researchers from using this method.

The attempt to produce a representative sample had not gone as well as hoped ...

Exam booster

Representativeness versus time

An easy way to remember the evaluation points of the four different sampling methods is by sorting them in terms of how long they will take to do and also how representative a sample they produce. For example, opportunity sampling is the least time consuming to do (a strength) but will give you the least representative sample (a weakness).

APPLY IT - Research Methods

A psychologist believed that eating chocolate made people happier. He recruited the 20 students in his psychology class on a Monday morning. After finding some initial support for his hypothesis, the researcher decided to carry out the study on a larger scale by taking a systematic sample of 100 people from the 10,000 students attending the university.

1. Identify the sampling method that the researcher first used at the start of this study. Explain your answer. **[2 marks]**

2. Describe how the researcher could have selected his systematic sample. **[2 marks]**

3. Explain why systematic sampling would be more suitable for this investigation. **[2 marks]**

KNOWLEDGE CHECK

1. What is meant by the term 'target population'? **[1 mark]**

2. What is the difference between a random and opportunity sample? **[3 marks]**

3. Outline **one** weakness of a stratified sample. **[3 marks]**

Sampling methods wordsearch

There are ten words related to sampling methods for you to find in the grid below. They could be vertical, horizontal or diagonal (but not backwards).

POPULATION

SAMPLE

BIAS

REPRESENTATIVE

GENERALISATION

RANDOM

OPPORTUNITY

SYSTEMATIC

STRATIFIED

PROPORTION

W	Y	D	W	M	B	J	P	S	G	A	F	P	U	Q
C	W	A	O	Y	G	F	O	R	I	J	W	S	T	U
R	E	P	R	E	S	E	N	T	A	T	I	V	E	Y
R	U	L	T	L	M	T	C	G	L	L	K	P	R	S
B	S	Q	P	R	O	P	O	R	T	I	O	N	N	Y
I	A	P	O	P	P	O	R	T	U	N	I	T	Y	S
A	M	A	O	M	M	I	S	M	V	G	J	R	W	T
S	P	R	N	P	D	O	F	E	I	W	E	D	Y	E
T	L	A	K	Z	U	B	I	B	E	L	G	P	D	M
G	E	N	E	R	A	L	I	S	A	T	I	O	N	A
F	S	D	S	V	K	H	A	F	W	M	T	G	N	T
C	V	O	M	N	Y	K	N	T	T	X	C	Z	M	I
W	Z	M	K	S	T	R	A	T	I	F	I	E	D	C
T	I	N	P	E	P	I	Q	H	I	O	C	W	X	J
T	G	K	P	W	Z	X	G	R	E	C	N	E	X	H

Draw your sample (geddit?!)

Drawing a picture is a really good way of helping you to remember the different sampling methods. Think about the main features of each method, and then have a go at illustrating them with a picture.

Another good way to remember something is to create a mnemonic – something that helps memory. Take the first letter of each method – R O S S – and try to create a memorable sentence of four words. Here's a suggestion: *Really Orange Satsumas Stink*. But you can do much better than that (make it rude – it usually helps).

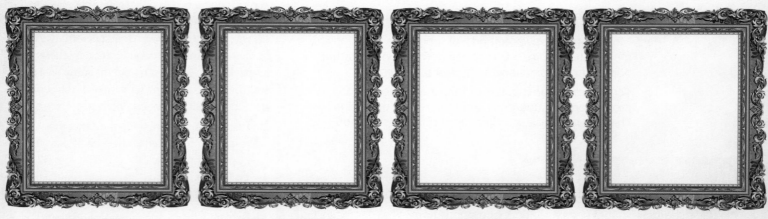

RANDOM   **OPPORTUNITY**   **SYSTEMATIC**   **STRATIFIED**

Description

Ethical issues in psychology	A conflict between participants' rights and well-being and the need for researchers to gain valuable findings. The well-being of participants needs to be protected at all times.
Informed consent	At the start of a study participants should be given information about the purpose of the study, so an informed decision can be made. Participants told they can leave at any time (right to withdraw). If the researcher doesn't reveal the aim at the start, participants must be informed at the end.
Deception	Participants should not be lied to or misled about the aims of the study without justification. Mild deception is justifiable. Major deception is used but only when the benefits outweigh the ethical cost.
Protection from harm	Participants' physical and psychological safety should be protected at all times. Stress and embarrassment are included in this. Participants must be reminded they can leave at any time.
Privacy	Participants have the right to control information about themselves. It is acceptable to observe people in public places but a public place can be quite private, e.g. a conversation in a restaurant.
Confidentiality	Personal data should be protected and respected.

Ways of dealing with ethical issues

The BPS guidelines	A code of conduct that every professional psychologist in the UK has to follow in order to deal with ethical issues in their research.
Dealing with informed consent	Participants (or guardians for children under 16) sign a form that outlines the research procedures. If this is not possible at the start, they sign a form at the end of the study (retrospective consent).
Dealing with deception and protection from harm	Participants offered right to withdraw during study and right to withdraw data at the end. Participants given a full debriefing at the end of an investigation to explain the true aims and/or reduce any distress. May be offered counselling.
Dealing with privacy and confidentiality	Keep data safe. All participants should be anonymous. They can be referred to by a number or initials.

KNOWLEDGE CHECK

1. What is meant by an 'ethical issue'? **[2 marks]**
2. Outline **two** ethical issues psychologists must consider when conducting their research. **[4 marks]**
3. Explain how researchers could deal with **one** ethical issue. **[3 marks]**

The specification says...

Ethical considerations:
Students should demonstrate a knowledge and understanding of:

- Ethical issues in psychological research as outlined in the British Psychological Society guidelines.
- Ways of dealing with each of these issues.

Exam booster

Don't forget the second part of the question

Research methods questions often come in two parts. For example, 'outline a particular ethical issue in psychological research and explain how the researchers could have dealt with it' [2 marks + 2 marks]. Make sure you answer both parts of the question.

When is a public place private?

APPLY IT – Research Methods

A study found that participants would eat disgusting flavoured biscuits if a recognised authority figure ordered them to do so. The participants thought the study was on food tasting when actually it was one into obedience to unjust commands.

1. Identify **two** ethical issues in this study and for each one explain how the researcher could have dealt with them.

[2 marks + 2 marks + 2 marks]

2. The researchers wanted to repeat the study with a group of 14 year olds to see if there were any age differences in obedience. Explain how they would have dealt with issues surrounding informed consent in this follow-up study.

[2 marks]

Broken ethics

Below are some sentences about the ethical considerations in psychology. They have become broken and muddled up, but you can put them back together again by matching the first half of each sentence in the left-hand column with the second half in the right-hand column.

1. Ethical issues arise because …	**A.** … they have the right to withdraw at any time.
2. Getting informed consent from participants means …	**B.** … they should be fully debriefed at the end of the study.
3. Even if participants consent to take part …	**C.** … avoiding causing them stress and embarrassment.
4. It is ethically acceptable to deceive participants …	**D.** … is one way of dealing with the issue of consent.
5. Protecting participants from physical and psychological harm includes …	**E.** … protected and kept confidential.
6. Participants can be observed in some public places but …	**F.** … giving them important information at the start of the study.
7. The data provided by participants should be …	**G.** … produces a code of conduct for psychologists in the UK.
8. The British Psychological Society …	**H.** … as long as the benefits of the study justify it.
9. Getting participants to sign a form at the start of the study …	**I.** … they also have a right to privacy.
10. If participants are deceived …	**J** … there is a conflict between participants' well-being and researchers' desire for useful findings.

Ethical mnemonic

There are a few ethical issues for you to remember, so this is an ideal topic for a mnemonic. The first table helps you to do this. Take the first letter of each issue and create a memorable sentence (or change the order if it helps).

Then have a go at the mini quiz below the first table.

Consent	C	
Deception	D	
Protection	P	
Privacy	P	
Confidentiality	C	

Give two ways to …	
… get consent.	
… protect participants from harm.	
… ensure confidentiality.	

The specification says...

Designing research: Interviews, questionnaires. Strengths and weaknesses of each research method and types of research for which they are suitable.

Interviews – Description and evaluation

Interviews	Face-to-face, real-time contact. Can take place over the phone or via text.
Structured interviews	Interviewer reads out a list of prepared questions. Follow-up questions may also be prepared beforehand.
Unstructured interviews	Interviewer has a general aim, but few if any questions are prepared in advance. New questions based on previous answers.
Semi-structured interviews	Some questions decided in advance. Follow-up questions emerge from the answers.
Evaluation	+ Interviews produce a lot of information from each person. Especially true of unstructured interviews. Means that unexpected results may occur.
	+ Insight can be gained into thoughts and feelings. Observations only show what people do. Interviews (and questionnaires) provide a different perspective.
	− Data can be difficult to analyse. This is because of the breadth of information collected. Clear conclusions difficult.
	− People are less comfortable giving personal information face-to-face. Especially if questions are on a sensitive topic. Limits information collected.

As the only interviewee, Norman felt he had an excellent chance of getting the job. Unfortunately – as would become all too clear six hours later – he had turned up on the wrong day.

Questionnaires – Description and evaluation

Questionnaires	A prepared list of written questions which can be completed face-to-face or in writing, over the phone or on the Internet.
Open and closed questions	Open questions tend to produce qualitative data as participants can answer them how they wish. Closed questions produce quantitative data – fixed range of possible answers, e.g. 'yes' or 'no'.
Evaluation	+ Researcher gets information from lots of people relatively quickly. This is because a questionnaire can be sent to many people. So generalisations easier to make.
	+ Data tends to be easier to analyse than interviews. This is when closed questions are used. Easier to draw conclusions.
These weaknesses apply to interviews as well.	− Respondents may not give truthful answers. This social desirability bias affects validity of responses. Reduces validity of data collected.
	− Questions may be unclear or leading. This makes it difficult to answer questions. So participants' responses may lack validity.

Exam booster

Design your own study

You could be asked to design a study in an exam question, so a good way to review any topic is to design a study. For example, design a questionnaire on the influence of social media on the mental health of young people. Not only will that give you practice on the 'design a study' questions but you will also revise what you know about questionnaires – and about mental health issues.

APPLY IT – Research Methods

A study investigated whether men or women in romantic relationships were more unfaithful to their partners. The researchers interviewed 50 participants and asked them the same ten questions about their relationships. The researchers then compared the various responses to each of the ten questions.

1. What feature of the above study suggests that the researchers were using a structured interview?   **[1 mark]**

2. Explain **one** problem of doing an unstructured interview in this study.   **[2 marks]**

3. Explain why a questionnaire would be a more suitable method of collecting data than an interview in this study.   **[3 marks]**

KNOWLEDGE CHECK

1. Outline **one** advantage and **one** disadvantage of using interviews in psychological research.   **[4 marks]**

2. Explain **one** difference between semi-structured and unstructured interviews.   **[2 marks]**

3. Describe and evaluate the use of interviews in psychological research.   **[9 marks]**

Self-report anagrams

Here are nine anagrams of words related to this topic. There are some clues to help you if you need them.

1.	UNCUREDSTRUT NEWERVISIT		Interviewer has a general aim but not many prepared questions.
2.	MIES-DUSTRRECTU		A combination of of two kinds of interview.
3.	THISGIN		Interviews provide _____ into thoughts and feelings.
4.	SIEVENITS		If the topic is _____, an interview could be a problem.
5.	SENORITASEQUIN		A self-report method that isn't an interview.
6.	NOPE NOSEQUITS		People can answer these as they wish.
7.	QUIETLATVIA		The kind of data produced when people express themselves in words.
8.	EASINGLIERATONS		These are possible because questionnaires are sent out to many people.
9.	OILSAC BIRDIESITALY		When people give you the answers they think make them look good.

Which is best?

First of all, identify a similarity and a difference between interviews and questionnaires, following the headings in the table (you can use a structured or unstructured interview).

Then explain which method would be best to use in the scenarios provided below.

An interview …	A questionnaire …	So the similarity is …
An interview …	A questionnaire …	So the difference is …

Scenario	Interview or questionnaire?	Why?
Finding out the difference in moral attitudes between males and females.		
Comparing the weekly average calorie intake for teenagers and over 60s.		
Collecting eyewitness testimony following an accident in school.		

Description and evaluation

Observation studies	A researcher watches or listens to participants, and records data.	
Types of observation	Naturalistic versus controlled	Naturalistic observation is recorded in a place where it would normally occur and nothing is changed in the environment.
		If a level of control is needed a controlled observation will be used, e.g. Zimbardo's prison study or Kendon's study of conversation.
	Covert versus overt	Covert observation = participants are not aware their behaviour is being recorded.
		Overt observation = participants are told in advance.
	Participant versus non-participant	Participant observation = researcher becomes part of the group s/he is studying.
		Non-participant observation = researcher remains separate from the people s/he is studying.
Categories of behaviour	The observer breaks the target behaviour into different types of behaviour.	
	Each type/category should be observable and obvious so that it can be counted each time it occurs.	
	For example, flirting behaviours could be broken down into four categories: eye contact, smiling, laughing, touching.	
Interobserver reliability	Two observers should produce same observations.	
	To establish interobserver reliability the researcher creates categories of behaviour, observers record the same sequence of behaviour, then they compare their data (correlate) and talk over differences and amend categories.	
Evaluation	+ Observation data are based on what people do rather than what they say they do! This enhances the validity of the conclusions.	
	+ Observation studies look at real-life behaviour. People may not be aware they are being observed. Therefore, the data collected will have greater validity.	
	− There may be ethical issues. You cannot always gain people's consent when observing them in public places. This means that some observations should not be conducted.	
	− There may be observer bias. Observer's expectations can influence what they see. Therefore, the observations may lack validity.	

KNOWLEDGE CHECK

1. Briefly explain why categories of behaviour are necessary in observation studies.   **[2 marks]**

2. Outline how psychologists could check interobserver reliability in their observation.   **[4 marks]**

3. Explain **one** weakness of using an observation to carry out research.   **[3 marks]**

The specification says...

Designing research: Observation studies (including categories of behaviour and interobserver reliability). Strengths and weaknesses of the research method and types of research for which it is suitable.

Something told Snowy the Police Dog that his cover had been blown.

APPLY IT – Research Methods

Some students investigated gender differences in driving behaviour. They hid behind a bush at the entrance to their school and noted the gender of the driver of each car that entered the campus.

1. Identify the type of observation in this study. Explain your answer.   **[2 marks]**

2. Explain why this would be regarded as a covert observation.   **[1 mark]**

3. Explain why a covert observation might be preferable to an overt observation in this study.   **[2 marks]**

4. The students looked at whether people indicated or not when turning. Suggest **two** other categories of behaviour that could represent driving ability.   **[2 marks]**

5. Explain how the students could have checked reliability of their observations.   **[2 marks]**

Put it right

*The passage below is a description of the observation method. Unfortunately, eight mistakes have crept into it.
Your task is to identify the errors and correct them.*

In an observation study a researcher watches or listens to participants and records data. There are several different types of observation.

For example, artificial observation takes place in a situation where the behaviour being observed would normally occur. The observer makes an attempt to alter the environment. On the other hand, Milgram's prison study is an example of a controlled observation.

In overt observation, participants are not aware they are being observed and their behaviour ignored. But in covert observation, participants know in advance they are being observed.

In participant observation, the observer is not part of the group she or he is studying. The participants might know this (overt) or they might not (covert). In non-participant observation the researcher stays apart from the people they are studying.

The observer breaks target behaviour down into participants. These must be observable and obvious with no overlap so the behaviour can be counted each time it happens.

Observe the differences

*For each observational study in the table, indicate what type you think it is.
But beware, for each study there are actually three answers (for example it could be non-participant, controlled and covert). Give a brief explanation of your response.*

Study	Type(s)?	Why?
1. A researcher secretly joins a religious cult to see if people are being brainwashed.		
2. A researcher watches primary school children in a special playroom with the same toys each time through a two-way mirror to investigate co-operation.		
3. A psychologist observes the crowd at a football match using footage from CCTV recordings. These were recorded by cameras that were obvious to the people in the crowd.		
4. A researcher observes student behaviour in class by enrolling on a psychology degree course and pretending to be a mature student.		
5. The head of a psychology department observes an A level class by watching the lesson at an agreed time, sitting at the back of the room.		
6. With the permission of the headteacher, two psychologists observe children in a local school playground, to measure the time they spent in various play activities.		

Description and evaluation

Association between two variables	Correlations show how things are linked together.
	They tell us the strength and direction of the association or relationship between co-variables.
Co-variables	Correlations are quantitative so co-variables are reduced to numbers.
	For example, aggression could be reduced to how aggressive a person is on a scale of 1–10.
Scatter diagrams	Correlations are plotted on a scatter diagram.
	One co-variable goes on the x-axis and the other one goes on the y-axis. A dot is placed where they meet.
	Shows direction and strength of the correlation.
Types of correlation	Positive correlation As one co-variable increases the other co-variable increases. For example, number of people in a room and noise.
	Negative correlation As one co-variable increases the other decreases. For example, number of people in a room and amount of personal space.
	Zero correlation No relationship between co-variables. For example, time taken to complete a crossword and number of packets of crisps sold in a local shop each week.

Evaluation

+ Correlations are a good starting point for research. If two variables are related this gives researchers ideas for future investigations.

+ Correlations can be used to investigate more complex relationships. For example, the curvilinear relationship between people's alertness and time of day. This means correlation has many uses.

− Correlations do not tell us whether one co-variable causes the other. This means it is not possible to show cause and effect. This limits the usefulness of the technique.

− Intervening variables may affect the co-variables. This is because there is no control of extraneous variables. This means it is possible to draw a conclusion that is wrong.

KNOWLEDGE CHECK

1. What is meant by a 'correlation'? **[2 marks]**

2. Outline how a scatter diagram used in a correlation is constructed and interpreted. **[3 marks]**

3. Explain **one** strength and **one** weakness of using a correlation. **[4 marks]**

The specification says...

Correlation:
An understanding of association between two variables and the use of scatter diagrams to show possible correlational relationships.
The strengths and weaknesses of correlations.
Computation of formulae is not required.

Exam booster

You don't need a ruler

If asked to sketch a scatter diagram, you will not be assessed on the neatness of your sketch but rather whether you have plotted the graph correctly and have labelled the axes and given an appropriate title.

APPLY IT – Research Methods

A researcher wanted to investigate whether people who believe in the paranormal are less afraid of death. He used a questionnaire to determine a score for the their paranormal beliefs and fear of death. In each case, a score closer to ten meant a greater belief or fear of death. The researcher found that those with a higher paranormal belief score had a lower fear of death score.

1. Name the **two** co-variables in this study. **[2 marks]**

2. What type of correlation did the researchers find in this study? Explain your answer. **[2 marks]**

3. Why was it *not* possible to conclude that belief in the paranormal causes people to have no fear of death? **[2 marks]**

Apparently there's a negative correlation between how much couples use their phones and how much time they spend speaking to each other. Apparently.

Positive or negative?

Can you tell the difference between a positive and a negative correlation? Identify which is which in the table below left. In the space on the right, roughly sketch four scattergrams as indicated in the boxes.

	Positive or negative
1. The hotter the temperature, the fewer clothes people wear.	
2. The fewer sweets you eat, the fewer fillings you have.	
3. The more people exercise, the less their risk of heart disease.	
4. The fewer hours of daylight, the more depressed people there are.	
5. The more anxious students are, the worse they do in exams.	
6. The more hungry you are, the more attractive food looks.	

Strong positive

Weak positive

Strong negative

Weak negative

The big fight: Experiments vs Correlations

Students sometimes get experiments and correlation studies mixed up, but it is important to know the difference.

So for each study below, decide whether it is an experiment or a correlation, and give a brief explanation of your choice.

Study	Experiment or correlation?	Why?
1. A psychologist investigated the relationship between spatial awareness and driving skill in sixth-form students. Each student gave scores on a spatial awareness test and a rally-driving computer game.		
2. A study investigated whether men or women are better at remembering mobile phone numbers.		
3. Some students conducted a study to investigate whether finding a romantic partner through a social network site is more successful than finding one through a 'lonely hearts' column of a local newspaper.		
4. A psychologist tested the hypothesis that 'the number of times people attend the cinema in a year is related to performance on a questionnaire about film knowledge'.		
5. A researcher conducted a study to see if time of day affects ability to remember.		
6. A psychologist looked at how people's mood affected how long they chatted to the checkout operator in a shop. Previous research showed that people in a good mood chat longer than people in a bad mood.		

The specification says...

Designing research:
Case studies.
Strengths and weaknesses of
the research method and types
of research for which it
is suitable.

Description and evaluation

Case studies	An in-depth investigation of a single individual, group, event or institution.
	Often involves unusual or unexpected people/events, but can also be used with everyday experiences, e.g. mother adjusting to going back to work after having a child.
A qualitative method	Mostly qualitative data which expresses people's experiences in words. Case studies often involve interviews with the person's friends or relatives.
	May include quantitative data, e.g. intelligence test score.
Longitudinal	Tend to take place over a long period of time.
	This may mean collecting data from the past or following a person/event for many years.
Evaluation	+ Researchers tend not to have a specific aim. This means they are often more open-minded and less blinkered by what they hope to discover. This increases the validity of the results.
	+ A good method for studying rare behaviour that can't be investigated using experiments because there are only one or two people who could be studied. This gives us a greater insight into topics that may not be studied by other research.
	− Often only focus on one individual or event. This means it is difficult to generalise the results beyond the particular person or event being studied. This reduces the validity of the results.
	− The analysis may be subjective. The information collected may be biased by the researcher's own 'reading' of the case. Therefore, conclusions drawn may lack validity.

Case studies sometimes involve unexpected events.

Case study of Glastonbury? That's our kind of research.

Exam booster

It's not just one person

Students often think that case studies are about one individual – but they can also be about one group, institution or event. For example, one school could be the focus of a case study on the education system. Such an institution consists of many people but is just an example of one of many schools in the country. Using one school permits the researcher to look in great detail at that case.

APPLY IT – Research Methods

A psychologist interested in addiction conducted a case study with a young man who had become addicted to playing fruit machines. The psychologist spent several years collecting data about the boy, David, and his family.

1. Explain how the psychologist could have collected the data in this case study. **[2 marks]**

2. Explain **one** strength and **one** weakness of using a case study to investigate the causes of aggression. Refer to the case study of David in your answer. **[4 marks]**

KNOWLEDGE CHECK

1. Outline **two** features of a case study. **[4 marks]**

2. Give an example of quantitative data that might be collected in a case study. **[1 mark]**

3. Describe and evaluate case studies as a method of conducting psychological research. **[9 marks]**

Fill in the blanks

Fill in the blanks in the following description of case studies. The words are given below if you get stuck, but try and do the activity without them first.

A case study is an in-depth investigation of a single _____, group, event or organisation. It is flexible because it can be used to study people going through _____ experiences, someone who is _____ or an unexpected event.

Case studies produce mostly _____ data because people express their experiences in words. They often include _____ with the individual and/or their family and friends. However, it is possible to collect quantitative data, for example by using _____ or tests.

An unusual feature of case studies is that they are often _____. This means they take place over a period of time, sometimes many years. Therefore they are ideal for studying the processes of _____ and change.

One strength of case studies is that they often do not have a specific _____ so are flexible. However, a weakness is that the focus on one person makes it hard to _____ findings to the wider population.

longitudinal   interviews   questionnaires   person   unusual

generalise   everyday   qualitative   development   aim

Strengths and weaknesses trigger phrases

Here are some 'trigger' phrases related to the strengths and weaknesses of case studies.
The first thing to do is decide which phrases go together by putting them into pairs in the table.
Then write a sentence explaining each pair of statements (or giving an example) without looking at your notes or elsewhere on the previous page.

1. **Hard to generalise findings.**

2. **Researcher is subjective.**

3. **Researcher is more open-minded.**

4. **Just one person, event, etc.**

5. **Good for when experiment can't be used.**

6. **No specific aim.**

7. **Open to bias.**

8. **Can study rare behaviour.**

Reliability

Reliability	Consistency. If you can repeat a measurement and get the same results, then the measurement is reliable.	
Quantitative methods	Experiments	Experiments can be controlled using standardised procedures, so each participant has exactly the same experience.
	Interviews and questionnaires	If same person answers same questions (with same ..interviewer) in the same way then the questionnaire/interview is reliable.
		Closed questions (compared to open ones) achieve reliability more easily as choices are fixed.
	Observations	An observer should produce the same observations if the same behaviour is watched/ listened to twice.
		Interobserver reliability is when two observers produce same data.
Qualitative methods	Less reliable. Unstructured interviews and case studies are difficult to repeat in the same way.	

Validity

Validity	Whether a result reflects 'real-world' behaviour.
Sampling methods	Sampling methods do not always produce a sample that is reflective of the target population.
	Opportunity sampling is less likely to produce a representative sample, stratified sampling is more likely to.
Experimental designs	Repeated measures design is influenced by order effects, and can be overcome by counterbalancing.
	Independent groups design is affected by participant variables, and can be overcome by random allocation.
Quantitative methods	Laboratory experiments often involve artificial tasks or settings which are not reflective of real life. Participants are aware of being studied. However, greater control enhances validity.
	In field experiments extraneous variables are not always controlled, tasks may be artificial and participants may be aware of being studied – all reduce validity.
	Methods producing numerical data (e.g. questionnaires and experiments) may lack validity as they reduce behaviour to a score.
Qualitative methods	Qualitative methods (e.g. case studies) have greater validity as they provide unrestricted information.
	Qualitative data depends on subjective interpretation, reducing the validity of conclusions.

The specification says...

How research should be planned, taking into consideration the reliability and/or validity of:

- Sampling methods.
- Experimental designs.
- Quantitative and qualitative methods.

The Sanders sisters were nothing if not consistent.

Exam booster

Validity means accuracy but ...

If you are asked: *What is meant by the term 'validity'? [2 marks]* make sure you say more than just 'accuracy'. There is a definition on the left but you could also say 'whether something measures what it intends to measure'.

APPLY IT – Research Methods

A questionnaire was designed by a group of students to investigate attitudes towards social media.

1. How might reliability be an issue for the students in their questionnaire? **[3 marks]**
2. The students gave the questionnaires out to just their close friends. How would this affect the validity of the data collected? **[2 marks]**
3. One of their questions in the questionnaire collected qualitative data. Explain why the data collected by this question might have high validity. **[2 marks]**

KNOWLEDGE CHECK

1. What is meant by the term 'reliability'? **[1 mark]**
2. Explain **one** factor that might reduce the validity of a laboratory experiment. **[2 marks]**
3. Explain **one** factor that might reduce the validity of a field experiment. **[2 marks]**
4. Explain why qualitative methods are generally regarded as less reliable than quantitative methods of gathering data. **[3 marks]**

Crossword time

Complete the crossword to see how familiar you are with terms relating to reliability and validity.

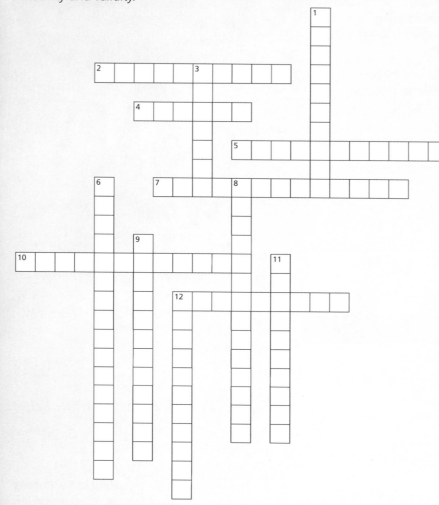

DOWN

1. Case studies rely on S_____ interpretation. (10)
3. Case studies give us I_____. (7)
6. A solution to order effects, C_____. (16)
8. Samples are more valid if they are R_____ of the population. (14)
9. Procedures are more reliable when they are S_____. (12)
11. These uncontrolled variables reduce validity of field experiments, E_____. (10)
12. This is another word for reliability, C_____. (11)

ACROSS

2. A_____ tasks reduce validity. (10)
4. This type of question is quite reliable, C_____. (6)
5. Methods producing Q_____ data are less reliable. (11)
7. The kind of reliability you need with two people watching, I_____. (13)
10. Methods producing Q_____ data tend to be more reliable. (12)
12. A method that investigates a single person/event, C_____ S_____. (4,5)

Reliability instant messaging

Two students are having an instant messaging conversation about the finer points of reliability. Some of the conversation has gone missing, but fortunately you are on hand to fill in the gaps. [You can have a similar conversation about validity.]

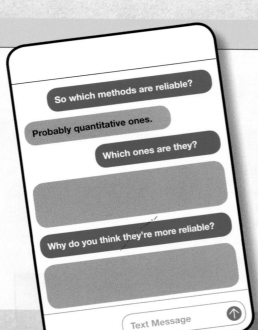

So which methods are reliable?

Probably quantitative ones.

Which ones are they?

Why do you think they're more reliable?

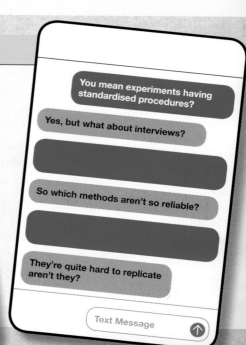

You mean experiments having standardised procedures?

Yes, but what about interviews?

So which methods aren't so reliable?

They're quite hard to replicate aren't they?

Text Message

The specification says...

Quantitative and qualitative data: The difference between quantitative and qualitative data.

Primary and secondary data: The difference between primary and secondary data.

Quantitative and qualitative data

Quantitative data	Quantities (numbers) – but can involve words and data about what people think and feel as long as the answers can be counted.
	+ Quantitative data can be easy to analyse. Data can be converted to averages and then graphs and charts. This means that groups of people can easily be compared.
	− A weakness is it lacks depth and detail. This is because we obtain little information about thoughts or abilities. Therefore, it doesn't reflect how complex things are in the real world.
Qualitative data	Words or pictures – but qualitative data can be turned into numbers. For example, in an interview about people about early childhood experiences, the number of times the words 'mother' or 'father' are said is counted.
	+ Qualitative data is in more depth and detail than quantitative data. The researcher can gain more insight as the participant is free to express their thoughts and feelings. This increases the validity of the data.
	− It is more difficult to analyse. It may be hard to summarise material and draw conclusions. This means conclusions may be based on the researcher's opinion.

Primary and secondary data

Primary data	Data obtained first hand by the researcher for the purposes of a research project.
	+ Primary data suits the aims of the research. It is authentic because it comes first hand from the participants themselves. This means the data may be more useful.
	− It takes more time and effort to collect primary data. The researcher must design and carry out a study rather than using readily available secondary data. This slows the process down and increases expense.
Secondary data	Second hand data from sources such as other studies or government statistics. It has been collected by someone else for a different set of research aims.
	+ Secondary data is convenient to use. This is because it has already been checked and collected. This reduces expense.
	− Secondary data may not quite fit what the researcher wants and/or it may come from a poorly designed study. This may reduce the validity of the research.

KNOWLEDGE CHECK

1. Outline the difference between primary and secondary data.   **[2 marks]**
2. Describe **one** strength and **one** weakness of using qualitative data.   **[4 marks]**
3. Using an example of something you have studied in Psychology, explain what quantitative data is.   **[3 marks]**

APPLY IT – Research Methods

A psychologist was investigating the amount of stress experienced in a local company. She used a questionnaire to calculate a stress score for each employee. She also used their absence record over the last year to give her more information on how they were coping with their job.

1. Identify the primary data and the secondary data in this study.   **[2 marks]**
2. Explain **one** weakness of using secondary data in this study.   **[2 marks]**
3. Explain **one** strength of using quantitative data in this study.   **[2 marks]**
4. In a follow-up study the psychologist wanted to gather qualitative data. Explain how she could do this.   **[2 marks]**

Primary data is sometimes called 'field research'. No, come back Ben, it's not what you think!

Three-column match-up

Link the terms in the left-hand column to the statements in columns 2 and 3.

Quantitative data	(1) Produced when people use their own words to express their thoughts and feelings.	(5) Difficult to analyse and summarise, leaving room for subjective interpretation.
Qualitative data	(2) From sources such as other research studies and government publications.	(6) The kind of data that exactly matches the aims of a study.
Primary data	(3) Usually in the form of numbers.	(7) Convenient because it has already been checked/verified by someone else.
Secondary data	(4) First-hand data obtained by research specifically for the project/study.	(8) Relatively easy to analyse, convert to graphs and use to compare groups.

One to another

Do you know the differences between quantitative and qualitative data?
Find out by reading the descriptions below of data collected in six studies.
For each study identify the type of data collected.
Then suggest what data could be collected instead.

Data description	Quantitative or qualitative data?	How could the other kind of data be collected instead?
1. Steve is interested in the career ambitions of his classmates. He asks them to discuss what jobs they might like to do and why.		
2. In a study of attractiveness, Harsa asks what qualities (such as kindness) make you fancy someone.		
3. On a questionnaire Alistair asks how many people go to the cinema more than once a week.		
4. Jon loves football but thinks it has a bad reputation. He asks his classmates for their opinion of players' behaviour on the pitch.		
5. Lucy counts how many items on a conveyor belt people can remember.		
6. During her work placement at a nursery, Ellie counts the number of boys and girls who play with building blocks.		

Topic 12 Descriptive statistics

Descriptive statistics	Express numbers in a way that gives an immediate impression of the overall pattern.

Descriptive statistics: Understand and calculate mean, median, mode and range.

Interpretation and display of quantitative data: Construct and interpret frequency tables and diagrams, bar charts, histograms and scatter diagrams for correlation.

Normal distribution: The characteristics of normal distribution.

Measures of dispersion and central tendency

Range		Represents spread. Tells us whether a set of data are close together or spread out. Arrange data in order and subtract lowest from highest score. + Easy to calculate. − Distorted by extreme scores.
Averages	Mean	Add up all the scores in a data set and divide by number of scores there are. + Uses all data values when calculated, so most sensitive measure. − Distorted by extreme scores, so less reflective of the 'typical' value.
	Median	The middle value in a set of data. Order numbers from lowest to highest and identify the middle number. + Not affected by extreme scores. − Less affected by extreme scores, so more reflective of the 'typical' value.
	Mode	The most common score in a set of data. + Very easy to calculate. − Quite unrepresentative overall.

Exam booster

Evaluating averages

An easy way to evaluate the mean, median and mode is by comparing them against each other. For example, the mean is less easy than the mode to calculate.

APPLY IT – Research Methods

A teacher analysed the results of a recent class test.

Test score (out of ten)	Number of students who obtained the score
3	8
4	3
5	2
6	3
7	2
8	7

1. Draw a histogram to represent the data. Label the axis and give it a suitable title. **[4 marks]**
2. Perform the following calculations:
   a) What was the mode of the test? **[1 mark]**
   b) What was range? **[2 marks]**
   c) What was the mean? **[2 marks]**

Interpretation and display of quantitative data

Scatter diagrams		To display correlation. One co-variable on x-axis, other on y-axis. A dot is placed where co-variables meet.
Frequency tables		A systematic way of representing data, organised in rows and columns. Displays how often an event occurred, using tallies.
Frequency diagrams Frequency represented on one axis	Histogram	Continuous data. No spaces between bars.
	Bar chart	Data not continuous, i.e. it could be placed in any order.
	Normal distribution	Symmetrical spread of frequency data that forms a bell-shaped curve. Mean, median, mode at same point.

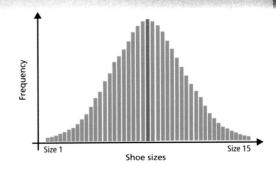

A normal distribution showing the shoe sizes of 2,000 men in the UK. The red line shows the mean, median and mode.

KNOWLEDGE CHECK

1. Explain how to calculate the median. **[3 marks]**
2. Explain **two** features of a normal distribution curve. **[4 marks]**
3. Outline **one** weakness of using the mean to interpret data. **[2 marks]**

Descriptive statistics unjumble

There is some useful information about descriptive statistics in the following sentences, but it has become jumbled up.
Put the sentences together correctly (the first half is in the first column, the second half is in the second column).

1. The range tells us …	**A.** … the most sensitive measure because it uses all the data values.
2. The range is calculated by …	**B.** … a bar chart.
3. The term average is …	**C.** … subtracting the lowest score from the highest.
4. A strength of the mean is that it is …	**D.** … how spread out (or close together) the data are.
5. A strength of the median is that it is …	**E.** … the most common score in a set of data.
6. The mode is …	**F.** … the normal distribution.
7. The name given to a symmetrical bell-shaped curve is …	**G.** … relatively unaffected by extreme scores.
8. The type of graph where the bars could be placed in any order is …	**H** … another term for measure of central tendency.

Right or wrong?

Indicate which of Rudi's and Trudi's decisions (in italics) are right and which are wrong.
Briefly explain your responses in the third column.

1. Rudi gave a memory test to ten of his friends. Their scores were 4, 6, 7, 10, 11, 14, 16, 17, 17, 20 *He calculated a mean score of 12.2.*		
2. *He also calculated the mode to be 16.*		
3. *He calculated the median as 11.*		
4. *Finally Rudi calculated the range as 16.*		
5. Rudi wondered which graph would be best to display his results. *He decided on a scatter diagram.*		
6. Trudi tested the cognitive development of 100 children of different ages. *She found that 22 were at the sensorimotor stage of development, 46 were at the preoperational stage, 24 were at the concrete operational stage, and 8 were at the formal operational stage.* She wondered what size of frequency table to use to display her results. *She chose a table 1 row by 4 columns.*		
7. She also thought about which graph would be best to present the figures. *She decided on a bar chart.*		

The specification says...

Computation:
Recognise and use expressions in decimal and standard form: use ratios, fractions and percentages, estimate results, find arithmetic means and use an appropriate number of significant figures.

Description

Decimals	A way to represent fractions out of 10, 100, 1,000, etc. In the number 36.02 the digit 2 represents two hundredths. 36.02 and 3.62 both have two decimal places. 36.351 has three decimal places, i.e. number of digits to right of the decimal point.
Fractions	A decimal is another way of writing a fraction. 0.12 is 12 out of 100 ($\frac{12}{100}$). To reduce to lowest form, identify a number that divides evenly into the top and bottom part of the fraction (called the highest common factor).
Ratios	Ratios are another way to express a fraction. 8 out of 10 did better in the audience condition = $\frac{8}{10}$ or $\frac{4}{5}$ 2 out of 10 did better in the no-audience condition = $\frac{2}{10}$ or $\frac{1}{5}$ Expressed as a ratio this would be 8:2 which can be reduced to 4:1
Percentages	Fractions out of 100. 12% means 12 out of 100. It is the same as 0.12 or $\frac{12}{100}$ or $\frac{3}{25}$.
Finding the arithmetic mean	Just the same as the mean: add up all the scores and divide by the number of scores there are.
Standard form	Mathematical shorthand to represent very large or small numbers. 1. Move the decimal point left or right to obtain a value between 1 and 10, e.g. 3.28 or 9.6, rounding off may be necessary. 2. Work out how many times you moved the decimal point to the right or the left. e.g. 3,280,000 can be written as 3.28×10^6 or 3×10^6 0.0000328 can be written as 3.28×10^{-5} or 3×10^{-5}
Significant figures	Another way to deal with very large or very small numbers. Round large numbers to the nearest thousand, ten thousand, hundred thousand, etc. … or nearest tenths, hundredths, etc. 2 significant figures: 32,462 becomes 32,000 0.003256 becomes 0.0033 (Note: zero does not count as a significant figure.)
Estimate results	This is a rough calculation.

I love to count.
(You have to be a Sesame Street fan to get the joke.)

Exam booster

Show your workings

Exam questions that involve calculations such as working out a percentage or the mean of a data set are always worth at least two marks. There is credit for your working out so, even if you get the answer wrong, you may still get some marks if your calculations are correct. Therefore, it is always a good idea to show your workings.

APPLY IT – Research Methods

Asch (1955) investigated conformity.

1. On many trials 6 out of 7 people in the group were confederates. Express this as a percentage. Give your answer to **one** decimal place and show your workings. **[3 marks]**

2. There were 18 trials of which 12 were critical trials. What was the ratio of standard trials to critical trials? Express this in the lowest form. **[2 marks]**

3. 75% of naïve participants conformed at least once. How many of the 123 naïve participants conformed at least once? Round your answer up to the nearest whole number. **[2 marks]**

KNOWLEDGE CHECK

1. Express 256,678 to **two** significant figures. **[1 mark]**

2. Using an example, explain how to express a very large number in standard form. **[3 marks]**

3. There are 15 cats and 12 dogs in a pet shop. What is the ratio of cats to dogs? Give your answer in its simplest form and show your workings. **[2 marks]**

Maths quiz

1. Express a quarter as a percentage.

2. Convert 0.65 to a fraction.

3. What was the highest common factor to use for the previous question?

4. In a study, 14 participants are women and 26 are men. Express the proportion of women to men as a ratio (suitably reduced).

5. In the study above, what fraction of the total participants are men?

6. In a study to investigate the capacity of short-term memory, six participants remembered 7 words, three remembered 6 words and one remembered 9. What is the mean number of words remembered?

7. Jon recorded the ratio of black to white mice in his study as 6:2. Reduce this ratio.

8. Round off the following numbers to 2 significant figures:
   a) 6.459   b) 0.00186
   c) 38,755

9. Asif's scores showed a normal distribution. Was the mode higher or lower than the mean or the same as it?

10. What is the range of the following numbers?
   10, 12, 12, 14, 16, 27, 28, 36, 39, 41, 45, 49, 52

11. In a survey, Sabiha asked a group of participants to classify themselves as being from one of 5 regions of the country. What measure of central tendency should she use with this information?

12. A health psychologist collected data on the number of calories eaten by participants. She expressed these in blocks of 0-499, 500-999, etc. What type of graph should she use?

Computation true or false?

Indicate which of the statements in italics are true and which are false. For the false statements, give the correct answer.

		True or false?	
1.	75% of people are on Facebook. So ¾ of people are on Facebook.		
2.	In a study of perception: 65% of the participants said their favourite visual illusion was the Ponzo illusion, 15% said it was the Müller-Lyer, the rest said it was Rubin's vase. So one-third (1/3) said their favourite was Rubin's vase.		
3.	The ratio of men to women in a care home is 1:3. There are 16 men. So there are 32 women.		
4.	A rat ran a maze in exactly 27.696 seconds. Another ran it in 22.385 seconds. So the difference between them is 5.3 seconds to two significant figures.		
5.	There could be 86,000,000,000 neurons in the human brain. So this is 8.6×10^8 neurons.		

Description

Aim	To investigate conformity through responses of participants to group pressure in an unambiguous situation.
Method	123 American male students tested in a group of six to eight confederates.
	Two large cards were shown, one with a single standard line and the other with three comparison lines. Participants were asked to select the matching line. The confederate went last or next to last.
	18 trials, 12 were 'critical' where confederates all selected the wrong line.
Results	On the 12 critical trials the participant gave the wrong answer 1/3 of the time, agreeing with the confederates.
	25% of the participants never gave a wrong answer.
Conclusion	This shows people are influenced by group pressure.
	Also shows a high level of independence as, despite group pressure, the majority went against group opinion.

Participants saw two large cards. On one was a 'standard line'. On the second card were three comparison lines. One of the three lines was the same length as the standard and the other two were always clearly different. The participant was asked to state which of the three lines matched the standard, after listening to answers given by others.

Evaluation

Child of the times	One weakness of Asch's study is it may only reflect conformity in 1950s America.
	Perrin and Spencer repeated Asch's study in 1980 in the UK and found just one conforming response in 396 trials.
	This suggests that the Asch effect is not consistent over time.
An artificial task	Another weakness is that the task and situation are artificial.
	Being asked to judge the length of a line (a trivial task) with a group of strangers doesn't reflect everyday situations where people conform.
	This means that the results may not explain more serious real-world conformity situations.
EXTRA: Cultural differences	A further weakness is that Asch's research is more reflective of conformity in individualist cultures.
	Studies conducted in collectivist countries such as China produce higher conformity rates than those carried out in individualist countries such as America and the UK (Bond and Smith).
	This suggests that Asch's findings cannot be generalised to collectivist cultures.

Exam booster

Don't forget the critical trials

When outlining Asch's study a common mistake students make when describing the results is that they just mention that participants conformed to the wrong answer a third of the time and forget to mention that this occurred in the critical trials only.

APPLY IT – Research Methods

Read the item below and then answer the questions that follow.

In 1961 the USA invaded Cuba in an attempt to overthrow the then leader Fidel Castro. However, the invasion was a failure. It later turned out that the US President's advisors had severe doubts about the invasion but no one spoke out because they believed everyone else thought it was a good idea. Therefore they all agreed on a course of action that they privately disagreed with!

1. What is meant by the term 'conformity'? Give an example from the above item in your answer. **[2 marks]**

2. How is the behaviour of the US President's advisors similar to that of Asch's participants? Refer to Asch's study in your answer. **[2 marks]**

KNOWLEDGE CHECK

1. Outline what Asch's study shows us about conformity. **[3 marks]**

2. Outline **one** way that research into conformity can be applied to everyday life. **[2 marks]**

3. Outline and evaluate Asch's study into conformity. **[9 marks]**

Classic study mix-up

Exam style question: Describe Asch's study of conformity.
[6 marks]

Here are some sentences relating to Asch's study. They could be useful to answer the exam-type question above, but they have become mixed up.

Put the numbers of the sentences in the right boxes below, in the order that makes the most sense.

Aim	Method	Results	Conclusion

1. Each group included just one genuine participant – the others were all confederates.

2. Genuine participants gave the wrong answer 1/3rd of the time on the critical trials.

3. As most participants did not conform most of the time, there was also a high level of independent behaviour.

4. Asch wanted to investigate participants' responses in an unambiguous situation.

5. The participants were tested in groups of between seven and nine people.

6. Each participant had to choose the comparison line that matched the length of the standard line.

7. One card showed a standard line and the other card showed three comparison lines.

8. The findings show that people are influenced to conform to the majority by group pressures.

9. 12 of the 18 trials were critical – confederates all chose the same incorrect line.

10. The participants were 123 American male students.

11. 25% of the participants never agreed with the confederates.

12. Each group was shown two cards alongside each other.

Elaborate your evaluation

Make the most of your AO3 points by elaborating them – extend, develop and explain them thoroughly, just like we do in this book. Use the trigger phrases in the table below to help you construct an elaborated evaluation of Asch's study.

One weakness	Asch's study is called a 'child of its time' because …	For example, when Perrin and Spencer replicated the procedure …	This suggests that …
Another weakness	Asch's participants had to …	This is artificial because …	This means that …
A further weakness	Asch's research only applies to one type of culture because …	For example, other studies in collectivist cultures (China) …	This suggests that …

The specification says...

Conformity:
Identification and explanation of how social factors (group size, anonymity and task difficulty) and dispositional factors (personality, expertise) affect conformity to majority influence.

Social factors

Social	'Social' means other people.
	Conformity occurs because of real or imagined pressure from others.
Group size	The more people there are in a group, the greater the pressure to conform.
	Asch found that with two confederates conformity was 13.6%, but three confederates was 31.8%.
	More than three confederates made little difference.
	Evaluation: Effect of group size depends on the task.
	When there is no obvious answer people don't tend to conform unless the group size is 8 or more people (Campbell and Fairey).
Anonymity	When participants could write down answers (they were anonymous) conformity was lower.
	Evaluation: If participants are friends expressing opinions anonymously they conform more (Huang and Li).
Task difficulty	If comparison lines are more similar to the standard, the task becomes harder and conformity increases.
	Evaluation: People with more expertise are less affected by task difficulty (Lucas *et al.*).

Linda was renowned for her high internal locus of control.

Dispositional factors

Dispositional	Characteristics of a person.
Personality	Internal locus of control leads to lower conformity.
	When asked to rate cartoons, Burger and Cooper found that participants with a high desire for control (internals) were less likely to agree with a confederate's ratings of the same cartoons.
	Evaluation: Control is less important in familiar situations (Rotter).
Expertise	More knowledgeable people tend to be less conformist.
	For example, self-confessed maths experts were less likely to conform to others' answers to maths problems (Lucas *et al.*).
	Evaluation: No single factor to explain conformity, e.g. maths experts may conform in a group of strangers in order to be liked.

Exam booster

How many factors?

You could be asked to describe and evaluate factors that affect conformity to majority influence for 9 marks. In answering this question, you don't need to outline all five factors on this spread but could get away with writing about any two in more detail. Providing you write about 100 words of description (AO1) and about 120 words of evaluation (AO3) and you include relevant information, you can still gain full marks for a 'two factor' answer.

APPLY IT – Research Methods

Use your knowledge of psychology to design an experiment that investigates how a social factor affects conformity. Refer to the following in your answer:

- A suitable alternative hypothesis.
- The experimental design you would choose with a justification of why it was chosen in your study.
- An explanation of how you would carry out your study.
- The results that would be expected. **[6 marks]**

KNOWLEDGE CHECK

1. Explain how expertise affects conformity.   **[3 marks]**
2. Explain the difference between a social and dispositional factor in relation to conformity.   **[3 marks]**
3. Describe and evaluate **two** factors that affect conformity to majority influence.   **[9 marks]**

Fill in the AO1

Fill in the blanks in the following description of social and dispositional factors in conformity. The words are given below if you get stuck, but try and do the activity without them first.

One social factor affecting conformity is group size. The bigger the group, the _____ pressure there is on the individual to conform. For example, in Asch's study conformity was _____ when there were two confederates. When there were three confederates conformity was _____. Having more than _____ confederates made little difference to the conformity rate.

A second social factor is _____. For example, when participants were allowed to write their answers down, conformity was _____.

A third social factor is _____ difficulty. Asch found that conformity _____ when he made the comparison lines more similar to the standard line.

One dispositional factor is personality. For example, _____ locus of control is linked to _____ conformity. Burger and _____ asked participants to rate cartoons. They found that participants who were internals disagreed with a _____ ratings.

Another dispositional factor is _____. People who have more knowledge are usually _____ likely to conform. Lucas *et al.* found that maths experts did not conform to other people's answers to maths problems.

| task |
| internal |
| lower |
| less |
| 31.8% |
| more |
| anonymity |
| confederate's |
| 13.6% |
| expertise |
| increased |
| three |
| lower |
| Cooper |

Instant messaging evaluation

Two students are having an instant messaging conversation about factors affecting conformity. There are some gaps in the conversation which you can fill in.

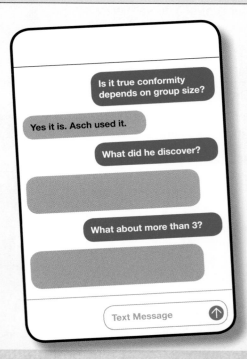

Description

Aim	To see if people would obey an unreasonable order (to deliver electric shocks).
Method	Forty males, aged 20–50, volunteered for a study on memory.
	'Teacher' paired with 'learner' (confederate).
	Learner was strapped in a chair and wired with electrodes which could give an electric shock.
	Teacher was instructed by the experimenter (in lab coat) to give a shock to the learner when a mistake was made. Experimenter gave 'prods' to continue. Intensity increased from 15 to 450 volts.
Results	No participants stopped below 300 volts.
	Five participants (12.5%) stopped at 300 volts when the learner pounded on wall.
	65% continued to 450 volts.
	Participants showed extreme tension, e.g. three had seizures.
Conclusion	Obedience has little to do with disposition.
	Factors in the situation made it difficult to disobey, e.g. the experimenter wearing a lab coat (authority figure), location (prestigious university), uncertainty (being in a novel situation).

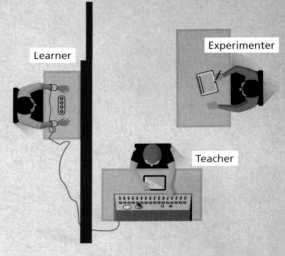

In Milgram's study the true participant played the role of the teacher. Confederates played the other two roles: The experimenter issued orders, and the learner answered questions sitting in a separate room.

Evaluation

Lacked realism	One weakness is that participants may not have believed that the shocks were real.
	Milgram's participants voiced suspicions about the shocks (Perry).
	This suggests that Milgram's participants just went along with the study but weren't really obeying orders.
Supported by other research	One strength is that other studies have found similar obedience levels.
	Sheridan and King found that 100% of females followed orders to give what they thought was a fatal shock to a puppy.
	This suggests that Milgram's results were not faked but represented genuine obedience.
EXTRA: Ethical issues	Another weakness is that Milgram's participants experienced considerable distress.
	He could have caused psychological damage to his participants because they thought they were causing pain to the learner.
	Such ethical issues question whether his research should have been carried out.

Exam booster

Learn this study!

Even though Milgram's study is not mentioned in the specification, it is important that you know it as you might be asked to 'describe and evaluate a study into obedience' or alternatively 'design a study into obedience'. Also, Milgram's agency theory relates to this study, so knowledge of this investigation will help you describe and evaluate agency theory.

APPLY IT

Read the item below and then answer the question that follows.

Michael: I like school trips. The teachers seem more relaxed and wear more casual clothes.

Rebecca: I don't enjoy them really. The students muck about more than when they are in lessons.

- Use your knowledge of research into obedience to explain why students misbehave on school trips. Refer to the conversation in your answer. **[4 marks]**

KNOWLEDGE CHECK

1. Using an example, outline what is meant by 'obedience'. **[3 marks]**

2. Use your knowledge of psychology to describe the method used in a study in which obedience was investigated. Your answer should include how the obedience was created and what was measured. **[4 marks]**

3. Describe and evaluate research on obedience. **[9 marks]**

Milgram true or false

In the table are some sentences about Milgram's study. In the middle column indicate which you think are true and which are false. For each false statement, write down the true version in the third column.

		True or false?	
1.	Milgram wanted to investigate conformity to the majority.		
2.	The participants were all males.		
3.	The participants were selected by random sampling.		
4.	The 'teacher' in the study was actually a confederate.		
5.	The learner was given an electric shock whenever they made a mistake on a task.		
6.	The highest shock available was 450 volts.		
7.	Ten participants disobeyed when the learner banged on the wall.		
8.	65% of the participants gave the highest possible shock.		
9.	Five participants had seizures because of the stress.		
10.	The results showed that how obedient you are depends on your personality.		

Milgram for a day

Imagine Stanley Milgram is with you now. What would you say to him to criticise his study? In the left-hand column write down three things you would say to criticise what he did. In the right-hand column write down what he might say in defence.

Alternatively, if you are working on your own, you can still do this activity. List on the left three key weaknesses of the study and on the right provide answers as if you were Milgram.

Criticism	Milgram's defence
1.	
2.	
3.	

The specification says...

Obedience:
Milgram's agency theory of social factors affecting obedience including agency, authority, culture and proximity.

Description

Milgram's agency theory	Explains obedience in terms of the power of others and social factors.
Agency	Agentic state: Person follows orders with no sense of personal responsibility.
	Autonomous state: Person makes their own free choices and feels responsible for their own actions.
Authority	The term 'agentic shift' is used to describe the change from autonomous to an agentic state.
	The shift occurs when a person sees someone else as a figure of authority.
Culture – the social hierarchy	Societies have a hierarchy with some people having more authority than others. This hierarchy is agreed on by all members.
	The culture we live in socialises us to respect the social hierarchy.
Proximity	In Milgram's further studies, if the teacher was physically closer to the learner, the teacher was less obedient.

Agency theory is all about passing responsibility to others.

Evaluation

Research support	One strength is that there is research support.
	Blass and Schmitt showed a film of Milgram's study to students who blamed the 'experimenter' rather than the 'teacher' for the harm to the learner.
	Therefore the students recognised the legitimate authority of the experimenter as the cause of obedience.
Doesn't explain all findings	One weakness is that agency theory can't explain why there isn't 100% obedience.
	In Milgram's study 35% of the participants didn't go up to the maximum shock of 450 volts.
	This means that social factors cannot fully explain obedience.
EXTRA: The obedience alibi	Another weakness is that agency theory gives people an excuse for 'blind' obedience.
	Nazis who were racist and prejudiced were doing more than just following orders.
	This means that agency theory is potentially dangerous as it excuses people.

Exam booster

How much detail?

It is not enough to be able to briefly explain what agency theory is as you could be asked questions on the specific parts of it as these are named in the specification. With this in mind, make sure you can write a couple of sentences on each of the four components named in the specification (i.e. agency, authority, culture and proximity).

APPLY IT - Research Methods

Milgram conducted many variations of his studies and he interviewed participants afterwards.

1. Explain the difference between a questionnaire and an interview.   **[3 marks]**
2. Use your knowledge of interviews to explain why Milgram used an interview rather than a questionnaire to gather information about the factors that affect obedience.   **[5 marks]**
3. Explain **one** weakness of using an interview to gather information.   **[3 marks]**

KNOWLEDGE CHECK

1. Briefly outline agency theory.   **[2 marks]**
2. With reference to Milgram's theory, explain how culture affects obedience.   **[3 marks]**
3. Describe and evaluate **one** social factor that affects obedience.   **[9 marks]**

Put it right

Below is a description of Milgram's agency theory. Sadly, it contains nine mistakes. Your task is to identify the errors and correct them.

Milgram devised his agency theory to explain conformity. It is a theory about the influence of personality factors and the power other people have over us.

Usually we are in an agentic state in which we can make our own choices. We behave independently and take responsibility for our actions. But sometimes we switch to an autonomous state in which we follow the orders of another person. We see this person as an authority figure and give up our sense of personal responsibility.

The change from an autonomous to an agentic state is called an agentic switch. The agentic switch occurs because we live in a society which is equal. This means that we all agree that some people should have authority over us. These people are entitled to expect conformity from us. We learn to respect the social hierarchy through a process of inheritance as children. For example, we obey parents and teachers from an early age.

Writing thoroughly

Here is a typical 9-mark exam question:

Describe and evaluate Milgram's agency theory of social factors affecting obedience. *[9 marks]*

Plan an answer by completing the table below.

For the describe part, identify 4 key points (each in a different colour):	For the evaluate part, identify 3 points:
1.	1.
2.	2.
3.	3.
4.	

Now use the framework above to write out your essay in full. Use the same colours to write out each description point. For AO1, add as much detail to your description as you can (use examples or explain things). For AO3, practise developing and explaining further any strength or weakness you write – you should never be satisfied with just one-sentence evaluations.

The specification says...

Obedience:
Explanation of dispositional factors affecting obedience including Adorno's theory of the authoritarian personality.

Description

Adorno's theory	Explaining obedience in people's personality.
The authoritarian personality	Some people have an exaggerated respect for authority. They are more likely to obey orders and look down on people of inferior status.
Cognitive style	'Black and white', rigid style of thinking. They believe in stereotypes and don't like change.
Originates in childhood	Originates from overly strict parenting and receiving only conditional love from parents. Child identifies with parents' moral values. Also feels hostility towards parents which cannot be directly expressed for fear of reprisals.
Scapegoating	Freud suggested that people who have hostility displace this onto others who are socially inferior in a process called scapegoating. You offload anger to something else, relieving anxiety and hostility.

Some people have exaggerated respect for authority.

Evaluation

Lack of support	One weakness is that the theory was based on a flawed questionnaire. The F-scale has a response bias because anyone who answered yes to each question would end up with a higher authoritarian score. This challenges the validity of the theory because it is based on poor evidence.
The results are correlational	Another weakness is that the evidence is based on correlational data. We cannot claim that an authoritarian personality causes greater obedience levels. Therefore, other factors may explain the apparent link between obedience and the authoritarian personality.
EXTRA: It's both social and dispositional	A further weakness is the authoritarian personality cannot explain all cases of obedience. Millions of Germans displayed highly obedient and prejudiced behaviour but didn't have the same upbringing and same personality. This means that there are probably social factors that affect obedience as well as dispositional ones.

Exam booster

Social or dispositional?

Remember you can use explanations to evaluate other explanations. For example, if you are evaluating dispositional factors then you can use the social factors as a way of criticising a dispositional explanation. Social factors suggest that it is other people that influence obedience rather than the personality of the individual who is given the order.

APPLY IT

Read the item below and then answer the question that follows.

David is the least popular drill sergeant in the Army. He seems to enjoy inflicting pain on the members of his unit. He resented his Dad for calling him a slacker but enjoys punishing those beneath him for behaving in a similar way.

- Identify characteristics of the authoritarian personality. Refer to examples of David's behaviour. **[4 marks]**

KNOWLEDGE CHECK

1. Outline what is meant by an 'authoritarian personality'. **[3 marks]**
2. Explain why someone with an authoritarian personality is likely to be more obedient than someone who does not have an authoritarian personality. **[3 marks]**
3. Describe and evaluate **one** dispositional factor that affects obedience **[9 marks]**

AO1 Adorno broken sentences

There is some useful information about Adorno's theory in the following sentences, but it has become jumbled up.
Put the sentences together correctly (the first half is in the first column, the second half is in the second column).

1. Adorno's theory explains obedience …	**A.** … only conditional love.
2. People with an authoritarian personality …	**B.** … rigid and 'black and white'.
3. They look down on people they believe have …	**C.** … have excessive respect for authority.
4. Authoritarian people do not like …	**D.** … in terms of someone's authoritarian personality.
5. In terms of cognitive style, their way of thinking is …	**E.** … relieved anxiety and hostility.
6. The origins of authoritarian personality are …	**F.** … hostility towards their parents.
7. Parents are overly strict and give their children …	**G.** … displaced onto people of inferior social status.
8. In childhood, people who develop an authoritarian personality feel …	**H.** … inferior social status.
9. The hostility cannot be expressed directly so it is …	**I.** … found in childhood.
10. Freud believed scapegoating …	**J.** … change.

Match-up the AO3

Fill in the missing information.
Match up the sentences to make three full evaluation points of three sentences each.

1. Because of this, it is not possible to claim that an authoritarian personality _____ people to be more obedient.	**2.** This is because there is a _____ bias in the F-scale – if you answer '_____' to all the items you get a high authoritian score.	**3.** For example, millions of people in Nazi _____ behaved very obediently even though they had _____ personalities and upbringings.
4. This means that _____ factors affect obedience as well as dispositional ones.	**5.** A weakness of Adorno's theory is that it was based on a _____ questionnaire.	**6.** This is a weakness because it means other _____ could explain the link between authoritarian personality and obedience.
7. This means the _____ of the theory is low because it lacks research support.	**8.** A further weakness of Adorno's theory is that it cannot explain all examples of _____.	**9.** Another weakness of Adorno's theory is that the evidence it is based on is _____.

The specification says...

Prosocial behaviour: Piliavin's subway study.

Description

Prosocial behaviour	Acting in a way that promotes the welfare of others and may not benefit the helper.
	Bystander behaviour (bystander effect) – the presence of others reduces prosocial behaviour.
Aim	To investigate if certain characteristics of a victim would affect whether people will help a bystander in a natural setting.
Method	A male confederate collapses on a New York City subway train, either appearing drunk or disabled (with a cane).
	103 trials.
	One confederate was a 'model' if no other help was offered.
	Two observers recorded key information.
Results	'Disabled' victim (with cane) was given help in 95% of the trials.
	'Drunk' victim was helped in 50% of the trials.
	Help was forthcoming as much in a crowded carriage as in a carriage with very few people.
Conclusion	Characteristics of the victim affect whether they will receive help.
	In a natural emergency willingness to help is not related to the number of witnesses.

Evaluation

High realism	One strength of this study is that participants did not know their behaviour was being studied.
	The subway train passengers did not know they were in a study and behaved naturally.
	So the results of the study are high in validity.
Urban sample	One weakness of the study is that the participants came mostly from a city.
	They may have been used to emergencies.
	This means that their behaviour may not have been typical of all people.
EXTRA: Qualitative data	Another strength of this study was that qualitative data was also collected.
	The two observers on each trial noted down remarks they heard from passengers.
	This offered a deeper insight into why people did or did not offer help.

KNOWLEDGE CHECK

1. Explain what Piliavin's subway study shows about prosocial behaviour. **[3 marks]**
2. Evaluate Piliavin's subway study. **[4 marks]**
3. Piliavin used a field experiment in his study into prosocial behaviour. Describe his study and evaluate the research methods used. **[9 marks]**

Psychology laboratory, waiting for participants.

Exam booster

Use maths to help you revise

Remembering the results of a study can be tricky so attempt to revise your maths skills at the same time to help you remember them. For example, bystanders helped a 'disabled' person on 95% of the trials but only helped a drunk person on 50% of the trials. The approximate ratio of those students who helped the 'disabled' person in comparison to those who helped the 'drunk' person was therefore about 2:1.

APPLY IT

Read the item below and then answer the question that follows.

Neche receives a nasty foul whilst playing football which causes him to fall and cry out in pain. An opposing player sees this and kicks the ball out of play so Neche can receive treatment from the physiotherapist. Later on in the same game Neche's team mate Corey falls to the floor after barely being touched by a defender who tackled him. This time, the opposition ignore him.

• Use your knowledge of Piliavin et al.'s study to explain why the other team were more willing to help Neche compared to Corey. **[3 marks]**

Classic study true or false

Here are some sentences about Piliavin et al.'s subway study. Identify which are true and which are false.
You can rewrite the false ones to make them correct.

		True or false?	
1.	Bystander behaviour refers to how the presence of other people increases the chances of a victim being helped.		
2.	Piliavin *et al.* wanted to study bystander behaviour in a fully controlled situation.		
3.	The person who collapsed was a male confederate.		
4.	The confederate sometimes appeared to be drunk and sometimes to be disabled.		
5.	There were 100 trials in total.		
6.	There was one observer in the carriage to record behaviour.		
7.	The 'drunk' victim was more likely to be helped than the 'disabled' victim.		
8.	The victim was just as likely to be helped in a crowded carriage as in one with few people.		
9.	The researchers concluded that the most important influence on helping was the number of people present.		

Classic study anagrams

Time to unjumble these words relating to the classic study on this spread. Can you do it without looking at the clues in the right-hand column?

1.	BRATSDENY AVIBEHOUR		Another term for what onlookers do.
2.	VINIPLIA		He and she did the study.
3.	SAWBUY RANIT		The procedure took place on this.
4.	KNURD		The victim was sometimes in this state.
5.	BALDSIDE		The victim sometimes carried a cane so appeared _____.
6.	DEFEATCRONE		Someone working for the researchers, pretending to be a victim.
7.	CIGAREAR		The train was made up of several of these.
8.	CITVIM		The person who needed help.
9.	MERCYGENE		The type of situation the researchers created.
10.	TEQUILAVITA		Type of data collected by the observers.

The specification says...

Prosocial behaviour:
Bystander behaviour: identification and explanation of how social factors (presence of others and cost of helping) and dispositional factors (similarity to victim and expertise) affect bystander intervention.

Social factors

Presence of others	Bystander behaviour/effect states that the more people are present the less likely that help is given.
	Darley and Latané asked participants to have a discussion on an intercom with others (confederates). One had an epileptic seizure and asked for help.
	If participants thought they were alone 85% reported the seizure compared to 31% if they thought four others were present.
	Evaluation: It depends on the situation and the cost of not helping. In very serious emergencies help is given (Faul *et al.*).
Cost of helping	Decision of whether to help depends on costs: • Cost of helping includes: danger to self or embarrassment. • Cost of not helping includes: guilt, blame, leaving another in need.
	Cost-reward model: Balance between costs and rewards of helping.
	Evaluation: Help also depends on how the situation is interpreted, e.g. man and woman arguing, 65% intervened when the woman shouted, 'I don't know you' but only 19% when shouting 'I don't know why I married you' (Shotland and Straw).

Dispositional factors

Similarity to victim	If you identify with a characteristic of the victim you are more likely to help.
	Manchester United football fans were more likely to help a runner who had fallen over if the runner was dressed in a Manchester United shirt as opposed to a Liverpool one (Levine *et al.*).
	Evaluation: Similarity may increase helping but, for example, if the costs are too high or the situation is ambiguous it is not sufficient to guarantee helping.
Expertise	People with specialist skills are more likely to help in emergency situations that suit their expertise.
	Registered nurses were more likely than non-medical students to help a workman who had fallen off a ladder (Cramer *et al.*).
	Evaluation: In contrast, people who had received Red Cross training were no more likely to help a victim who was bleeding a lot than people who had received no training – though the Red Cross people gave higher quality help (Shotland and Heinold).

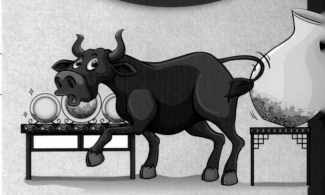

Though his efforts to lend a hand were well-intentioned, Billy couldn't help thinking that he was about to make things worse.

Exam booster

Names and dates

Don't worry too much about remembering names and dates of studies. It is acceptable in the exam to say, 'a research study was carried out where they found ...' as long as you describe the research in an accurate way to show that you understand it, you will not lose any marks in the exam.

APPLY IT – Research Methods

A psychologist plans to review research conducted by other researchers who have investigated the social and dispositional factors related to prosocial behaviour. He finds 25 studies, seven of these studies concluded that the presence of others is the main factor in prosocial behaviour, four found most support for the cost of helping, eleven found similarity of the victim was most important and three found that expertise was most significant.

1. Explain whether the psychologist has used primary or secondary data in his study. **[2 marks]**

2. Draw a bar chart of the data. Label the axes carefully and give it a suitable title. **[4 marks]**

3. Calculate the results as a percentage. Show your workings. **[4 marks]**

KNOWLEDGE CHECK

1. What is meant by the term 'bystander behaviour'? **[2 marks]**

2. Explain how similarity to the victim can be used to explain bystander behaviour. **[3 marks]**

3. Describe and evaluate research into social and dispositional factors that affect bystander behaviour. **[9 marks]**

Using examples for detailed AO1

You can add detail to your descriptions by using examples. To practise this, start by writing definitions of the social/dispositional factors in the left-hand column in the table below.

Then add examples to explain your definitions further in the right-hand column. Use examples from the previous page, but write them in your own words.

The presence of others is a social factor affecting prosocial behaviour. The bystander effect …	Darley and Latané investigated this by … They found that …
Another social factor is the cost of helping, which means …	The costs of helping include … The costs of not helping include …
Similarity is a dispositional factor that affects prosocial behaviour. This means …	Levine *et al.* investigated this and found that …

AO3 Prosocial unjumble

In the following sentences you will find an evaluation of social and dispositional factors in prosocial behaviour.

First, put the sentences together correctly (the first half of each sentence is in the first column, and the second half is in the second column).

Then, once you have nine complete sentences, put them together into three elaborated points of three sentences each.

1. For example, social factors such as high costs and an ambiguous situation can lead to…	A. … 65% of onlookers intervened in an argument between a man and a woman when the woman shouted, 'I don't know you', but only 19% intervened when she shouted 'I don't know why I married you'.
2. This shows that there is more to the decision to help than …	B. … how the bystander interprets the situation.
3. For example, Shotland and Straw found that …	C. … can outweigh the role of similarity in the decision to help.
4. This means that social factors may be …	D. … no helping taking place, even if the victim and bystander are similar.
5. A weakness is that the cost of helping depends on …	E. … makes little difference.
6. For example, Shotland and Heinold found that …	F. … not enough on its own to guarantee helping.
7. This is a weakness because other factors (especially social ones) …	G. … more important influences on prosocial behaviour than dispositional factors such as expertise.
8. A weakness is that some research shows that expertise …	H. … people with Red Cross training were no more likely to help a bleeding victim than people with no training.
9. A weakness is that similarity is …	I. … just weighing up costs and rewards.

The specification says...

Crowd and collective behaviour: Prosocial and antisocial behaviour in crowds: Identification and explanation of how a social factor (deindividuation) affects collective behaviour.

Description

Crowd and collective behaviour	Le Bon suggested that being in a crowd creates anonymity, leading to antisocial behaviour.
	Behaviour is ruled by social norms. When not identifiable (deindividuated) we lose our sense of responsibility and behave irrationally/aggressively.
Aim	Zimbardo aimed to investigate deindividuation in a study similar to Milgram's.
Method	Four female undergraduates had to deliver a fake electric shock to another student.
	Group 1: Individuated group – Person delivering the shock wore their normal clothes, name tags and could see each other.
	Group 2: Deindividuated group – Person delivering the shock wore large coats with hoods, never referred to by name.
Results	The deindividuated group was more likely to press the button to shock the 'learner' in the other room.
	They held the shock button down twice as long as the individuated group.
Conclusion	This supports the view that both anonymity and deindividuation increase the likelihood of antisocial behaviour.

Evaluation

Not always antisocial	One weakness is that deindividuation doesn't always lead to antisocial behaviour.
	Johnson and Downing found that participants dressed as a nurse gave fewer and milder shocks than those dressed in a KKK outfit but more shocks than those in their own clothes.
	This shows that people take on group norms.
Real-world application	One strength is that understanding deindividuation can be used to manage crowds.
	At sporting fixtures crowd control can be achieved through using video cameras so people are more self-aware.
	This can then reduce aggressive behaviour of the crowd.
EXTRA: Crowding	Another weakness is that antisocial behaviour may be due to crowding rather than collective behaviour.
	When animals are packed together they feel stressed and act aggressively (Freedman).
	So it may be overcrowding that creates antisocial behaviour as well as deindividuation.

KNOWLEDGE CHECK

1. Distinguish between prosocial and antisocial behaviour. **[3 marks]**

2. With reference to an example, explain what is meant by the term 'deindividuation'. **[4 marks]**

3. Describe and evaluate deindividuation as an explanation for antisocial behaviour. **[9 marks]**

Exam booster

Don't forget to use an example

Consider this exam question: *What is meant by the term deindividuation? [2 marks].* When writing your definition it is good to use an example as this demonstrates your knowledge and understanding and could also provide you the extra detail to gain the second mark for the question in the exam. Therefore, a suitable answer to the question would be ... *Deindividuation relates to the loss of personal identity people experience in situations where they are anonymous* for example, *people acting more antisocially when in a crowd.*

APPLY IT

Read the item below and then answer the question that follows.

Darren was sentenced to two years in prison for a theft. His parents were worried about how he would cope as he was never 'tough'. So they were shocked to find out that he had spent a week in solitary confinement after beating up another prisoner. When Darren was asked to explain his actions to his parents, he said that being treated as a number rather than a person just changed him.

• Identify **one** social factor that could have affected Darren's behaviour and explain why it might have caused him to act more antisocially. **[3 marks]**

Ku Klux Klan (KKK) outfit – not something for Halloween.

Crossword time

How familiar are you with the deindividuation explanation? Complete the crossword to find out.

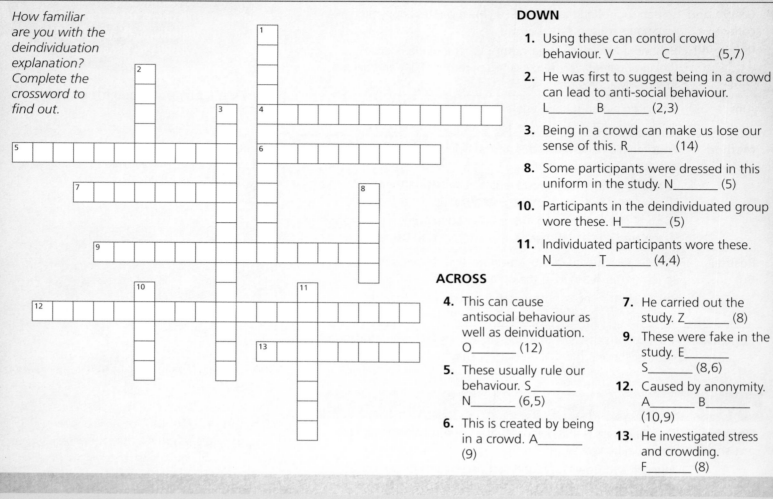

DOWN

1. Using these can control crowd behaviour. V_____ C_____ (5,7)

2. He was first to suggest being in a crowd can lead to anti-social behaviour. L_____ B_____ (2,3)

3. Being in a crowd can make us lose our sense of this. R_____ (14)

8. Some participants were dressed in this uniform in the study. N_____ (5)

10. Participants in the deindividuated group wore these. H_____ (5)

11. Individuated participants wore these. N_____ T_____ (4,4)

ACROSS

4. This can cause antisocial behaviour as well as deinividuation. O_____ (12)

5. These usually rule our behaviour. S_____ N_____ (6,5)

6. This is created by being in a crowd. A_____ (9)

7. He carried out the study. Z_____ (8)

9. These were fake in the study. E_____ S_____ (8,6)

12. Caused by anonymity. A_____ B_____ (10,9)

13. He investigated stress and crowding. F_____ (8)

AO3 – Fill in the blanks

Complete the passage by filling in the missing words from this evaluation of the deindividuation explanation. Try to complete the activity without referring to your notes or this spread. The words you need to choose from are on the right if you really get stuck.

A weakness is that antisocial behaviour is not always the outcome of _____. Johnson and

_____ found that participants dressed in a _____ uniform gave fewer and lower electric

shocks than people dressed in a KKK outfit. This shows that deindividuation can lead to prosocial behaviour when

people take on prosocial _____.

A strength is that deindividuation can help us to manage _____ behaviour. For example, using video

cameras at sporting events can increase people's _____ of their own behaviour. This is a strength

because it is a real-world _____ that can reduce the aggression of crowds.

A weakness is that there are alternative theories. For example, _____ showed that when animals

are crowded together they become _____ and behave aggressively. This is a weakness because

deindividuation may not be enough on its own to explain _____ behaviour.

awareness

nurse's

antisocial

Downing

Freedman

application

deindividuation

stressed

crowd

norms

The specification says...

Crowd and collective behaviour: Prosocial and antisocial behaviour in crowds.

Description

Aim	Reicher aimed to investigate the behaviour of a crowd to see if their behaviour was ruly or unruly.
Method	Analysed newspaper, TV, radio and police reports of the St Pauls riots (Bristol) in 1980.
	Interviewed 20 people immediately after the riots to understand what happened, including six interviews in depth.
Results	The riots were triggered by policemen raiding a café for drugs, an action which was seen as unjustified.
	A crowd of 300–3000 gathered and attacked the police and other properties, throwing stones and bricks and burning police cars. The attack intensified and spread.
	When the police left, rioters calmed down and never moved beyond the St Pauls area.
Conclusion	This shows that the crowd's behaviour was rule-driven and anger was only expressed towards predictable targets, based on the social attitudes of the area.

Evaluation

Supported by research	One strength is that other research has come to similar conclusions about crowd behaviour.
	Research on football hooligans also found that violence didn't escalate beyond a certain point (Marsh).
	This supports the view that crowd behaviour is rule-driven and not out of control.
Issues with methodology	One weakness is that the case study is based on subjective data.
	Reicher based his account on eyewitness testimony of reporters and members of the crowd who may have had a biased perspective of the events they witnessed.
	This means that the conclusions may lack validity.
EXTRA: Real-world application	Another strength of this research is that it provides ideas about how best to police such riots.
	Reicher's analyses suggest that increasing the police presence in riots does not always lead to a decrease in violence so it may be better to let local communities 'police' themselves.
	This shows that this research can have a positive effect in the real world.

Crowd behaviour doesn't always have to be antisocial – assuming you're a fan of expressive dance!

Exam booster

Don't forget prosocial behaviour

Crowds are often linked to antisocial behaviour but this does not mean that all crowd behaviour is negative. You may also be asked to comment on examples of prosocial behaviour in crowds. For example, in the study to the left, some rioters helped direct traffic through the area which shows that people in crowds will also act to benefit others.

KNOWLEDGE CHECK

1. What is meant by the term 'collective behaviour'? **[2 marks]**
2. Describe the method of **one** study that investigated behaviour in crowds. **[2 marks]**
3. Describe and evaluate how research into crowd behaviour has increased our understanding of antisocial behaviour. **[9 marks]**

APPLY IT – Research Methods

Reicher conducted a case study to investigate crowd and collective behaviour in St Pauls in Bristol.

1. Explain in what way Reicher's study was a case study. **[2 marks]**
2. Reicher gathered both primary and secondary data in his case study. Briefly outline what is meant by primary and secondary data and give an example of each in Reicher's study. **[4 marks]**
3. Explain **one** strength and **one** weakness of the case study method, using examples from this case study. **[4 marks]**

Storyboarding the case study

Using visual images can be useful, because converting the details of a study into a picture helps you process the meaning of the information. This makes it easier to remember. Try to outline Reicher's case study in pictures. Take the main elements of the study and represent them with drawings, like a film director might do with a 'storyboard', a series of images that tell the story of the film (or study) from start to finish. Here's a template to help you along.

Evaluate with trigger phrases

On the right are some 'trigger' phrases related to the case study in crowd and collective behaviour.
First of all, decide which phrases go together and put them into pairs in columns 1 and 2 of the table.
Next, write a sentence in column three for each pair without looking elsewhere.
Finally, write a further sentence in column 4, to explain why your first sentence is a strength/weakness.

1. **This case study uses data that is subjective rather than objective.**

2. **The case study gives us some ideas about how riots can be policed effectively.**

3. **Research support.**

4. **Methodological problem.**

5. **Other studies draw similar conclusions to this one about crowd behaviour.**

6. **Real-world application.**

Social factors

Deindividuation	Group norms (social factors) determine the behaviour of the crowd – either prosocial or antisocial.
	Evaluation: Antisocial effects may be due to being packed together in a small space (crowding), as researched by Freedman with rats.
Social loafing	In a group, people individually put in less effort.
	Being in a group reduces personal identity (deindividuation) so individual effort not known.
	Latané *et al.* found participants made less noise individually when shouting in a group of six than when on their own.
	Evaluation: Social loafing is not a problem for creative tasks – in fact more people mean greater individual output.
Culture	Individualist cultures (e.g. US, UK) focus on individual needs. Collectivist cultures (e.g. China, Korea) focus on the needs of the group.
	Social loafing lower in collectivist cultures, e.g. Earley found Chinese but not US people put in the same amount of effort on a group task regardless of whether they could or could not be identified.
	Evaluation: Making generalisations about cultures may be a simplification of the way people behave since they are influenced by multiple factors.

Dispositional factors

Personality	People with an internal locus of control are less likely to be influenced by others in a crowd.
	Evaluation: Not all research shows that personality matters. For example, in one study 'whistle-blowers' had similar scores on a personality test as non-whistle-blowers (Bocchiaro *et al.*).
Morality	Morals are our sense of right and wrong. Those with greater moral strength are more likely to have their behaviour guided by these morals than be influenced by the opinions/behaviour of others.
	Evaluation: Supported by history when the German Sophie Scholl was executed for distributing anti-Nazi literature. She resisted the group norm and was willing to sacrifice her life for her moral values.

KNOWLEDGE CHECK

1. Identify **three** factors that affect crowd and collective behaviour. [3 marks]
2. Explain how personality affects crowd and collective behaviour. [3 marks]
3. Describe and evaluate the effect of social factors on collective behaviour. [9 marks]

The specification says...

Crowd and collective behaviour: Identification and explanation of how social factors (social loafing, deindividuation and culture) and dispositional factors (personality and morality) affect collective behaviour.

Always gonna be tough when the rest of your group are a bunch of social loafers.

Exam booster

Be prepared to describe and evaluate factors

You could be asked to *describe and evaluate social and/or dispositional factors that affect collective behaviour* for 9 marks. In order to prepare effectively for this question, make sure that you can provide a definition, a piece of relevant research and one evaluation point for each of the five factors that are named on the specification, i.e. social loafing, deindividuation, culture, personality and morality.

APPLY IT

Read the item below and then answer the question that follows.

Chris and Mike are two teachers.

Chris: My students are less productive when doing group work and actually work better on their own.

Mike: I see what you mean but also I find that some students work really well in groups whereas others are just lazy. It depends on the student really.

• Identify **two** factors that influence collective behaviour and explain how these may have affected the behaviour of Chris's and Mike's students. [4 marks]

Crowd behaviour match-up

Match up the statements across the four columns.

1. Deindividuation	**2.** Dispositional factor	**3.** People put in less individual effort when they work in groups.	**4.** People with strong moral sense are less likely to be influenced by crowd behaviour.
5. Social loafing	**6.** Dispositional factor	**7.** Includes characteristics such as locus of control.	**8.** Latané *et al.* studied noises made by people in groups of six.
9. Culture	**10.** Social factor	**11.** Involves loss of personal identity, awareness and responsibility.	**12.** People who are internals are less likely to be influenced by crowd behaviour.
13. Personality	**14.** Social factor	**15.** Concerns our sense of right and wrong.	**16.** Earley found social loafing was lower in Chinese people than in Americans.
17. Morality	**18.** Social factor	**19.** Focus in USA and UK on individual needs, focus in China on needs of the group.	**20.** Leads to prosocial or antisocial behaviour through adherence to group norms.

Collective behaviour wordsearch

There are ten words related to collective behaviour for you to find in the grid on the right. They could be vertical, horizontal or diagonal (but not backwards).

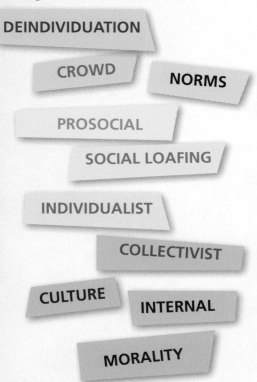

DEINDIVIDUATION

CROWD

NORMS

PROSOCIAL

SOCIAL LOAFING

INDIVIDUALIST

COLLECTIVIST

CULTURE

INTERNAL

MORALITY

D	S	A	I	Q	O	S	V	O	Y	O	H	J	U	U
H	E	O	O	R	V	M	R	T	D	T	H	B	U	C
T	S	I	C	Z	Z	W	N	S	G	Q	K	H	N	O
B	A	N	N	I	D	E	J	I	F	N	R	L	H	L
S	D	D	X	D	A	I	I	N	T	E	R	N	A	L
D	C	I	C	Q	I	L	E	Y	Z	P	P	O	L	E
P	F	V	K	U	M	V	L	C	B	Y	X	Q	A	C
R	J	I	Q	L	L	O	I	O	N	O	R	M	S	T
O	K	D	D	C	H	T	R	D	A	J	J	J	R	I
S	D	U	X	N	J	V	U	A	U	F	L	Q	V	V
O	L	A	C	A	U	R	L	R	L	A	I	Y	S	I
C	K	L	R	W	B	F	B	Z	E	I	T	N	X	S
I	E	I	O	Y	J	R	M	R	A	F	T	I	G	T
A	H	S	W	T	D	B	H	Z	L	B	P	Y	O	B
L	P	T	D	A	R	L	F	L	F	E	A	T	W	N

The specification says...

The possible relationship between language and thought.
Piaget's theory: Language depends on thought.

Description

Piaget's theory	Piaget's theory of cognitive development concerns how our thinking develops. He proposed that we learn by developing schemas about the world.
Language depends on thought	Children develop language by matching the correct word to their knowledge. Thought and understanding come first, language develops after.
Young children	Children only understand words when they have reached the correct stage of development and are ready. They can have language without understanding but will not be able to use it effectively.
The development of language	Sensorimotor stage: Children speak towards the end of their first year. Pre-operational stage: From 2 years they talk about things not present.
Logical thinking	Concrete operational stage: By 7 years children's language becomes mature and logical as they question things and create their own ideas.

Evaluation

Supporting evidence	One strength is that early language is not random. When children start talking they use two-word phrases like 'Mummy sock', which shows they can see how objects relate to each other. This suggests that children only start to use language when they have some understanding of it.
Language comes first	One weakness is the Sapir–Whorf hypothesis challenges Piaget. Evidence (e.g. Roberson *et al.*) suggests that language does come before thought because Berinmo people didn't have certain colour words and couldn't distinguish between colours. This suggests that Piaget may have been wrong.
EXTRA: Schema	Another weakness is that schema cannot be scientifically measured. It is very difficult to know if schema exist as we cannot directly measure them. This shows that Piaget's theory of language and thought is not based on solid scientific evidence.

KNOWLEDGE CHECK

1. Outline Piaget's view that language depends on thought. **[3 marks]**
2. Explain **one** evaluation of Piaget's theory of language. **[3 marks]**
3. Describe and evaluate Piaget's theory of language development. **[9 marks]**

Her Dad's quick camera work meant that the day Mavis projectile vomited alphabetti spaghetti would never be forgotten ...

Exam booster

More Piaget

It is important to not get this theory on language mixed up with Piaget's theory on cognitive development (see page 51). Make sure when you answer a question in this area that you specifically comment on how Piaget explained the relationship between language and thought.

APPLY IT

Read the item below and then answer the question that follows.

Toby is learning how to speak. At the age of one and a half he uses the word 'sharp' when referring to anything that is dangerous. By the age of two and a half he now uses it only in relation to objects that have an edge that can cut something, such as a knife.

- Use your knowledge of Piaget's theory to explain Toby's language development. **[3 marks]**

AO1 – Anagrams

Here are ten anagrams of words related to this topic. There are some clues to help you if you need them.

1.	ANJE TAGPIE		It's his theory!
2.	GIVETONIC		This is the kind of development the theory is about.
3.	SCAMSHE		Mental structures that help us learn about the world.
4.	ALGAEGUN		This develops after.
5.	GOTHHUT		This develops before.
6.	PELTEDVENOM		Growth.
7.	STOREROOMSIN		The stage in which children begin to speak.
8.	OPTIONALREAPER		The stage in which children can talk about things that are not present.
9.	TENCEROC AIRPLANETOO		The stage that occurs by about seven years.
10.	GOLILAC		The kind of thinking that develops in the above stage.

Elaborate to evaluate

Here's some more practice for you at developing, extending and elaborating your AO3 points.

Use the trigger phrases in the 2nd, 3rd and 4th columns to prompt you to write some sentences and construct a thorough evaluation.

A strength is that the theory is supported by evidence.	Early language …	For example, …	This shows that …
A weakness is that language may come first.	Piaget's theory is challenged by …	This argues that …	This suggests that …
A weakness concerns the nature of schema.	We cannot …	If we cannot measure schema …	This suggests that …

The specification says...

The possible relationship between language and thought.
The Sapir–Whorf hypothesis: Thinking depends on language.

Description

The hypothesis	Sapir and Whorf suggested it is not possible to think about something you don't have words for.
Thinking depends on language	Language comes first and thought afterwards. There are two versions of the hypothesis: one which believes words *determine* our thoughts and one which says that words just *influence* thoughts.
The strong version: language determines thought	If there are no words for a thought, object or idea then you can't think about it. This is why it is difficult to translate ideas from one language to another.
The weak version: language influences thought	Words help to 'carve up' the world. However, you can still imagine something with no words for it.
Which version is better?	Weaker version preferred. If the words we have for a concept or idea are limited, our ability to notice or recall that idea will be limited.

Researchers Sapir and Whorf today sensationally claimed that we cannot think about an object or a concept unless we have words for them.

Committed to the concept of snow, slush is no use.

Evaluation

The differences are exaggerated	One weakness is that differences between cultures may have been exaggerated by Boas. There are really only two words for snow in Inuit culture and actually English has other words for different types of snow. This shows that the differences aren't great and challenges the conclusion language may determine thought.
Thoughts come before language	Another weakness is that having more words for snow doesn't mean the words came first. The Inuit language may have more words for snow because there is always lots of snow. This suggests that language develops because of the way we perceive our environment, which supports Piaget's view that thinking influences language.
EXTRA: Restricted and elaborated code	One strength is that the hypothesis explains the link between language and intelligence. Bernstein suggested that working-class children will always fall behind in school because their use of the restricted code will have a negative effect on their ability to think. This shows that language influences a particular type of thinking (intelligence).

KNOWLEDGE CHECK

1. Explain what is meant by the phrase 'thinking depends on language'. **[2 marks]**
2. Explain **two** versions of the Sapir-Whorf hypothesis. **[4 marks]**
3. Describe and evaluate the Sapir-Whorf hypothesis. **[9 marks]**

Exam booster

Structuring your answer

In the exam you will not be asked to distinguish between the stronger and weaker version of the Sapir-Whorf hypothesis (because those terms are not in the specification). However, they may be a useful way to structure any answer.

APPLY IT – Research Methods

A researcher investigated the relationship between language and intelligence (as a measure of thought) with a group of students. The students took a language test and an intelligence test.

Participant	Language score	Intelligence score
1	20	40
2	10	15
3	80	70
4	50	65
5	35	45
6	30	35
7	90	85
8	65	60
9	50	45
10	10	20

1. Draw a scatter diagram of the results. **[4 marks]**
2. Describe the relationship between the two co-variables. **[2 marks]**
3. Explain **one** weakness of using correlational analysis in this study. **[2 marks]**

Fake headlines

Fake news is everywhere these days, but we're not going to stand for it. Here are some fake headlines about the Sapir-Whorf hypothesis. Rewrite them so they are true, and then write the first sentence of an imaginary article to explain the headline.

Language depends on how we think, claim researchers Sapir and Whorf.	LATE NEWS: Language comes before thinking	Researchers Sapir and Whorf today sensationally claimed that we cannot think about an object or a concept unless we have words for them.
Only one version of the Sapir-Whorf hypothesis, psychologists discover.		
Language determines thought, says weak version of S-W hypothesis.		
Strong version of S-W hypothesis much better than weak, say researchers.		

Writing thoroughly

For AO1 (on the left), describe the Sapir-Whorf hypothesis in as much detail as you can (use examples or explain things).

For AO3, practise developing and explaining further any strength or weakness you write – never write an evaluative point in just one sentence.

Complete the table by responding to the statements in each box.

In your own words, summarise the theory in no more than five sentences – one for each of the main AO1 points on the previous page.	
	Explain a weakness of the theory in three sentences – Point / Example / Conclusion
	Explain a weakness (or a strength) of the theory in three sentences – Point / Example / Conclusion
	Explain a weakness (or a strength) of the theory in three sentences – Point / Example / Conclusion

The specification says...

The effect of language and thought on our view of the world.
Variation in recall of events and recognition of colours, e.g. in Native American cultures.

Variation in recall of events

Native American cultures	Whorf studied Native American cultures to investigate whether language influences the way people think.
Native Americans: The Hopi	Hopi language doesn't distinguish between past, present and future. This influences the way they think about time.
	Evaluation: Only one individual was studied. Some argue that Hopi and European languages describe the passing of time similarly. So Whorf's conclusions lacked a firm basis in fact.
Language affects recall of events	Carmichael et al. gave two groups of participants the same pictures but each group heard different descriptions. When they were asked to draw them, the pictures drawn reflected the labels they had heard. This suggests that language influences memory.
	Evaluation: The materials used were ambiguous. Usually we would be less influenced by labels. So we may not be able to generalise the findings to everyday life.

Variation in recognition of colours

Native Americans: The Zuni	Brown and Lenneberg found that the Zuni people have only one word for shades of yellow and orange and had difficulty recognising and recalling these colours compared to English speakers. Their lack of words for those two colours affected their ability to distinguish between them.
	Evaluation: The language barrier could have affected how well the Zuni people communicated their understanding of colour to the researchers. This means the research lacks validity.
Language affects recall of colour	Roberson et al. found that the Berinmo people of New Guinea had only five words for different colours and had difficulty recalling and distinguishing between a variety of colours. Supports the Sapir–Whorf hypothesis because cognitive processes are influenced by language.
	Evaluation: Some researchers have found the opposite. The Dani people have only two words for colour but were still as good as English-speaking participants on a colour-matching task (Heider and Olivier). So their lack of colour words did not influence their ability to think about colour.

KNOWLEDGE CHECK

1. Psychologists have studied the recall of events in different cultures. Describe **one** finding from such research.   [2 marks]
2. Explain **one** criticism of research into the variation in recall of events.   [3 marks]
3. Describe and evaluate research into the recognition of colours in Native American cultures.   [9 marks]

Exam booster

Be creative when evaluating

Remember that you can use studies in other areas of the specification if they are relevant to the research you are writing about. For example, Bartlett's study supports the idea that recall of events is influenced by culture – in his study, Western participants' recall of the Native American folk story was influenced by knowledge from their own culture.

Picture shown to participants	Figure drawn by participants who saw:	
	List 1 words	List 2 words
◯━◯	Eyeglasses ◯◯	Dumbell ◯━◯
⋈	Hourglass	Table ⋈
⊓	Seven 7	Four 4
◁━	Gun ◁━	Broom

Example of material used by Carmichael et al. to test how language affects recall.

APPLY IT

Read the item below and then answer the question that follows.

A group of psychology students were given a task where they had to read a personality profile of a man. Half of the students were also told he was a father whereas the others were not. An hour later, the students were asked to recall the man's details. Students who had been told that the man was a father were more likely to recall characteristics relating to him being caring and responsible than those who were not told he was a father.

- Use your knowledge of the effect of language and thought on our view of the world to explain these results.   [3 marks]

AO1 – Fill in the blanks

Fill in the blanks in the following description of how language and thought affect our view of the world. The words are given below if you get stuck, but try and do the activity without them first.

Whorf studied Native American cultures, including the _____. These people think

about _____ in an unusual way. This is because their language does not distinguish

between past, present and _____.

Carmichael *et al.* studied how language affects _____ of events. They gave

two groups of participants identical pictures. But the labels given to the pictures were _____

for each group. The participants drew the pictures from _____. Their drawings were

affected by the labels they had heard.

Brown and _____ studied the Zuni people. Their language has _____ word for

all shades of yellow and orange. They could not recognise or recall these colours as well as

_____ speakers. The lack of words made it hard for them to distinguish between colours.

Roberson *et al.* also found that the _____ people found it hard to recall different

colours they did not have words for.

These findings all support the _____ hypothesis.

Lenneberg

different

one

recall

future

Berinmo

Sapir-Whorf

Hopi

time

English

memory

The view of the world cube

Make a small cardboard cube using the template on the right. Roll the cube and whichever phrase comes up, provide a detailed explanation of it. You can do this on your own, but if you're with other students you can take turns to explain to each other. Keep the explanation going until everyone understands it.

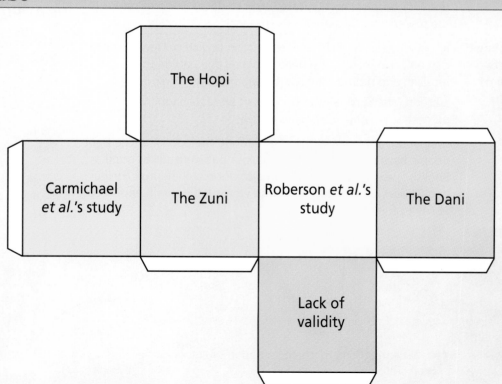

The Hopi

Carmichael *et al.*'s study

The Zuni

Roberson *et al.*'s study

The Dani

Lack of validity

The specification says...

> Differences between human and animal communication: von Frisch's bee study.

Description

The study	This study changed the way scientists thought about animal communication.
Aim	To describe the dance of the honey bee as a means of communicating information to each other.
Method	von Frisch put a food source close to the hive (within about 10–20 metres), as well as one further away (up to 300 metres). Over 20 years he made more than 6000 observations.
Results	Worker bees tell the others where pollen is located by two types of dance: • Round dance: Bee moves in a circle to indicate food is less than 100 metres away. • Waggle dance: Moving in a figure of eight, bee waggles its abdomen on the straight line in the 'middle' of the eight. This line points at the source of pollen. Speed indicates distance. 60% of bees went to food sources at the distance indicated by the dances.
Conclusion	Bees use a sophisticated form of animal communication. The signalling system has evolutionary value as it helps their survival.

Evaluation

Scientific value	One strength is that von Frisch's work made an important contribution to science. People knew that bees 'danced' but had no understanding of the meaning of the movements. This shows how valuable his research was.
Sound matters too	One weakness is the importance of sound was overlooked. When bees did dances in silence, other bees would not then go on and investigate food sources (Esch). This shows that sound-based signals also play a part in directing other bees.
EXTRA: Other factors are important	Another weakness is that bees do not always respond to the waggle dance. Bees did not use the information from the waggle dance to fly to nectar if it was placed in a boat in the middle of a lake (Gould) – perhaps not liking to fly over water. This shows von Frisch's account was incomplete.

KNOWLEDGE CHECK

1. What is meant by the term 'animal communication'? [2 marks]
2. Describe the method von Frisch used in his bee study. [3 marks]
3. Describe and evaluate the study into bees by von Frisch. [9 marks]

Exam booster

Know the task

Sometimes you have to answer an exam question that requires you to design a study – and this may include having to describe the task that participants (in this case the bees) would do. Use your knowledge of studies in the specification to do this, i.e. you might basically describe the method that von Frisch used.

Round dance (left), waggle dance (right).
There was always a buzz down at the local bee dance club.

APPLY IT - Research Methods

A researcher studied the distance 50 bees flew from their hive, giving distances to the nearest 10 metres: 60, 40, 30, 70, 50, 40, 80, 70, 30, 60, 60, 80, 30, 50, 90, 20, 40, 20, 70, 10, 90, 50, 40, 50, 70, 50, 40, 40, 60, 20, 30, 70, 20, 80, 40, 50, 60, 50, 80, 50, 70, 60, 30, 50, 40, 60, 30, 40, 40, 60.

1. Construct a frequency table from the above data. Use appropriate headings. [4 marks]

2. Draw a histogram for the data. Include a title and label the axes. [4 marks]

3. The researcher was interested in doing the study on a larger scale but did not have the resources to do it as there were approximately 4,150,000,000 bees in the UK which were too many to study. Express the total number of bees in the UK:

   a) To **one** significant figure. [1 mark]

   b) In standard form. [1 mark]

Classic study mix-up

Describe von Frisch's bee study.

Below are some sentences that will help you answer the question above. Unfortunately the sentences have become jumbled up so are in the wrong order.

Write down the right order in the boxes below so that the answer makes sense.

Aim	Method	Results	Conclusion

1. The bee moves around in a circle.

2. von Frisch made about 6000 observations over a period of 20 years.

3. The bee moves in a figure of 8, waggling its abdomen.

4. The bees' dances have evolutionary value because they promote survival.

5. 60% of the bees successfully located the food sources from the dances.

6. This indicates the food is less than 100 metres away.

7. von Frisch placed a food source about 10 to 20 metres from the hive.

8. Another type of dance is the waggle dance.

9. One type is the round dance.

10. von Frisch wanted to observe and describe the dance of the honey bees as a form of communication.

11. This points to the source of the pollen and the speed of the movement indicates distance.

12. Bees are able to use a complex form of communication.

13. He also placed another food source about 300 metres away from the hive.

14. von Frisch found that worker bees use two types of dance to communicate the location of pollen.

Match-up the AO3

Fill in the missing information.
And match up the sentences to make three full evaluation points of three sentences each.

1. Before the study, people had no idea what the _____ of the bees' movements was.	2. This suggests that von Frisch's explanation is _____ because it did not take account of this factor.	3. Another weakness is that von Frisch did not consider other important factors.
4. For example, Gould found that bees did not respond to a _____ dance if the food source was in the middle of a _____, perhaps because they didn't like to fly over water.	5. This means von Frisch's research was valuable because it gave important insights into a form of animal _____.	6. A weakness of the study is that von Frisch did not consider the role of _____.
7. For example, _____ later found that when bees dance in silence, other bees fail to go and explore for _____.	8. A strength of von Frisch's study is that it had _____ value.	9. This shows that bee communication is even more _____ because sound also plays a part.

Topic 5   Human versus animal communication

The specification says...

Differences between human and animal communication.

Limited functions of animal communication (survival, reproduction, territory, food).

Properties of human communication not present in animal communication, e.g. plan ahead and discuss future events.

Functions of animal communication

Survival	Vervet monkeys use sounds for danger (alarm calls). A specific sound warns other monkeys close by.
	Rabbits use visual signals. They lift their tail and pin ears back to communicate danger to other rabbits.
	These signals increase the survival of members of the signaller's species.
Reproduction	Animals use mating displays.
	Peacocks stretch their feathers to attract females.
	Mating displays communicate genetic fitness through brightly coloured and plentiful feathers.
Territory	Animals mark territory through spreading scents.
	Rhinos produce 20–30 piles of dung to communicate that an area is occupied.
	This has evolutionary value as it takes less energy than fighting.
Food	Animals use signals to show location of food.
	Ants leave a pheromone trail to communicate the location of a food source.

Show off.

Properties of human communication not present in animal communication

Plan ahead and discuss future events	Humans can use their language to plan ahead and discuss future events (displacement).
	In contrast, animal communication tends to focus on things that are physically present in the environment, such as food sources or predators.
	Therefore, displacement is not a part of animal communication in the same way as it is part of human communication.
Creativity	Animal communication is a closed system as the gestures, sounds and movements refer to specific events.
	Human language is an open system as words can be combined together in an infinite number of ways.
	This means that human communication has endless potential, i.e. it is creative.
Single versus multiple channels	Human language can be expressed using a whole range of different channels such as spoken, written or sign language.
	This is not a feature of animal communication which tends to use single channels such as pheromones.

Exam booster

Be creative when evaluating

If you were asked to describe differences between human and animal communication in the exam, you would not get full marks if you just state how animals and humans communicate. Instead, you must choose an area of behaviour on which they differ and explain how they differ. For example, if the area of behaviour relates to channels of communication, animals tend to use just one such as pheromones *whereas* human communication uses many channels such as speech and gestures.

APPLY IT

Read the item below and then answer the question that follows.

Donny prefers the company of his dog Max to that of people as he finds it easier to understand the dog's behaviour. For example, when Max is happy he wags his tail whereas some people will smile even when they are talking about how unhappy they are.

* Explain **one** difference between animal and human communication. Refer to Donny's experience in your answer   **[3 marks]**

KNOWLEDGE CHECK

1. With reference to a specific type of animal, explain how communication is related to survival.   **[2 marks]**
2. Outline how animals communicate their territory to other animals.   **[2 marks]**
3. Describe **two or more** properties of human communication not present in animal communication.   **[6 marks]**

AO1 – Broken sentences

Below are some sentences about human versus animal communication. They have become broken and muddled up, so put them back together again by matching the first half of each sentence in the left-hand column with the second half in the right-hand column.

1. Animals use signals to warn …	**A.** … signal that it is their territory.
2. Using warning signals …	**B.** … lifting their tails and pinning back their ears.
3. Vervet monkeys use …	**C.** … increases survival chances of members of the species.
4. Rabbits use visual signals by …	**D.** … a pheromone (chemical) trail for other ants to follow to a food source.
5. Animals increase their chances …	**E.** … communicates his genetic fitness to attract females.
6. The male peacock's spectacular tail-feather display …	**F.** … different alarm calls to warn other monkeys of specific dangers.
7. A rhino can spread 20 to 30 piles of dung over an area to …	**G.** … of danger.
8. Marking territory with scents has evolutionary value because …	**H.** … it uses less energy than fighting.
9. Animals can communicate the location of …	**I.** … of reproducing by using mating displays.
10. Ants leave …	**J.** … a food source by using signals.

Explaining the differences

Humans and animals both use communication, but in quite different ways. This activity helps you to explain and organise these differences to (hopefully) make them more memorable. You can do this by just completing the table.

Plan ahead and discuss future events	In humans …	But animals …	So the difference is …
Creativity	Human language …	Animal communication …	So the difference is …
Single versus multiple channels	Humans …	Animal communication …	So the difference is …

Non-verbal communication: Definitions of non-verbal communication and verbal communication.

Functions of eye contact including regulating flow of conversation, signalling attraction and expressing emotion.

Description

Verbal and non-verbal communication	Verbal communication is any communication involving spoken or written words.
	Only part of communication is verbal and the other half is non-verbal communication (NVC).
Eye contact	When two people look at each other's eyes at the same time.
Regulating flow of conversation	Kendon found that speakers looked away when they were about to speak and gave prolonged eye contact when about to finish.
	Shows eye contact encourages turn-taking in conversation.
Signalling attraction	Conway *et al.* found that people who use eye contact are judged as more attractive even with a negative facial expression.
Expressing emotion	Adams and Kleck found that participants judged emotions of joy and anger as more intense when shown a picture of someone gazing straight at them as opposed to gazing away.
	In contrast, they judged emotions of fear and sadness as more intense when the gaze in the picture was averted.

Evaluation

Real-world application	One strength is that studies can explain an important feature of autism.
	People with autism may have difficulty communicating with others because they avoid eye contact.
	Knowing the importance of eye contact means that people with autism could be taught these skills.
Use of rating scales	One weakness is the use of rating scales to make judgements.
	Studies in this area rely on people rating their views of 'attractiveness' and 'intensity of emotion', and these are open to bias and interpretation.
	This suggests that studies of eye contact may produce subjective evidence.
EXTRA: Artificial studies	Another weakness is that studies of eye contact involve quite artificial tasks.
	In Kendon's study, participants were asked to get to know someone as part of the experiment.
	This means the conclusions may lack validity as they do not reflect what would happen in everyday life.

She was aiming for 'flirty', but 'starey and slightly sinister' was probably nearer the mark.

Exam booster

Contextualise your evaluation

In order to gain top marks in the exam for evaluation you need to link the point that you make to the research you are evaluating. If you say that a weakness of a study is that rating scales were used you will get few marks – you need to explain why this feature is an issue for research on eye contact.

APPLY IT – Research Methods

In a study on the role of eye contact in conversation, two people have a conversation. In one condition the listener looks at the floor, whilst in the other condition they maintain eye contact with the speaker. Two independent observers judge how many speech errors the speaker makes.

1. Identify **two** categories of behaviour that could be used to represent speech errors.   **[2 marks]**

2. Explain how the researcher could check interobserver reliability in the study.   **[2 marks]**

3. Explain **one** way that the researcher could standardise the procedure in this study.   **[2 marks]**

KNOWLEDGE CHECK

1. What is meant by 'eye contact'?   **[2 marks]**

2. Using an example, explain what is meant by 'non-verbal communication'.   **[3 marks]**

3. Describe and evaluate the function of eye contact.   **[9 marks]**

AO1 – Eye contact wordsearch

There are ten words related to eye contact for you to find in the grid on the right. They could be vertical, horizontal or diagonal (but not backwards).

NONVERBAL

COMMUNICATION

EYE CONTACT

KENDON

CONVERSATION

TURNTAKING

CONWAY

ATTRACTION

EMOTIONS

GAZE

I	T	Z	E	V	K	K	L	D	Z	N	Q	O	P	D
R	P	J	Y	Y	V	K	S	G	T	O	E	R	F	B
T	A	T	V	K	E	N	X	Z	X	N	I	W	T	A
U	T	U	Q	E	V	C	U	R	V	V	Z	R	P	Y
R	T	V	N	Q	M	V	O	I	D	E	A	V	W	S
N	R	V	D	Z	H	O	F	N	K	R	W	L	D	D
T	A	H	R	E	I	K	T	U	B	L	N	U	Y
A	C	C	O	M	M	U	N	I	C	A	T	I	O	N
K	T	E	Y	G	C	K	C	V	O	L	C	W	H	K
I	I	C	W	T	O	K	G	G	V	N	W	T	I	E
N	O	U	M	Z	N	J	P	S	E	J	S	Z	F	N
G	N	N	W	R	W	G	W	M	B	M	Z	O	Z	D
Q	T	K	K	J	A	A	E	N	T	F	U	S	K	O
A	Q	W	U	C	Y	Z	T	Z	P	K	T	O	Y	N
F	Z	C	O	N	V	E	R	S	A	T	I	O	N	E

Evaluate with trigger phrases

On the right are some 'trigger' phrases related to research into eye contact. The first thing to do is decide which phrases go together by putting them into pairs in the table. Then write a sentence in column 3, explaining each pair of statements (or giving an example) without looking at your notes or on the previous page. Finally, in column 4, write a further sentence, to explain why your first sentence is a strength/weakness.

The first one is done for you.

People indicate their views of attractiveness and 'emotional intensity'.

Difficulty in communicating.

For example, in Kendon's study.

Artificial tasks.

Uses rating scales.

Explains autism.

Explains autism.	Difficulty in communicating.	People with autism find it hard to communicate with others because they have difficulty using eye contact appropriately.	This is a strength of eye contact research because it means people with autism can be helped to develop communication skills.

The specification says...

Non-verbal communication: Body language including open and closed posture, postural echo and touch.

Description

Body language	Communication through unspoken movements and gestures.
Open and closed posture	Closed posture = crossing your arms and/or legs, communicates rejection or disagreement.
	Open posture = arms and legs not crossed, communicates approval and acceptance.
	McGinley *et al.* found that participants were more likely to change their opinions in line with a female confederate if she had adopted an open posture when discussing her views, not a closed posture.
Postural echo	Copying each other's body position.
	Tanner and Chartrand found that participants had more positive feelings towards a new drink if the researcher had used postural echo during the interview, than if there was no postural echo.
Touch	'Touch' in a social interaction includes high fives, slapping, putting hand on a shoulder.
	Fisher *et al.* found that students handed books by a librarian who touched them on the hand were more positive about the librarian than those who were not touched.

Evaluation

Real-world application	One strength is that the research can be applied to real-world situations.
	People who are trying to create a good relationship with others should use an open posture, postural echo and touch.
	This shows the research is useful in everyday life.
Body language studies lack control	One weakness is that the studies are not always well controlled.
	For example, in the library study (Fisher *et al.*) there may have been other reasons why the participants liked or disliked the librarian aside from the presence or absence of touch.
	This is a problem for the validity of the results.
EXTRA: Body language studies are unethical	Another weakness is that research in this area raises ethical issues.
	For example, field experiments on postural echo and touch involved a lack of informed consent. It is also unclear if participants were debriefed.
	This could affect the trust people have in psychologists.

Exam booster

Defining key terms

Make sure you do not use the word you are defining when writing a definition. For example, if defining the term 'body language', don't say 'communication using your body' but instead replace the word 'body' with an alternative word/phrase such as 'movements and gestures'.

APPLY IT

Study the item below and then answer the question that follows.

- Identify and briefly describe **one** feature of body language shown by the people in the picture which might indicate that they like each other. Refer to the method and results of **one** psychological investigation to support your answer. **[5 marks]**

KNOWLEDGE CHECK

1. What is meant by the term 'postural echo'? **[2 marks]**
2. Use your knowledge of psychology to explain how people use open posture in an everyday situation. **[2 marks]**
3. Describe and evaluate research into body language. Refer to 'touch' in your answer. **[9 marks]**

Use examples to boost your AO1

Using examples is a great way to add detail to your descriptions. In the boxes below, write down definitions of the four body language terms from this topic. Add examples to take your definitions further. Try to think of different examples from the ones on the previous page.

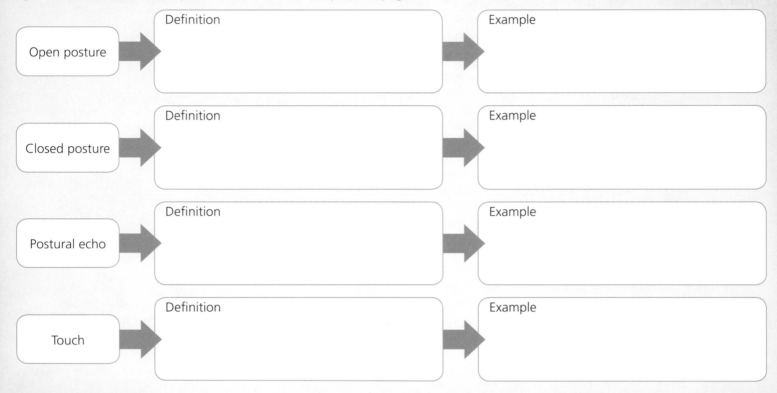

| Open posture | → | Definition | → | Example |

| Closed posture | → | Definition | → | Example |

| Postural echo | → | Definition | → | Example |

| Touch | → | Definition | → | Example |

AO3 – Fill in the blanks

Complete the evaluation by filling in the missing words. Try to avoid looking at the words below unless you get really stuck.

One strength of research is that it has practical _____. For example, it can help people form romantic relationships – adopt an _____ posture, echo the other person's _____ and use (safe) touch carefully. This is a strength because it means the research has validity in the real _____.

However, a weakness is that research studies do not have much control. For example, Fisher *et al.* could not control all the _____ in their library study, so _____ was not the only reason why the participants liked or disliked the librarian. This is a weakness because it means the findings of studies lack _____.

Another weakness is that body language research raises ethical issues. For example, it is difficult to gain informed _____ from participants in field experiments and to carry out _____. This is a weakness because people become wary of _____ psychologists if their studies are unethical.

debriefing

world

touch

applications

open

trusting

validity

consent

posture

variables

128

The specification says...

Non-verbal communication: Personal space including cultural, status and gender differences.

Description

Personal space	The distance we keep between ourselves and others.
	We feel uncomfortable when it is invaded and try to defend it by moving away.
Cultural differences	Sommer found that English people's personal space is 1–1.5 metres whereas Arabs' is much less.
	Collett found that Englishmen who stood closer and gave more eye contact were better liked by Arabs.
Gender differences	Men prefer a larger social distance when interacting with men than women talking to other women.
	Fisher and Byrne found that women felt more uncomfortable when a confederate invaded their personal space from the side whereas with men it was from the front.
Status differences	Status is someone's rank within society or the workplace.
	Zahn found that people with a similar status maintain a closer personal space than those with unequal status.

The estate agent had described it as 'a compact flat with potential' but Simon wasn't convinced.

Evaluation

Real-world application	One strength is that this research has proved useful in everyday life.
	For example, doctors could use knowledge about cultural differences.
	Therefore it has a positive impact on the real world.
Over simplistic	One weakness is that research into personal space only looks at one factor at a time.
	In reality, several factors may be affecting personal space distances at the same time such as culture, gender and status.
	This makes research in this area too simplistic.
EXTRA: Unrepresentative samples	Another weakness is that studies may use unrepresentative samples.
	It is difficult to use a sample of people in a personal space experiment that reflects all people within a culture, or all males and all females.
	This means we should be cautious in generalising the findings to everyone in that culture.

Exam booster

Identifying a factor

Exam questions may ask you to identify a factor that affects personal space and then design a study that investigates the factor. Make sure you choose wisely, it is best to choose a factor for which you know a study.

APPLY IT – Research Methods

A study looked at gender and personal space in a local park. A female confederate sat on a park bench next to 10 participants who were female and 9 who were male. The researcher timed (in seconds) how long it took the person (participant) to move away from the bench:

Same gender: 59, 75, 60, 45, 70, 49, 52, 62, 75, 40.

Different gender: 20, 15, 28, 32, 12, 25, 38, 15, 19.

1. Identify the experimental design used in this study. Explain your answer. [2 marks]

2. Explain **one** strength of the design you have identified in question 1. [2 marks]

3. Calculate the mean for each condition. Show your workings. [4 marks]

4. Draw a conclusion about the role that gender plays on personal space. Refer to the results of the above study in your answer. [2 marks]

KNOWLEDGE CHECK

1. What is meant by the term 'personal space'? [2 marks]

2. Outline the way status affects personal space. [3 marks]

3. Describe and evaluate how cultural differences and gender affect personal space. [9 marks]

Three-column AO1 match-up

Match up the statements across the three columns.

Personal space	1. Sommer: Arab people prefer much smaller personal space than English people.	5. Collett: Arab people liked English people who stood closer and gave more eye contact.
Cultural differences	2. This refers to how people vary in their position in society or the workplace, etc.	6. Zahn: people who have similar status interact more closely than people who have unequal status.
Gender differences	3. This refers to the distance we prefer to maintain between ourselves and other people.	7. Fisher and Byrne: men felt uncomfortable when personal space invaded from the front, whereas women more uncomfortable when space invaded from the side.
Status differences	4. Women interacting with other women prefer a shorter social distance than men interacting with other men.	8. When this is invaded we feel uncomfortable and will move away to increase it.

AO3 – Broken sentences

There is an evaluation of personal space research in the following sentences, but it has become jumbled up. Put the sentences together correctly (the first half is in the first column, the second half is in the second column). Then take the completed sentences and put them together into three elaborated points of three sentences each (Point / Explanation or Example / Conclusion).

1. In real-life situations, personal space preferences are affected by …

A. … generalise the findings of studies to everyone.

2. This is a strength because …

B. … are unrepresentative.

3. For example, participants in personal space experiments rarely reflect …

C. … cultural differences in personal space preferences when dealing with patients.

4. One strength of personal space research is that …

D. … several interacting factors (e.g. culture, gender, status).

5. This is a weakness because it means that research often ignores …

E. … it means the research has validity in the real world.

6. This is a weakness because it makes it difficult to …

F. … all people within a culture, or all males and all females.

7. A weakness of research is that it only investigates …

G. … it has uses in everyday life.

8. Another weakness is that the samples of participants in studies …

H. … important factors, making it simplistic.

9. For example, it is useful for doctors to know about…

I. … the role of one factor at a time.

> **Explanations of non-verbal behaviour: Darwin's evolutionary theory of non-verbal communication as evolved and adaptive.**

Description

Darwin and evolution	Darwin proposed the theory of natural selection: The genes for any behaviour that improves an animal's chances of survival and reproduction are more likely to be passed to the next generation. Therefore the genes have been naturally selected.
Non-verbal communication as evolved and adaptive	Non-verbal behaviours that are beneficial (adaptive) are naturally selected. Baring teeth in a fight causes the attacked animal to get scared and leave, and therefore both animals in the fight are more likely to survive. This means the behaviour is adaptive – it helps protect survival.
Comparisons with human behaviour	Opening eyes wide indicates surprise because it evolved from animal behaviour – it would help animals under threat to see an escape route. This behaviour is passed down to humans and continues to express surprise.
Serviceable habits	Behaviours adaptive to our distant ancestors (e.g. wrinkling the nose and baring teeth). These behaviours still show how we feel but may not serve the original adaptive purpose.

The number of times I need to bare my teeth to get what I want.

Exam booster

Apply Darwin to non-verbal communication

If you are asked to describe Darwin's theory in the exam, remember to explain the adaptiveness of behaviour rather than physical characteristics (such as a giraffe's long neck). Examples of why non-verbal behaviours are adaptive would be good ones to use.

Evaluation

Research into facial expressions	One strength is the theory is supported by research. Ekman *et al.* identified six primary emotions: surprise, fear, disgust, anger, happiness and sadness that are found in all people. If a behaviour is universal this suggests it is in our genes, supporting Darwin's evolutionary theory.
Research into newborns	Another strength is support from newborn baby studies. Babies are born with the ability to smile or maintain eye contact, which suggests that, because these behaviours are present at birth, they are innate. If these behaviours are innate this supports the idea that they have been selected by evolution to help the child's survival.
EXTRA: Cultural differences in non-verbal communication	One weakness is that Darwin's theory can't explain cultural differences in non-verbal communication. Personal space and gestures differ from culture to culture, This suggests the theory doesn't explain all non-verbal communication.

APPLY IT – Research Methods

Past research has suggested that people with dilated pupils are seen as more attractive. A lab experiment was carried out to investigate this. Participants were shown two pictures of the same woman. In one condition, the woman's pupils were of normal size whilst in the second condition, they were dilated. Each participant had to rate the attractiveness of each picture.

1. Write a suitable hypothesis for this investigation. **[2 marks]**

2. Explain **one** strength of using a repeated measures design in this study. **[2 marks]**

3. Order effects are an issue with studies like the one above. Explain how counterbalancing could have been carried out to reduce the impact of order effects in the above study. **[3 marks]**

KNOWLEDGE CHECK

1. What is meant by the term 'adaptive'? **[2 marks]**

2. Explain what is meant by the phrase 'non-verbal communication has evolved'. **[2 marks]**

3. Describe and evaluate Darwin's evolutionary theory. **[9 marks]**

Evolutionary theory crossword

Complete the crossword to see how familiar you are with terms relating to Darwin's evolutionary theory.

DOWN

1. Behaviours that protect survival of the species are A_____. (8)

5. A behaviour babies are born with. S_____. (7)

6. What Darwin's theory is all about. E_____. (9)

7. These are passed on. G_____. (5)

9. This emotion has often been studied. Well I never!! S_____. (8)

11. He identified six primary emotions. E_____. (5)

ACROSS

2. Some behaviours improve our chances of survival and R_____. (12)

3. Darwin talked about S_____ habits. (11)

4. Darwin's explanation of how evolution happens. N_____ S_____. (7,9)

8. If a behaviour is in our genes, it is U_____. (9)

10. The theory can't explain C_____ differences. (8)

11. Faces express this. E_____. (7)

AO3 – Match-up

Work out which statements in the first column go with the statements in the second column.

1. There is some research support for Darwin's evolutionary theory.	**A.** These include different preferences for personal space distances and uses of gestures.
2. There are six primary emotions, including fear, disgust and surprise.	**B.** This shows that Darwin's theory does not explain all forms of non-verbal behaviour.
3. Babies are born with the ability to smile and maintain eye contact.	**C.** For example, the findings of the study by Ekman.
4. There are some cultural differences in non-verbal behaviour.	**D.** These behaviours are adaptive because they promote the baby's survival, suggesting they are innate.
5. Darwin's evolutionary theory has difficulty explaining these differences.	**E.** These are found in all cultures, suggesting this behaviour is innate.

The specification says...

Explanations of non-verbal behaviour: Evidence that non-verbal behaviour is innate, e.g. in neonates and the sensory deprived.

Evidence that non-verbal behaviour is learned.

Evidence that non-verbal behaviour is innate

Neonate research	Neonate = a newborn baby.
	If non-verbal behaviour is shown at birth it is likely to be innate.
Social releasers	These are non-verbal behaviours like smiling which make others want to look after babies (Bowlby).
	This is adaptive because it means that a young baby will be looked after and the genes passed on.
Facial expressions	Rosenstein and Oster found that young babies' faces showed disgust with novel foods like citric acid (found in lemons).
	This suggests such facial expressions as a way of communicating emotions are innate.
Sensory deprived	An animal or human without a sensory ability, such as hearing or sight. If they show the same non-verbal behaviour as people with normal hearing or vision this suggests the behaviours are innate.
	Thompson found similarity in blind children and children with normal vision in terms of facial expressions such as surprise.

'You can't learn to be this cute', boasted Tibbles. *'You've either got it or you ain't.'*

Evidence that non-verbal behaviour is learned

Cross-cultural research	Comparing behaviours between cultural groups. If behaviours are different this suggests that they are learned rather than innate.
Contact versus non-contact cultures	One cultural difference in non-verbal behaviours is in terms of personal space.
	People from contact cultures (the Mediterranean and Latin America) are comfortable with smaller personal space.
	People from non-contact cultures (the UK and the US) maintain a larger distance between themselves and others.
Gestures	Pointing one's index finger is acceptable in Western culture to emphasise what is being said but offensive in Hindu culture where people tend to point with their thumbs (Black).
Explaining cultural differences	Social learning theory can explain cultural differences (observing and imitating others).
	People observe what other people in their culture are doing (e.g. personal space) and copy those behaviours.

Exam booster

Don't outline the whole study when evaluating

If you are writing an evaluation point and using a study as support for a theory then you don't need to describe the whole study. For example, if you are asked to evaluate the view that non-verbal behavior is innate [3 marks], write a sentence briefly summarising the method and results of a relevant study and then explain how the study's results show that we are born with our non-verbal behaviour.

APPLY IT

Study the conversation below and then answer the question that follows.

Kim: I think non-verbal behaviour is instinctive as neonates can show different facial expressions which they couldn't have learned.

Karen: I am not so sure as I have friends from Italy who have different mannerisms from me and my friends. For example, they stand much closer when talking to us.

• Identify evidence from the above item that non-verbal behaviour is innate and/or learned. Use research to support your answer.   **[4 marks]**

KNOWLEDGE CHECK

1. What is meant by the term 'neonate'?   **[1 mark]**
2. Outline evidence that non-verbal behaviour is learned.   **[4 marks]**
3. Outline evidence that non-verbal behaviour is innate.   **[4 marks]**

Put it right

The passage below is a description of the evidence that non-verbal behaviour is innate. Unfortunately eleven mistakes have crept into it. Your task is to identify the errors and correct them.

A lot of research into non-verbal behaviour has been carried out with neonates. A neonate is a child aged between one and two years. If a non-verbal behaviour such as eye contact is present at birth, this means it is probably learned.

Smiling is an example of a social reliever – these are non-verbal behaviours that encourage adults to look after babies, according to Darwin. This behaviour is adaptive because if the baby is not looked after its genes will not be passed on.

Rosencrantz and Guildenstern found that young babies expressed happiness when they were fed novel foods like citric acid (found in crisps). This suggests that using facial expressions to communicate must be learned.

An animal is sensory deprived if it lacks the ability to move. Thompson found that blind and sighted children differed in their ability to use facial expressions. This suggests that the behaviour is innate.

Evaluate with trigger phrases

There is some evidence that non-verbal behaviour is innate. And there is some evidence that it is learned. But which is which? Place the evidence into the correct columns (in any order).

Evidence it's innate	Evidence it's learned

1. Rosenstein and Oster's research.

2. Black's research into gesturing.

3. Cross-cultural research.

4. Role of social releasers (Bowlby).

5. Social learning theory.

6. Research with neonates.

7. Contact versus non-contact cultures.

8. Thompson's study with blind children.

The specification says...

Explanations of non-verbal behaviour: Yuki's study of emoticons.

Description

The study	Comparing cultural understanding of non-verbal behaviour can show whether it is universal or learned.
Aim	To find out if there is a difference in how emoticons are understood by people in the East (Japan) and the West (America).
Method	95 students from Japan and 118 students from America – an independent groups design. Six emoticons were shown with different combinations of eyes and mouths (sad, happy or neutral). Participants rated the emoticons for happiness using a 9-point scale.
Results	The Japanese gave higher ratings to faces with happy eyes than the Americans, even when the mouth was sad. Americans gave higher ratings when mouths were happy even when the eyes were sad.
Conclusion	This suggests that cultural groups interpret facial expressions differently, which may be due to cultural norms and expectations.

(1)   (2)   (3)   (4)   (5)   (6)

From left to right: (1) happy eyes + neutral mouth, (2) neutral eyes + sad mouth, (3) happy eyes + sad mouth, (4) neutral eyes + happy mouth, (5) sad eyes + neutral mouth, (6) sad eyes + happy mouth.

Emoticons. Why bother using precious facial muscles when you can say it with the touch of a button?

Evaluation

Artificial materials	One weakness is that emoticons may not represent human faces. Emoticons do not include those tell-tale lines on people's faces which give us further information of how to interpret their eyes and mouth. This means the results of the study may lack relevance to everyday life.
Only tested one emotion	Another weakness is the study only investigated two types of emotion. In everyday life, faces express a whole range of emotions – fear, surprise, disgust, etc. Therefore, the study does not give us insight into how the full range of emotional expressions are interpreted by people of different cultures.
EXTRA: Using rating scales	A further weakness is that rating scales may not be the best method of measurement. Emotions are very complex and rating scales reduce emotion to a single score. Therefore Yuki *et al.* may have measured the interpretation of emotions in too simple a way.

KNOWLEDGE CHECK

1. What is meant by an 'emoticon'? **[2 marks]**
2. Outline the method used in Yuki's study into emoticons. **[3 marks]**
3. Describe and evaluate Yuki's study of emoticons. **[9 marks]**

Exam booster

Including ...

If a question asks you to include something then you must write about it. For example, *Describe Yuki's study of emoticons. Include in your answer the method used, the results obtained and conclusion drawn.* If you just described the aim, method and results you would not get full marks, even if you mentioned a lot of relevant detail, as you have not fully answered the question.

APPLY IT – Research Methods

A researcher wanted to investigate whether students preferred teachers that smiled more than those that didn't. Twenty A level students were approached in their common room and asked to take part. They were each given 30 pictures to look at, 15 of which had teachers smiling, whilst the other 15 had teachers not smiling. For each picture students had to state how much they liked the teacher on a scale of 1 to 10.

1. Explain how randomisation could have been used to reduce bias in this study. **[2 marks]**
2. Identify the sampling method used and explain a weakness of this sampling method in relation to this study. **[3 marks]**
3. Write a null hypothesis for this investigation. **[2 marks]**
4. Identify **one** extraneous variable that might have been a problem in this study and explain how it could have been controlled. **[3 marks]**

Classic study – true or false?

Here are some sentences about Yuki's study of emoticons. Indicate whether you think each one is true or false. For the false statements, write down the true versions in the spaces provided.

		True or false?	
1.	The study involved comparing people from different cultures.		
2.	Yuki wanted to investigate differences in how Japanese and American people understand body language.		
3.	The study was an experiment using a repeated measures design.		
4.	213 students participated in the study.		
5.	The participants were shown seven different emoticons.		
6.	The participants rated the emoticons for anger using a 7-point scale.		
7.	Japanese students gave higher scores to faces with happy eyes than American students did.		
8.	Japanese students gave higher ratings to the faces with happy mouths than American students did.		
9.	Yuki concluded that how we interpret facial expressions is probably due to nature rather than nurture.		
10.	The study used materials that represented human faces very realistically.		
11.	A weakness of the study is that it only tested one emotion.		
12.	The rating scale used in the study was highly valid.		

Storyboarding Yuki's study

Visual images can be useful, so why not outline Yuki's study in pictures? Take the main elements of the study and try to represent them with drawings, like a film director might do with a 'storyboard', a series of images that tell the story of the film (or study) from start to finish. Here's a template to help you along.

The specification says...

The divisions of the human nervous system: central and peripheral (somatic and autonomic), basic functions of these divisions.

Structure

The nervous system	Collects and responds to information in the environment. Controls working of different organs and cells including the brain.
Subdivisions	CNS + PNS CNS = brain and spinal cord PNS = ANS + SNS ANS = sympathetic and parasympathetic

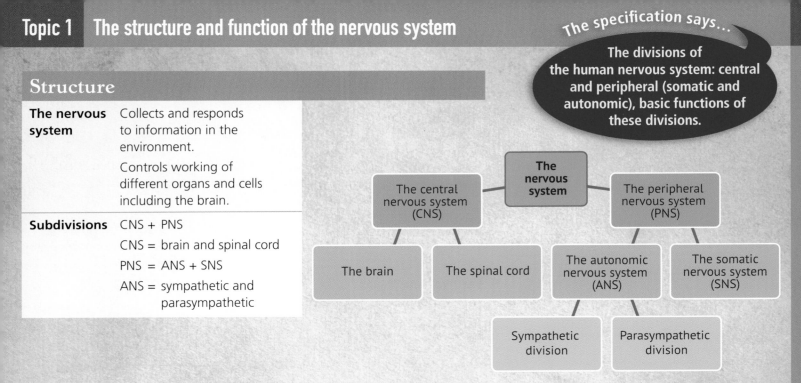

Function

Central nervous system (CNS)	The brain is divided into two halves (hemispheres). Right hemisphere controls the left side of body and vice versa. The brain is the centre of conscious awareness and where all decision making takes place. The brain stem governs some automatic functions (e.g. heartbeat) and reflex responses.
Peripheral nervous system (PNS)	Receives messages from the CNS. Sends messages to the CNS. Messages sent via neurons.
Autonomic nervous system (ANS)	Governs automatic (involuntary) functions. For example, breathing, heart rate, digestion and the body's response to stress.
Somatic nervous system (SNS)	Sends information from the brain to muscles, voluntary control of our muscles plus reflex responses. Takes in information from sensory organs, such as the eyes and the skin.

Exam booster

Can I use abbreviations?

Yes – but it is best to spell out the abbreviation the first time you use it as a way of showing off your knowledge of key terminology. For example, when mentioning the *autonomic nervous system*, write (ANS) after the term when you first mention it. You can then refer to it as the ANS in future. However, if you can't remember the full version then the abbreviation is acceptable (as long as it is well-known).

KNOWLEDGE CHECK

1. What is meant by the term 'somatic nervous system'? **[1 mark]**
2. Explain the function of the peripheral nervous system. **[3 marks]**
3. Draw a diagram showing how the nervous system is structured. Include in your diagram: central nervous system, peripheral nervous system, somatic nervous system, autonomic nervous system. **[4 marks]**

APPLY IT - Research Methods

A study on how prisoners responded to traumatic situations used a systematic sample of 50 prisoners from a prison population of 500. They had their heart rate measured whilst being shown a film of someone being murdered. They were also interviewed afterwards about how stressful they found the film.

1. Explain how the researcher would have recruited a systematic sample for this study. **[2 marks]**
2. Explain the difference between qualitative and quantitative methods in psychology. Refer to the above study in your answer. **[3 marks]**

Nervous system match-up

Match up the statements in the three columns.

1. Receives information from sensory organs.

2. Autonomic nervous system (ANS)

3. Sends information to voluntary muscles.

4. Includes centre of conscious awareness.

5. Consists of brain and spinal cord.

6. Central nervous system (CNS)

7. Consists of sympathetic and parasympathetic branches.

8. Has two hemispheres.

9. Left controls right side of body, and vice versa.

10. Connects to brain via brain stem.

11. Somatic nervous system (SNS)

12. Controls involuntary functions.

13. Brain

14. Spinal cord

15. Important role in reflex behaviour.

Nervous system maths

Complete up the following 'equations' by filling in the blank boxes.

Nervous system	=	☐	+	☐
Brain	=	2	×	☐
Spinal cord	=	CNS	−	☐
PNS	=	☐	+	☐
ANS	=	☐	+	☐

The specification says...

The autonomic nervous system and the fight or flight response.

The autonomic nervous system

Homeostasis	Keeping the body in a constant and balanced internal state. For example: • Levels of carbon dioxide in the blood controlled through regular breathing. • Body temperature maintained at 37 degrees centigrade by monitoring activity of the body's organs.
An 'automatic' system	We don't have to consciously direct the ANS. Breathing, our heart beating, etc., is vital to life so it needs to be involuntary.
Sympathetic nervous system	Works in opposition to the parasympathetic nervous system. A state of physiological arousal (e.g. heart beats faster) to prepare for the *fight or flight response*.
Parasympathetic nervous system	Parasympathetic nervous system produces the opposite effect to sympathetic nervous system. This *rest and digest response* returns the body to normal resting state once the threat has gone.

The fight or flight response

Brain detects threat	The hypothalamus identifies a threatening event (a stressor). Triggers the sympathetic division of the ANS to act.
Release of adrenaline	The ANS changes from resting state (parasympathetic) to an aroused (sympathetic) state. The stress hormone adrenaline is released from the adrenal glands into the bloodstream.
Fight or flight response	Immediate and automatic. Adrenaline targets the cardiovascular system, increasing heart rate and breathing. Also inhibits digestion and inhibits saliva production. Prepares the body to confront the threat (fight) or provide energy to run away (flight).
Once the threat has passed	Parasympathetic division returns body to normal 'rest and digest' state. Digestion and hunger stimulated.

KNOWLEDGE CHECK

1. Identify **three** bodily changes that occur during the fight or flight response.   **[3 marks]**
2. Explain what happens in the fight or flight response.   **[5 marks]**
3. Explain the function of the autonomic nervous system.   **[2 marks]**

APPLY IT

Read the item below and then answer the question that follows.

Holly sees herself as a bit of a practical joker and decides to surprise her friend Tom by jumping out from behind the door when he walks into the room. Tom's reaction makes Holly feel bad as his face goes red and he starts breathing more heavily.

• Use your knowledge of the autonomic nervous system and the fight or flight response to explain Tom's reaction to Holly's surprise.   **[4 marks]**

Sympathetic state	Parasympathetic state
Increases heart rate	Decreases heart rate
Increases breathing rate	Decreases breathing rate
Dilates pupils	Contracts pupils
Inhibits digestion	Stimulates digestion
Inhibits saliva production	Stimulates saliva production
Contracts rectum	Relaxes rectum

Learn the big picture

An exam question may review your knowledge of more than one section of the specification so it is important to know how everything links together. For example, you may be asked to *use your knowledge of the actions of both the central nervous system and the autonomic nervous system* to explain a person's behaviour. The first part of the task would relate to the information on the previous spread so it is important that you learn how all parts of the nervous system work together.

Exam booster

Complete the table

Match up the statements across the three columns.

Organ/function	Sympathetic response	Parasympathetic response
Heart rate		
Pupils		
Digestion		
Saliva production		
Breathing rate		
Rectum		

Decreases   Stimulates   Increases   Constricts   Inhibits   Relaxes

Dilates   Decreases   Inhibits   Increases   Contracts   Stimulates

Fight or flight – true or false?

What do you know about the fight or fight response? Find out by identifying which of the following statements are true and which are false. For the false ones, write them so that they are true.

		True or false?	
1.	A threatening event is detected in the brain by the spinal cord.		
2.	This triggers activity in the sympathetic division of the CNS.		
3.	Before the stressor, the ANS was in a parasympathetic state.		
4.	Now it switches to an aroused (sympathetic) state.		
5.	This triggers the adrenal glands to release the hormone insulin into the bloodstream.		
6.	Fight or flight occurs eventually once we decide how to act.		
7.	Adrenaline affects the cardiovascular system, for example by decreasing heart rate and breathing rate.		
8.	These physiological changes prepare the body to confront the threat (fight) or provide the energy to run away (flight).		
9.	After the stressor is over, the body switches from parasympathetic arousal to a sympathetic state of 'vest and detest'.		

Description

The theory	Physiological arousal comes first and emotion after.
	Two similar theories were proposed and combined.
Physiological arousal first	An event causes physiological arousal in the following way:
	Hypothalamus arouses the sympathetic division of the ANS.
	Adrenaline is released and creates physiological arousal (heart rate increased, etc. = fight or flight response).
Emotion afterwards	Brain *interprets* the physiological activity.
	Causes emotions, e.g. fear, excitement, love.
An example	Seeing a bear activates the sympathetic division.
	Muscles tense, heart pounds.
	These physiological changes interpreted as fear.
	Person runs away.
No physical changes = no emotion	If no physiological changes occur then emotions are not experienced.
	For example, if you stand in front of your class and your heart rate doesn't increase, then you do not feel scared because there are no physiological changes.

Evaluation

Evidence that emotions do come after arousal	One strength of the theory is real-life examples.
	A phobia of public situations can develop as a result of the anxiety (emotion) of falling down in public.
	This shows that emotional responses are a result of physiological arousal such as increased heart rate.
Challenged by the Cannon–Bard theory	One weakness is the challenge by Cannon–Bard.
	We experience some emotions (e.g. embarrassment) at the same time as physiological arousal and not one after the other.
	Therefore the Cannon-Bard theory can explain emotional situations that the James–Lange theory cannot.
EXTRA: James–Lange theory may be too simple	Another weakness is that the James-Lange theory is challenged by the two-factor theory.
	We need arousal *plus* social cues to correctly label the emotion we are feeling (Schachter and Singer).
	So the James–Lange theory does not explain how a person 'decides' the emotion they are experiencing.

KNOWLEDGE CHECK

1. Explain the role of the autonomic nervous system in the James–Lange theory of emotion. **[3 marks]**

2. Explain **one** criticism of the James–Lange theory of emotion. **[4 marks]**

3. Outline and evaluate the James–Lange theory of emotion. **[9 marks]**

Exam booster

How much description?

When describing psychological knowledge in the exam, you should use the number of marks available for the question as a guide for how much to write. For example, if you were given a 4-mark question asking you to *describe the James–Lange theory of emotion* then you should aim to write four relevant points about the theory and about 25 words for each point. So if you make as many relevant points as there are marks, you can't go far wrong!

No, don't run, I didn't mean it.

APPLY IT – Research Methods

A study investigated how physiological arousal affects judgements of attractiveness. One group of participants were asked to run on the spot as they rated 10 photos for attractiveness (on a scale of 1 to 5). A second group were asked to rate attractiveness while swaying gently.

1. Explain why the second group had to sway gently while completing the task. **[3 marks]**

2. Explain how the researcher could have standardised the procedures. **[3 marks]**

3. Explain **one** weakness of measuring attractiveness using a questionnaire. **[2 marks]**

Put it right

The passage below is a description of the James–Lange theory of emotion, but it contains 11 errors.
Your task is to identify the errors and correct them.

According to the theory, we experience an emotion before physiological arousal. Arousal occurs when the hypothalamus of the brain stimulates the parasympathetic division of the CNS. This releases the hormone oestrogen and creates physiological arousal, for example increased heart rate, sometimes called the fright and flight response.

The brain then interprets this physiological activity which causes us to experience an emotion such as fear or excitement.

To take an example, if you see a bear about to attack you, this activates the parasympathetic division. Your muscles relax and your heart rate slows down. Your brain interprets these changes as 'happiness'. You might then run away.

If there are no physiological changes in the body, then you will still experience the emotion. For example, if you stand in front of your class to give a presentation, your heart rate might stay the same and you would still feel scared.

Elaborate to evaluate

Don't waste your AO3 points. Make the most of them by elaborating – develop and explain them fully, just like we do in this book. You can do this in this activity by using the trigger phrases to help you construct an evaluation.

A strength	Evidence supporting the theory …	For example …	This shows that …
A weakness	An alternative theory …	This states that …	This suggests that …
Another weakness	The James–Lange theory is also challenged by …	This states that …	This suggests that …

Neurons and electrical transmission

What are neurons?	Nerve cells send electrical and chemical signals. There are 100 billion of them in the human body.
Types of neuron	*Sensory* neurons: PNS to CNS. **L**ong dendrites, **S**hort axons (LS). *Relay* neurons: Sensory neurons to motor neurons. **S**hort dendrites, **S**hort axons (SS). *Motor* neurons: CNS to muscles and glands. **S**hort dendrites, **L**ong axons (SL).
Structure of neurons	Cell body: Nucleus with genetic material (DNA). Axon: Carries signals from the cell body down the neuron, covered in myelin sheath. Myelin sheath: Fatty layer acts as insulation and gaps (nodes of Ranvier) speed up signal. Terminal button: End of axon (part of synapse).
Electrical transmission	Resting state: Inside has a negative charge compared to outside. When it fires: Changes to a positive charge which causes an action potential.

Synapses and chemical transmission

The synapse	Neurons communicate using neurotransmitters, released from presynaptic to postsynaptic neuron across the synaptic cleft.
Release of neurotransmitters	Neurotransmitters stored in vesicles at terminal buttons of presynaptic neuron. Electrical signal releases neurotransmitters into the synaptic cleft.
Reuptake of neurotransmitter	Neurotransmitters attach themselves to the next neuron at postsynaptic receptor sites. The chemical message is turned back to an electrical impulse. Neurotransmitters in synaptic cleft broken down by enzymes, reabsorbed by presynaptic neuron.
Excitation and inhibition	Excitatory neurotransmitters increase the postsynaptic neuron's positive charge and make it more likely to fire. Inhibitory neurotransmitters increase the postsynaptic neuron's negative charge and make it less likely to fire.
Summation	Summation occurs if there are more excitatory signals than inhibitory signals. Makes neuron fire, causing an electrical impulse.

The specification says...
Neuron structure and function: sensory, relay and motor neurons. Synaptic transmission: release and reuptake of neurotransmitters. Excitation and inhibition. An understanding of how these processes interact.

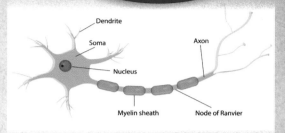

A neuron.

Exam booster

Can you draw it?

If you are asked to explain the function of a synapse, you can use a drawing to help you but make sure you also explain all of the labels.

APPLY IT

- Use your knowledge of synaptic transmission to explain how SSRI drugs work. Refer to the release and reuptake of neurotransmitters in your answer. **[4 marks]**

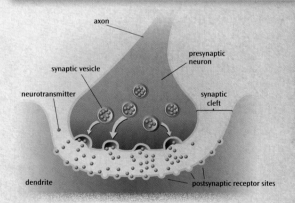

A synapse.

KNOWLEDGE CHECK

1. Explain the function of a motor and a relay neuron. **[2 marks]**
2. Outline how excitation and inhibition work together. **[3 marks]**
3. Describe the process involved in synaptic transmission. Refer to the release and reuptake of neurotransmitters in your answer. **[4 marks]**

AO1 – Broken sentences

Below are some sentences that describe the structure and functions of the neuron. They have become broken and muddled up, so put them back together again by matching the first half of each sentence in the left-hand column with the second half in the right-hand column.

1. The signals sent by neurons are …	**A.** … a nucleus with genetic material.
2. Relay neurons have …	**B.** … make the postsynaptic neuron more likely to fire.
3. Motor neurons connect …	**C.** … found at the end of an axon.
4. The cell body contains …	**D.** … short dendrites and short axons.
5. The axon is …	**E.** … is broken down by enzymes.
6. The terminal buttons are …	**F.** … the CNS to muscles and glands.
7. When a neuron 'fires' …	**G.** … vesicles in terminal buttons of the presynaptic neuron.
8. Neurotransmitters are stored in …	**H.** … electrical and chemical.
9. Neurotransmitter left in the synaptic cleft …	**I.** … it produces an action potential.
10. Excitatory neurons …	**J.** … covered in a myelin sheath.

Synaptic transmission flowchart

Representing the description of synaptic transmission in a different format can help you to remember it. With that in mind, use the information on the previous page to put the following events in the correct order by writing the letters into the table below.

A. On the other hand, if there are more excitatory signals than inhibitory ones …

D. An electrical signal arrives down the axon of the presynaptic neuron.

G. Neurotransmitter is released into the synaptic cleft.

B. The electrical signal activates vesicles in the terminal buttons of the presynaptic neuron.

E. … the postsynaptic neuron fires, creating an electrical impulse.

H. If there are more inhibitory signals than excitatory ones …

C. … the postsynaptic neuron does not fire.

F. Excess neurotransmitter in the synaptic cleft is broken down by enzymes and recycled into the presynaptic neuron.

I. Neurotransmitter molecules attach to receptors on the postsynaptic neuron.

1	2	3	4	5	6	7	8	9

Description

The brain is plastic	Synaptic connections in the brain become stronger the more they are used. The brain has the ability to change and develop.
The brain adapts	The brain changes structure and connections in response to new experiences (= learning). Any learning – at any age – will do this.
Learning produces an engram	Learning leaves a trace (engram). This can be made permanent if we practise and rehearse what we are learning.
Cell assemblies and neuronal growth	Cell assemblies are groups of neurons that fire together. The more they fire, the more the synaptic connections grow and strengthen. Neuronal growth occurs as the cell assemblies rewire to manage new learning.

Evaluation

Hebb's theory is scientific	One strength of Hebb's theory is that it is scientific. Hebb explained learning in terms of brain function which provided an objective basis for understanding behaviour. This shows that learning can be studied through brain processes.
Real-world application to education	Another strength of Hebb's theory is it can be applied to education. He found that rats raised in stimulating settings were better able to find their way through mazes as adults. This could be applied to education by creating more stimulating environments to encourage learning.
EXTRA: Reductionist theory	One weakness with Hebb's theory is that it reduces learning to a neuronal level. This means that other levels of understanding are ignored, such as Piaget's ideas about how accommodation moves learning forwards. This is an issue because a more complete account of learning should discuss non-biological factors as well.

Five women behind bars – how's that for a 'cell assembly'? Get it?? Oh never mind.

Exam booster

Using quotes

Quotes can be useful when it comes to explaining theory. For example, this quote is often used when describing Hebb's theory: 'Cells that fire together, wire together'. Explaining how this quote links to Hebb's theory will not only help your explanation but also show evidence of the wider reading which characterises the high-achieving student.

APPLY IT – Research Methods

A researcher wanted to see the effect of environment on learning. One group (group 1) of rats were brought up in a stimulating environment that promoted neuronal growth whilst the other group (group 2) were brought up in an unstimulating environment. Both groups were then timed on how quickly they could escape from a maze.

1. Write a suitable alternative hypothesis for this study. **[2 marks]**
2. Explain how the researcher might allocate rats to group 1 or group 2. **[2 marks]**

KNOWLEDGE CHECK

1. What is meant by the term 'neuronal growth'? **[2 marks]**
2. Outline Hebb's theory of learning. **[4 marks]**
3. Describe and evaluate Hebb's theory of neuronal growth. **[9 marks]**

Anagrams

Time to unjumble these words relating to Hebb's theory. Can you do it without looking at the clues?

1.	CATLISP		An important property of the brain, like Lego!
2.	RENALGIN		This takes place as a result of new experiences.
3.	MANGER		Another term for a memory trace.
4.	EARSHERE		What we do when we practise what we are learning.
5.	CLEE ABLEMISSES		Groups of neurons that fire together.
6.	ALONERUN THROWG		This occurs as the brain rewires to manage new learning.
7.	ICETICFINS		A strength of Hebb's theory is that it is _____.
8.	AUNTIECOD		Hebb's theory can be applied to this.
9.	ZESMA		What rats have to learn in experiments.
10.	EROTICNUDIST		A weakness of the theory is that it is _____.

Write it thoroughly

An excellent way to boost your AO3 marks is to make sure your evaluation is thorough. So every time you make a point of evaluation, such as a strength or weakness, you should develop and explain it. The same goes for description – add detail to increase your AO1 marks (using examples is good for this). Fortunately, you can learn these skills with plenty of practice.

Here's a typical 9-mark question: Describe and evaluate Hebb's theory of learning and neuronal growth.

Complete the table below by responding to the statements in each box. Remember – make sure you explain each part of your answer thoroughly.

In your own words, summarise the theory in about five sentences, covering the main AO1 points on this topic.	**Explain a weakness/strength of the theory in three sentences – Point / Example / Conclusion.**
•	
•	**Explain a weakness/strength of the theory in three sentences – Point / Example / Conclusion.**
•	
•	**Explain a weakness/strength of the theory in three sentences – Point / Example / Conclusion.**
•	

Structure and function

Two hemispheres, four lobes of cerebral cortex	The brain is divided into two hemispheres. The cerebral cortex covers the brain and is divided into four lobes.	
	Frontal lobe	Front (anterior) of the brain = thinking, planning. *Motor area* at the back (posterior).
	Parietal lobe	Behind frontal lobe. *Somatosensory area* at front (anterior).
	Occipital lobe	Back (posterior) of the brain. *Visual area.*
	Temporal lobe	Behind frontal lobe and below occipital lobe = memory. *Auditory/language area* (though Broca's area is in frontal lobe).
Cerebellum	Receives information from spinal cord and brain. Main role is movement, coordination and balance. Also involved in attention and language.	

Localisation of function

Localisation	Specific brain areas do particular jobs.
Motor area	Damage to the motor area in the left hemisphere affects the right side of the body, and vice versa.
Somatosensory area	The most sensitive body parts take up most 'space', e.g. sensations for face and hands use over half of the neurons available in the somatosensory area. Damage means less ability to feel pain and temperature.
Visual area	Right visual field of each eye sends information to visual area in the left hemisphere, and vice versa. Damage in left hemisphere may cause blindness in the right visual field of both eyes, and vice versa.
Auditory area	Damage can lead to deafness.
Language area	Language areas in the left hemisphere only. Damage to Broca's area leads to difficulty remembering and forming words. Damage to Wernicke's area leads to difficulty understanding and producing language.

KNOWLEDGE CHECK

1. Identify the location and the basic function of the occipital lobe.   **[2 marks]**
2. Use your knowledge of localisation of function to state what would happen if a person damaged the somatosensory area of their brain   **[2 marks]**
3. Explain how knowledge about localisation of function has contributed to our understanding of behaviour.   **[6 marks]**

The specification says...

Brain structure: frontal lobe, temporal lobe, parietal lobe, occipital lobe and cerebellum.
Basic function of these structures.
Localisation of function in the brain: motor, somatosensory, visual, auditory and language areas.

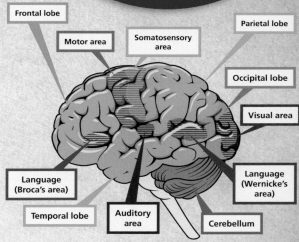

Frontal lobe · Motor area · Somatosensory area · Parietal lobe · Occipital lobe · Visual area · Language (Broca's area) · Language (Wernicke's area) · Temporal lobe · Auditory area · Cerebellum

'If the human brain were so simple that we could understand it, we would be so simple that we couldn't' Emerson M. Pugh.

Exam booster

Where is it and what does it do?

This topic involves looking at where different brain areas are located (structure) and what they do (function). Easier exam questions will ask you to label diagrams or answer multiple choice questions, whilst more challenging ones may get you to explain what certain areas do or even ask you to sketch the brain. Produce a detailed well-labelled diagram of the brain as part of your revision so that you are prepared for all of the types of questions that you could be asked.

APPLY IT

Read the item below and then answer the question that follows.

An accident meant that Fred's brain was damaged. He struggles to think clearly at times and finds it difficult to make future plans. He also can no longer move his right arm.

• Use your knowledge of psychology to identify which area of his brain Fred damaged and on which side of his brain this damage occurred. Explain your answers.   **[4 marks]**

Crossword

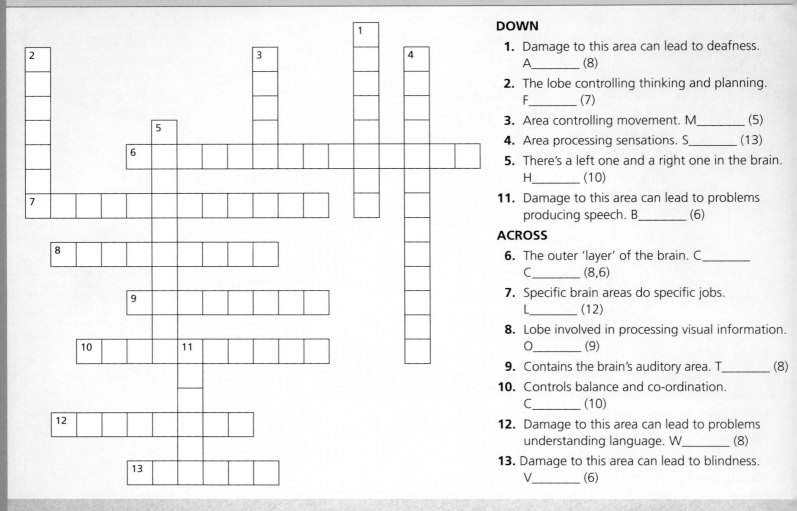

DOWN

1. Damage to this area can lead to deafness.
    A_____ (8)

2. The lobe controlling thinking and planning.
    F_____ (7)

3. Area controlling movement. M_____ (5)

4. Area processing sensations. S_____ (13)

5. There's a left one and a right one in the brain.
    H_____ (10)

11. Damage to this area can lead to problems
    producing speech. B_____ (6)

ACROSS

6. The outer 'layer' of the brain. C_____
    C_____ (8,6)

7. Specific brain areas do specific jobs.
    L_____ (12)

8. Lobe involved in processing visual information.
    O_____ (9)

9. Contains the brain's auditory area. T_____ (8)

10. Controls balance and co-ordination.
    C_____ (10)

12. Damage to this area can lead to problems
    understanding language. W_____ (8)

13. Damage to this area can lead to blindness.
    V_____ (6)

Draw it, colour it, label it

This is quite a challenging task, but it should really help you to remember the different areas of the brain.

Start by drawing a rough outline of the brain as viewed from the side. It doesn't have to be a work of art (even though there is a frame for you to use on the right). Have a look at a couple of examples to help you, but try to draw it from memory. Then use different colours to shade in and label the areas indicated in the in the boxes on the far right. You could draw a bigger version to stick on your bedroom wall for revision.

Frontal lobe

Parietal lobe

Occipital lobe

Temporal lobe

Cerebellum

Motor area

Somatosensory area

Visual area

Auditory area

Language area

Description

Aim	To investigate patients' responses when their brains were electrically stimulated.
Method	Penfield operated on people to treat their severe epilepsy. His technique meant that a conscious patient's brain was exposed and areas could be electrically stimulated. Patients could then report their thoughts and sensations.
Results	With temporal lobe stimulation, patients recalled experiences or recalled feelings associated with the experiences, including experiences of déjà vu (a sense of having seen something before). The same memory was recalled each time the same area was stimulated.
Conclusion	Suggests that memories of previous experiences are stored in the temporal lobe. An associated area stores the personal meaning of the experience. Penfield called this the *interpretive cortex*.

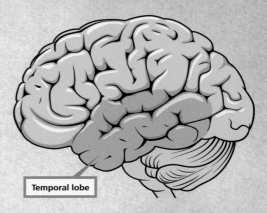

Temporal lobe

The temporal lobe is a part of the cerebral cortex – the orange peel that covers your brain. This contains the area that Penfield called the 'interpretative cortex'.

Evaluation

Precise method	One strength is that Penfield used a very precise method of studying the brain. He could stimulate the exact same area of the brain repeatedly and patients could report their experiences. This enabled him to produce an accurate 'map' of brain function.
Unusual sample	One weakness is that the participants in the study made up an unusual sample. The patients were suffering from severe epilepsy. This could mean that any findings produced were not reflective of people with non-epileptic brains.
EXTRA: Mixed results in later research	Another weakness is that Penfield's later research did not always support his original findings. In fact only 40 of the 520 patients he studied reported vivid memories when their temporal lobe was stimulated. This suggests that the interpretive cortex does not always respond in the same way.

Exam booster

Don't get mixed up

A common issue for students is that they get studies and theories mixed up. A theory in psychology is used to explain the causes of behaviour whilst a study is an investigation that is carried out to support or challenge a theory. For example, Penfield's study could be used to support Hebb's theory as the study shows that memory has a physical basis.

APPLY IT

Read the item below and then answer the question that follows.

When I smell bacon it triggers a memory of having breakfast at home as a child.

- Use your knowledge of Penfield's study of the interpretive cortex to explain this experience. **[3 marks]**

KNOWLEDGE CHECK

1. What is meant by the 'interpretive cortex'? **[2 marks]**
2. Explain what Penfield's study of the interpretive cortex can tell us about localisation of function. **[3 marks]**
3. Describe and evaluate Penfield's study of the interpretive cortex. **[9 marks]**

Classic study – true or false?

Here are some sentences about Penfield's study of the interpretive cortex. Indicate whether you think each one is true or false. For the false statements, write down the true versions in the spaces provided.

		True or false?	
1.	The aim of Penfield's study was to investigate how patients responded when their brains were stimulated by drugs.		
2.	Penfield performed brain operations to research the brain.		
3.	Penfield's patients were unconscious during surgery.		
4.	The patients could explain to Penfield what they experienced when he stimulated their brains.		
5.	Penfield was especially interested in the occipital lobe.		
6.	Patients could recall experiences and feelings associated with them when their temporal lobes were stimulated.		
7.	Patients reported experiencing déjà vu.		
8.	When the same area was stimulated repeatedly, patients reported recalling different memories.		
9.	Penfield concluded that memories of previous experiences are stored in the frontal lobe.		
10.	The personal meaning of the experience is stored in the interpretive cortex.		

Evaluation match-up

Fill in the missing information where necessary in the sentences below. Then match the sentences up to make three full evaluation points (three sentences each).

1. For example, the participants were people who were suffering from severe _____ that could not be treated.	2. For example, he studied 520 patients in total, but only _____ reported vivid memories when Penfield stimulated their _____ lobes.	3. This meant he was able to stimulate exactly the _____ brain areas repeatedly and could see if patients reported the same experiences.
4. This is a weakness because it suggests that the _____ cortex does not respond in a consistent way to stimulation.	5. A weakness of Penfield's study is that it used an unusual _____.	6. This is a weakness because it means that the study's findings may not be _____ to the majority of the population who do not have epilepsy.
7. This is a strength because it allowed Penfield to produce a very accurate _____ of the brain's functions.	8. One strength is that Penfield used a _____ method to study the brain.	9. Another weakness is that these findings were contradicted by Penfield's _____ research.

The specification says...

Cognitive neuroscience: How the structure and function of the brain relate to behaviour and cognition.

A basic understanding of how neurological damage, e.g. stroke or injury, can affect motor abilities and behaviour.

Cognitive neuroscience

What is it?	Scientific study of the influence of brain structures on mental processes. Aims to create a detailed map of localised functions in the brain.
Structure and function of the brain relates to behaviour	Frontal lobe includes the motor area which controls and coordinates movement. Temporal lobe includes the amygdala which processes emotion and has been linked to aggression.
Structure and function of the brain relates to cognition	'Cognition' refers to the mental processes of the mind – like memory and perception. Different types of long-term memories are located in different areas of the brain.
Cognitive neuroscience and mental illness	Low serotonin affects thinking (e.g. suicidal thoughts) and behaviour (low mood, depression).

Mapping the brain. A world of possibilities.

Neurological damage

The importance of localisation	The effect of any damage depends on the area of the brain affected because functions are *localised*.
The effects of stroke	When the brain is deprived of oxygen because of disruption to its blood supply, the specific areas affected will die. The effects may not be permanent if other parts of the brain take over localised functions.
Effects of neurological damage on motor ability	Damage to the motor area can lead to the person struggling with fine and complex movements. Damage to the left hemisphere affects the right side of the body, and vice versa.
Effects of neurological damage on behaviour	Brain damage can lead to 'aphasia' – an inability to understand and use language. Broca's aphasia leads to problems producing speech. Wernicke's aphasia affects understanding of speech.

Exam booster

Double up

This topic is similar to the spread on the structure and function of of the nervous system (page 137). So remember to use examples from page 137 when explaining what is meant by cognitive neuroscience and the role of neurological damage in cognition and behaviour. For example, damage to the frontal lobe affects our ability to think clearly (cognition) and also our movement (behaviour).

KNOWLEDGE CHECK

1. What is meant by the term 'cognitive neuroscience'? **[2 marks]**
2. Briefly outline how stroke or injury can affect motor abilities and behaviour. **[4 marks]**
3. Describe how the structure and function of the brain relates to behaviour and cognition. **[6 marks]**

APPLY IT – Research Methods

A man fell off a ladder, landing on his head. Afterwards, he experienced memory difficulties and was studied in depth by a psychologist.

1. Explain why a case study would have been suitable to investigate this person's brain damage. **[2 marks]**
2. Explain **one** weakness of using case studies like this one to study topics such as memory. **[2 marks]**
3. Explain how qualitative data could have been collected in this study. **[2 marks]**

Cognitive neuroscience fill in the blanks

Complete the passage by filling in the missing words from this description of cognitive neuroscience. Try to complete the activity without referring to your notes on the previous page. The words you need to choose from are below if you really get stuck.

Cognitive neuroscience is the scientific study of how brain structures influence mental _____. It aims to create a detailed _____ of the localised _____ of brain areas.

The structures and functions of the brain are associated with behaviours. For example, the motor area is found in the _____ lobe and is involved in co-ordinating _____. The _____ is found within the temporal lobe. It processes emotions and research has linked it to _____ behaviour.

Brain structures and functions are also associated with _____. This refers to the mental processes of the mind, for example memory and perception. Studies have found that different types of _____-term memory are localised to different areas of the brain.

Finally, cognitive neuroscience has also investigated the links between the brain and mental _____. For example, a low level of the neurotransmitter _____ is associated with depression. It affects both thinking (suicidal thoughts) and behaviour (emotional behaviours such as low _____).

frontal   **mood**   **aggressive**   **functions**   **illnesses**   **amygdala**

serotonin   **processes**   **cognition**   **movement**   **map**   **long**

Use examples to boost your AO1

Giving examples is a great way to add detail to your descriptions. In the boxes below, explain what is meant by the terms and phrases provided. Add examples to take your explanations further. Try to think of different examples from the ones on the previous page.

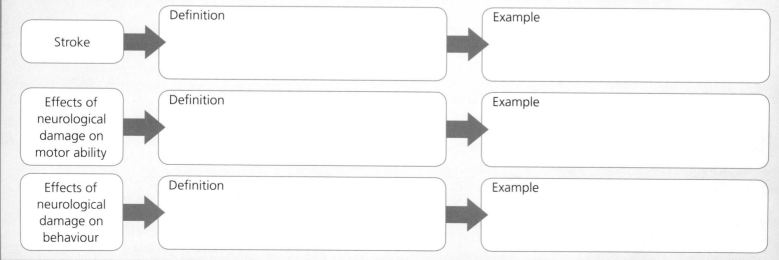

	Definition	Example
Stroke		
Effects of neurological damage on motor ability	Definition	Example
Effects of neurological damage on behaviour	Definition	Example

Description and evaluation

CT scans	Large doughnut-shaped scanner rotates around the person to take lots of X-rays of the brain. Images are taken from different angles and are combined to build up a detailed picture.	
	Strengths	Useful for revealing abnormal structures such as tumours. Quality of the images provided is higher than traditional X-rays.
	Weaknesses	Requires more radiation than X-rays. Only produces still images.
PET scan	Patient is injected with a radioactive substance such as glucose. Brain activity shown on a computer screen.	
	Strengths	Shows brain in action. Shows localisation of function when person asked to perform a specific task.
	Weaknesses	Expensive. Images difficult to interpret. Ethical issues due to the injection of radioactive substance.
fMRi scan	Measure changes in blood oxygen levels in the brain. Brain activity displayed as 3D images produced on a computer screen.	
	Strengths	Shows brain in action. Clear images. No radiation.
	Weaknesses	Expensive. Person must stay very still. Time lag between activity and image appearing.

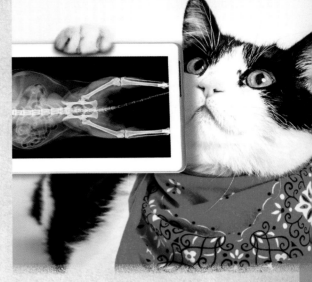

Cat scan.

Go compare

Comparing the different brain scanning techniques will help you to evaluate them more effectively. Select three criteria to use when looking at their similarities and differences. For example, how safe they are, whether they are expensive and also the accuracy of the images that they produce. Learning about them in this way will also help you for other question types such as those where you must explain the difference between two brain scanning techniques.

Exam booster

APPLY IT

Read the item below and then answer the question that follows.

Misha is discussing which type of brain scan would be best to investigate the cause of her 5-year-old son's learning difficulties. Ultimately she wants a technique that is safe but one that will also give her the most precise images of her son's brain. She is a wealthy woman who is happy to fund her son's treatment.

- Identify a brain scanning technique that Misha could use and explain the strengths and weaknesses of using it to investigate the cause of her son's learning difficulties. **[5 marks]**

KNOWLEDGE CHECK

1. Outline **one** difference between a PET and an fMRI scan. **[3 marks]**
2. Explain what is involved in taking an fMRI scan and how it has been used to identify brain functioning. **[4 marks]**
3. Describe and evaluate CT and PET scans as techniques used to identify brain functioning. **[9 marks]**

Brain scan wordsearch

Can you find the words related to the topic of scanning techniques? There are 11 of them, and they could be horizontal, vertical or diagonal (but not backwards).

SCANNING

XRAYS

RADIOACTIVE

PET

LOCALISATION

FMRI

OXYGEN

SCREEN

IMAGE

COMPUTER

DOUGHNUT

J	G	O	O	X	I	N	M	L	E	G	U	N	T	Z
R	D	Q	X	N	N	F	U	O	F	B	R	N	X	H
A	J	O	M	J	D	E	A	C	E	B	J	S	M	Y
D	J	O	U	T	X	R	O	A	Y	G	B	Y	R	O
I	D	X	N	G	I	D	C	L	L	D	Z	B	S	E
O	W	Y	P	G	H	A	C	I	M	X	N	W	C	I
A	J	G	U	E	V	N	X	S	M	J	P	A	A	B
C	I	E	I	F	T	J	U	A	X	A	E	A	N	V
T	P	N	Y	D	K	O	C	T	R	B	G	J	N	H
I	T	O	Q	F	K	O	Y	I	A	M	L	E	I	S
V	J	L	Y	W	Y	L	N	O	Y	F	E	W	N	C
E	S	C	T	S	O	T	G	N	S	K	F	V	G	R
K	U	X	C	O	M	P	U	T	E	R	M	Q	S	E
C	L	T	Q	V	Z	U	W	H	J	Y	R	S	S	E
X	G	T	C	C	P	I	H	Y	K	T	I	E	M	N

AO3 – Broken sentences

Here is an evaluation of brain scanning techniques, which is jumbled up. Put the sentences together correctly (the first half is in the first column, the second half is in the second column).

1. CT scans are useful for …

2. CT scans give …

3. CT scans use more …

4. A weakness of CT scans is that they …

5. PET and fMRI scans both show …

6. PET and fMRI scans help us to understand …

7. A strength of fMRI scans is that they …

8. Because PET scans involve injection of a radioactive substance …

9. A weakness of fMRI is …

A. … only produce still images.

B. … they raise ethical issues.

C. … higher-quality images than traditional X-rays.

D. … localisation of brain function.

E. … revealing abnormal structures such as tumours.

F. … do not use radiation.

G. … the time lag between the brain activity and the image appearing.

H. … radiation than traditional X-rays.

I. … the brain in action (e.g. when performing a task).

The specification says...

Tulving's 'gold' memory study.

Description

Aim	To investigate whether thinking about episodic memories produces different blood flow patterns from those produced when thinking about semantic memories.
Method	Six participants were injected with radioactive gold. Repeated measures design, each participants did: • Four episodic trials – thought of personal experiences. • Four semantic trials – thought of facts. Blood flow in the brain was monitored on a PET scan.
Results	Different blood flow patterns found in three out of six participants. Semantic memories created a greater concentration of blood flow in the posterior cortex (i.e. parietal and occipital lobes). Episodic memories created greater flow in the anterior cortex (i.e. frontal and temporal lobes).
Conclusion	Episodic and semantic memories are localised in different parts of the brain. Memory has a biological basis.

Evaluation

Objective evidence	One strength is that the study produced scientific evidence. It used evidence from brain scans that is difficult to fake, unlike other psychological investigations where you can be less sure that participants are behaving genuinely. This means that Tulving produced unbiased evidence.
Problems with the sample	One weakness is that the sample was restricted. Only six participants (including Tulving) were used and differences in blood flow for episodic and semantic memories were seen in only three participants. This means the results were inconclusive.
EXTRA: Are there different types of memory?	Another weakness is that episodic and semantic memories are often very similar. Memories for personal events also contain facts and knowledge about the world so it is difficult to work out which type of memory is being studied. This may explain why the evidence from Tulving's study was inconclusive.

KNOWLEDGE CHECK

1. Outline the results of Tulving's 'gold' memory study. **[3 marks]**
2. Describe what Tulving's 'gold' study can tell us about neuroscience. **[3 marks]**
3. Describe and evaluate Tulving's 'gold' memory study. **[9 marks]**

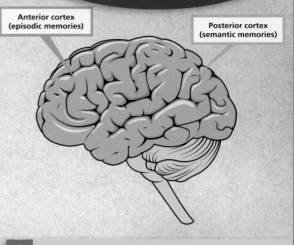

Anterior cortex (episodic memories)

Posterior cortex (semantic memories)

Exam booster

Don't get mixed up

A useful revision technique is to condense a study down to just one sentence. It will help you learn it and will also mean you have less to remember. For example, Tulving found that six participants injected with radioactive gold had greater blood flow in their posterior cortex for semantic memories whilst more blood flow in their frontal lobe for episodic memories.

APPLY IT – Research Methods

A psychologist used brain scans to investigate the location of different types of long-term memories in the brain. He interviewed his participants about the terrorist attack on the World Trade Centre in America in 2001. He measured their brain activity in relation to two types of questions: those that related to what they were doing when they heard about the event (episodic memory) and also facts about the event (semantic memory).

1. Write a suitable question that could provide the researcher with quantitative data about episodic memory. Explain why it would produce this type of data. **[3 marks]**

2. Explain **one** strength and **one** weakness of using an interview for this investigation. **[2 marks + 2 marks]**

3. In total 20 questions were asked about episodic memories and on 17 of these there was greater blood flow in the frontal lobe than in the posterior cortex. Express this as a percentage. Show your workings. **[2 marks]**

Classic study mix-up

Describe Tulving's 'gold' memory study.

Below are some sentences about the study by Tulving. You can use them to help you answer the exam-type question above, but they have become mixed up.

Put the numbers of the sentences in the right boxes below so that the answer makes sense.

Aim	Method	Results	Conclusion

1. Four of the trials involved thinking about personal experiences and four thinking about facts.

2. The study was a laboratory experiment using a repeated measures design.

3. Episodic and semantic memories are localised in different parts of the brain.

4. Semantic memories were associated with increased blood flow in the posterior cortex.

5. Tulving wanted to find evidence for a physical difference in the brain between two types of memory.

6. Each participant's brain blood flow was measured using PET scanning.

7. Tulving's results show that memory has a biological basis in the brain.

8. Each participant carried out eight trials in total.

9. Tulving wanted to find out if episodic memories produced different blood flow patterns in the brain from semantic memories.

10. Tulving found that blood flow patterns differed between semantic and episodic memories in three participants.

11. The participants were injected with radioactive gold.

12. Episodic memories were associated with increased blood flow in the frontal lobe.

Evaluate with trigger phrases

Here are some 'trigger' phrases related to Tulving's 'gold' study. The first thing to do is decide which phrases go together by putting them into pairs in the table (columns 1 and 2). Then write a sentence (in column 3) for each pair without looking at your notes or elsewhere on the previous page. Finally, in column 4, write a further sentence, to explain why your first sentence is a strength/weakness.

1. Findings about memory differences came from brain scans.

2. Tulving used a restricted set of participants.

3. Objective scientific evidence.

4. Episodic and semantic memories are often similar.

5. Sampling issues.

6. Different types of memory?

Understanding mental health and illness

Incidence of mental health problems	MIND – Incidence rates per 100 people: • Anxiety: 4.7 • Depression: 2.6 • Eating disorders: 1.6. 1 in 2 people experience mental health problems in their lifetime.
How incidence changes over time	In 2007 24% of adults were accessing treatment. Rising to 37% in 2014. It's estimated that by 2030 two million more adults will have mental health problems than in 2013. More women are treated than men and the gap is widening.
Increased challenges of modern living	Those in lower income households are more likely to have mental health problems (e.g. 27% of men) compared to higher income households (e.g. 15% of men). Greater social isolation due to city living increases loneliness and is linked to increased depression.
Cultural variations in beliefs about mental health problems	In Western society hearing voices is a symptom of mental health problems such as schizophrenia, but it is a positive experience In India and Africa. Some syndromes are culture-bound, occurring only in certain cultures, e.g. eating disorders were relatively rare for many years outside the Western world.
Characteristics of mental health	The signs and symptoms relating to mental illness are subjective, e.g. behaviours such as difficulty sleeping and problems socialising are hard to measure.
Increased recognition of the nature of mental health problems	Signs and symptoms are focused on illness instead of health. Jahoda suggested we look for signs of mental health. She listed six characteristics, e.g. accurate perception of reality and autonomy (independence).
Lessening of social stigma	Labelling a person as 'mentally ill' or a 'schizophrenic' develops expectations about their behaviour. These labels act as a stigma and can be harmful. The preferred term is 'mental health', which has less stigma and is focused on health.

KNOWLEDGE CHECK

1. Describe how the incidence of significant mental health problems changes over time. **[3 marks]**

2. Briefly outline **two** cultural variations in beliefs about mental health problems. **[4 marks]**

3. Explain how increased challenges of modern living, such as isolation, have led to mental health problems. **[2 marks]**

The specification says...

An introduction to mental health.
How the incidence of significant mental health problems changes over time.
Characteristics of mental health, e.g. positive engagement with society, effective coping with challenges.
Cultural variations in beliefs about mental health problems.
Increased challenges of modern living, e.g. isolation.
Increased recognition of the nature of mental health problems and lessening of social stigma.

Hearing voices.

Exam booster

Don't get (too) hung up on statistics

It is acceptable to remember general findings rather than focusing on specific numerical detail. For example, it is almost as good to recall that about twice as many people suffer from anxiety than depression (as opposed to knowing 4.7% and 2.6%).

APPLY IT

Read the item below and then answer the question that follows.

Javid has schizophrenia, a mental problem. In the past he may have been called 'a lunatic', resulting in people treating him a negative way. Nowadays he would be said to have a mental health problem – a label that causes others to treat him more favourably as they view him as having a problem that can be treated.

• What is meant by the phrase 'lessening of social stigma' in relation to mental health? Refer to Javid in your answer. **[4 marks]**

Three-column match-up

Match up the statements across the three columns.

(1) Incidence of mental health problems.	**(5)** For example, hearing voices is a symptom of schizophrenia in Western societies but a more positive experience in India and African countries.	**(9)** Depression is linked to social isolation in cities which increases loneliness.
(2) Increased challenges of modern living.	**(6)** Labelling someone as 'mentally ill' creates expectations about their behaviour that can be harmful.	**(10)** 1 in 2 people experience mental health problems in their lifetime.
(3) There are cultural variations in beliefs about mental health problems.	**(7)** According to MIND, 2.6 out of 100 people suffer from depression.	**(11)** Therefore, a less stigmatising label is 'mental health problem', which focuses positively on health rather than illness.
(4) It is important to lessen social stigma.	**(8)** 27% of men in lower income households have mental health problems compared with 15% of men in higher income households.	**(12)** This is evidence that some mental health problems are culture-bound.

Mental health unjumble

There is a description of mental health issues in the following sentences, but it has become jumbled up. All you have to do is put the sentences together correctly (the first half is in the first column, the second half is in the second column).

1. According to MIND, the incidence rate per 100 people is …	**A.** … are treated for mental health problems.
2. 1 in every 2 people experience …	**B.** … is viewed more positively in African countries than it is in European.
3. Compared with 2013 …	**C.** … leads to stigma and can be harmful.
4. More women than men …	**D.** … subjective and hard to measure.
5. People in lower income households …	**E.** … mental health problems in their lifetime.
6. Hearing voices …	**F.** … focus positively on signs of mental health, not illness.
7. An example of a culture-bound syndrome is …	**G.** … are more likely to have mental health problems than people in higher income households.
8. Signs and symptoms of mental illnesses are …	**H.** … eating disorders.
9. According to Marie Jahoda we should …	**I.** … 1.6 for eating disorders.
10. Labelling someone as mentally ill …	**J.** … two million more adults will have mental health problems by 2030.

Individual effects

Individual effects	The way that mental health problems affect the person who is experiencing them.
Damage to relationships	Mental health problems: • Affect the ability to talk to others, which affects relationships because communication is important. • Are isolating as people avoid being in social situations because they feel bad about themselves and fear judgement.
Difficulties coping with day-to-day life	Mental health problems are linked to difficulties with getting dressed, socialising, cleaning the house, etc. This may cause a patient little distress but it could be distressing to others.
Negative impact on physical well-being	If you are anxious or stressed, the body produces cortisol. This prevents the immune system functioning properly, so physical illness is more likely.

Social effects

Social effects	The way that mental health problems affect others in society.
Need for more social care	Taxes are used to fund social care, offering people who are in need the basic necessities, i.e. food, warmth, human company. Social care includes helping people to learn how to look after themselves and teaches new social and work skills. We should all feel more personally responsible.
Increased crime rates	There is an increased risk of violence in people with mental health problems (up to four times greater). However, this may be explained by co-occurring problems, e.g. substance abuse. It was found that only 1 in 20 crimes of violence were linked to mental health problems (Fazel and Grann).
Implications for the economy	The McCrone report estimates that mental health care costs £22 billion a year. Cheaper drug treatments should be researched more. Increase in dementia is also an issue.

The specification says...

Effects of significant mental health problems on individuals and society.

Individual effects, e.g. damage to relationships, difficulties coping with day-to-day life, negative impact on physical well-being.

Social effects, e.g. need for more social care, increased crime rates, implications for the economy.

Exam booster

Research mental illness

A good way of learning this topic area is to research a mental illness (e.g. depression) and then explain how this illness affects people on an individual level and affects society as a whole. Try to comment on each of the eight criteria on your left.

APPLY IT – Research Methods

[Graph showing a distribution curve with Performance on the y-axis and Anxiety score on the x-axis, bell-shaped distribution]

1. What type of distribution is displayed in this graph? **[1 mark]**
2. What is the relationship between performance and anxiety shown in this graph? **[3 marks]**
3. Give the graph a suitable title. **[1 marks]**

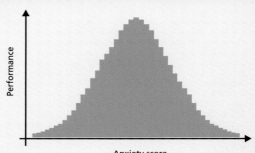

Mental health care costs over £20 billion but education and defence each cost twice as much.

KNOWLEDGE CHECK

1. Explain why mental health problems may have a negative impact on relationships. **[3 marks]**
2. Explain the effect that mental health problems can have on a person's physical well-being. **[3 marks]**
3. Describe the effects that significant mental health problems can have on society. **[4 marks]**

Mental health wordsearch

Can you find the words related to the topic of scanning techniques? There are 10 of them, and they could be horizontal, vertical or diagonal (but not backwards).

RELATIONSHIPS

COMMUNICATION

COPING

DISTRESS

CORTISOL

IMMUNE SYSTEM

SOCIAL CARE

SUBSTANCES

ECONOMY

MCCRONE

P	C	R	J	F	S	T	E	Z	D	X	N	N	Z	V
T	Q	O	E	P	M	O	M	F	B	W	E	N	F	C
P	G	I	M	L	Y	F	C	R	C	P	H	I	C	O
M	P	K	M	M	A	B	M	I	V	M	L	U	T	P
R	E	K	Y	M	U	T	S	C	A	Q	H	I	F	I
X	C	C	Q	P	U	N	I	Z	C	L	Q	U	C	N
V	O	C	U	N	V	I	O	R	R	C	Y	A	G
U	N	F	O	B	P	G	E	C	N	S	O	A	J	P
G	O	D	C	R	I	G	D	S	A	S	B	N	R	E
P	M	U	K	N	T	T	C	T	Y	T	H	J	E	E
R	Y	X	O	R	L	I	Y	S	C	S	I	I	L	C
D	I	S	T	R	E	S	S	P	R	J	T	O	P	G
W	G	O	S	G	W	W	K	O	I	M	K	E	N	S
I	F	A	O	L	J	Z	L	U	L	G	D	T	M	T
R	S	U	B	S	T	A	N	C	E	S	W	C	G	V

Which is which?

Mental health problems have serious effects on both the individual and wider society. But which effect is which? Place the following effects into the correct columns (in any order).

1. Greater need for social care resources.

2. Negative impact on physical well-being.

3. Causes damage to relationships.

4. Causes an increase in crime rates.

5. Reduces ability to communicate.

6. Co-occurring problems more likely.

7. Expensive for the economy.

8. Hard to cope with everyday life.

Effects on the individual	Effects on wider society

Topic 3 Depression

Types of depression

Clinical depression	Clinical depression is the name for depression as a medical condition.
Sadness and depression	Sadness is a 'normal' emotion where you can still function. Depression involves an enduring and all-encompassing sadness that stops the ability to function.
Unipolar depression	One emotional state (depression).
Bipolar depression	Depression alternates with mania, and also periods of normal mood. Mania is an exaggerated state of intense well-being.

Diagnosing unipolar depression

ICD	Mental health problems are diagnosed in the same way as physical illnesses. Symptoms are agreed by professionals. The International Classification of Diseases (ICD-10) lists symptoms of different disorders and a person is diagnosed with any one disorder if a clinician observes the symptoms.
Number and severity of symptoms	A diagnosis of mild unipolar depression requires two of the three key symptoms plus two others. A diagnosis of 'moderate depression' requires five or six symptoms, 'severe depression' requires seven or more. Symptoms should be present all or most of the time, and for longer than two weeks.
Key symptoms	1. Low mood: Depressed mood most of the day and nearly every day. 2. Loss of interest and pleasure: Diminished interest or pleasure in most activities most of the day. 3. Reduced energy levels: This has a knock-on effect on work, education and social life.
Other symptoms	4. Changes in sleep patterns: Reduced sleep (insomnia), early waking, or more need for sleep (hypersomnia). 5. Changes in appetite levels: This may increase or decrease, leading to weight gain or loss. 6. Decrease in self-confidence: May have a sense of self-loathing (hating themselves). 7-10. Four further symptoms: guilt, pessimism, ideas of self-harm or suicide, reduced concentration.

KNOWLEDGE CHECK

1. Distinguish between depression and sadness. **[3 marks]**

2. Explain how the International Classification of Diseases is used to diagnose unipolar depression. **[4 marks]**

3. Describe **two** characteristics of depression. **[4 marks]**

The specification says...

Characteristics of clinical depression.

Differences between unipolar depression, bipolar depression and sadness.

The use of International Classification of Diseases in diagnosing unipolar depression: Number and severity of symptoms including low mood, reduced energy levels, changes in sleep patterns and appetite levels, decrease in self-confidence.

Unipolar Bipolar

Exam booster

Learn the specification

Make sure you know, and can explain, any term on the specification, especially the key symptoms listed for depression. There are other relevant symptoms you could describe but being able to explain these three would be sufficient to get full marks for a question that asks you to describe symptoms of depression.

APPLY IT

Read the conversation below and then answer the questions that follow.

John: I am worried about Ivy as she hasn't seemed like her normal self lately. She usually loves playing hockey with her friends but last time she played she looked bored and had to go home early as she felt tired and 'flat'.

Daisy: I agree, I watched a TV programme about someone with depression and they acted in a similar way to Ivy.

1. Identify **two** symptoms of depression. Refer to Ivy's behaviour in your answer. **[4 marks]**

2. Which type of depression is Ivy experiencing? Explain your answer. **[3 marks]**

Depression true or false

What do you know about depression? Find out by identifying which of the following statements are true and which are false. For the false ones, write them so that they are true.

		True or false?	
1.	Clinical depression is a relatively mild form of depression.		
2.	Sadness and depression are similar because you can still function.		
3.	In unipolar depression only one abnormal emotional state is experienced.		
4.	There is another condition called bipolar depression.		
5.	In mania, the person is even more depressed than in unipolar depression.		
6.	Mental health problems are diagnosed very differently from physical illnesses.		
7.	The classification system is called ICD-10.		
8.	There are three key symptoms of depression.		
9.	A diagnosis of severe depression requires five or six symptoms.		
10.	Symptoms have to be present for one week.		

Increase or decrease?

The symptoms of depression involve changes of some kind, but in which direction? For each symptom identified in the table, indicate whether a diagnosis requires an increase or decrease or either.

Write a brief explanation in the space provided.

Finally write a sentence about any pattern you can see to the direction of the symptoms [HINT: which are 'key' and which are 'other'?].

SYMPTOM	Increase or decrease or both?	Explanation	Key or other?
Mood			
Interest/pleasure			
Energy levels			
Sleep			
Appetite			
Self-confidence			
ANY PATTERN?			

Theories of depression: Biological explanation

Theories of depression: Biological explanation (influence of nature): Imbalance of neurotransmitters, e.g. serotonin in the brain.

Sir tone in. May sound silly but bet you won't forget it!

Description

Biological and psychological	Biological explanations focus on physical influences (nature). Psychological explanations focus on other factors, e.g. other people's influence (nurture).
Neurotransmitters	Messages travel along a neuron electrically and are transmitted chemically across a synapse via neurotransmitters. Serotonin is a neurotransmitter, linked to several behaviours including depression.
Serotonin	High levels of serotonin in synaptic cleft stimulate postsynaptic neuron, improving mood. Low levels mean less stimulation of the postsynaptic neuron, resulting in a low mood.
Other effects of serotonin	Serotonin affects memory, sleep and appetite. These are linked to the characteristics of depression, e.g. lack of concentration, disturbed sleep and reduced appetite.
Reasons for low serotonin levels	Genes may cause low serotonin levels. Diet (environmental influence) may cause low levels of tryptophan, an ingredient of serotonin.

Exam booster

Show off what you know

Synaptic transmission crops up in many topics. Make sure you know this process well. You can then make reference to key terms in relation to how neurons communicate, which will provide detail in your description of the biological explanation of depression.

Evaluation

Research support	One strength of the biological explanation of depression is supporting research evidence. McNeal and Cimbolic found lower levels of serotonin in people with depression. This suggests that there is a link between low levels of serotonin and depression.
Cause or effect?	One weakness is low levels of serotonin could be an effect of being depressed. Thinking sad thoughts and having difficult experiences could cause low serotonin levels. So low levels of serotonin may be an effect of psychological experiences rather than the cause.
EXTRA: Alternative explanations	Another weakness is that depression may not be solely caused by abnormal levels of neurotransmitters. Some people with low levels of serotonin don't have depression and some people with depression don't have low levels of serotonin. This means that the neurotransmitter explanation isn't enough on its own.

APPLY IT – Research Methods

A study was carried out to see whether eating foods that raise serotonin levels would decrease depression. A group of 80 patients diagnosed with depression were recruited for the study and their depression level was measured at the start of the study. Half of the patients were given a high serotonin diet for six months. At the end of six months all patients' depression levels were measured again.

1. Identify a sampling method that could be used in this study and explain **one** strength of using this method. **[3 marks]**

2. Explain how the participants could have been allocated to each condition. **[3 marks]**

3. Identify **one** extraneous variable that could affect the outcome of the study and explain how it could be controlled. **[3 marks]**

KNOWLEDGE CHECK

1. Explain what is meant by the term 'serotonin'. **[2 marks]**

2. With reference to depression, explain what is meant by an 'imbalance of neurotransmitters'. **[4 marks]**

3. Describe and evaluate the biological explanation of depression. Refer to the influence of nature in your answer. **[9 marks]**

Broken sentences description

Below are some sentences about the biological explanation of depression. They have become broken and muddled up, but you can put them back together again by matching the first half of each sentence in the left-hand column with the second half in the right-hand column.

1. Physical influences are the focus of …	**A.** … less stimulation of the postsynaptic neuron and low mood.
2. Psychological explanations focus on …	**B.** … chemically across synapses.
3. Nurture is emphasised by …	**C.** … genes.
4. Neurotransmitters transmit signals …	**D.** … a neurotransmitter linked to depression.
5. Serotonin is …	**E.** … an ingredient of serotonin and low levels are caused by diet.
6. High serotonin levels in the synaptic cleft …	**F.** … factors such as the influence of other people.
7. Low serotonin levels mean …	**G.** … also affected by serotonin.
8. Memory, sleep and appetite are …	**H.** … psychological explanations.
9. Low serotonin can be caused by …	**I.** … biological explanations.
10. Tryptophan is …	**J.** … stimulate postsynaptic neurons and improve mood.

Instant message evaluation

Two students are having an instant messaging conversation about the biological explanation of depression (as you do). They are building evaluation points step by step. Some of the conversation has gone missing, so you need to fill in the gaps.

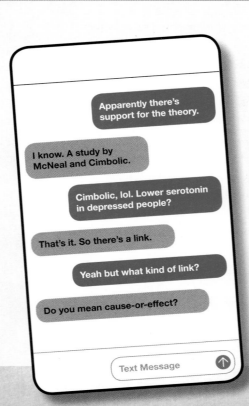

Apparently there's support for the theory.

I know. A study by McNeal and Cimbolic.

Cimbolic, lol. Lower serotonin in depressed people?

That's it. So there's a link.

Yeah but what kind of link?

Do you mean cause-or-effect?

Text Message

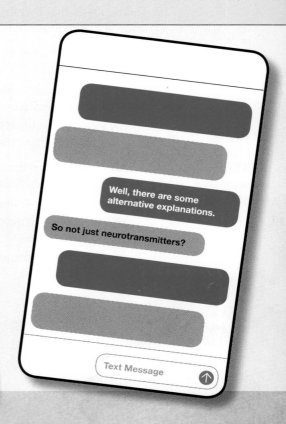

Well, there are some alternative explanations.

So not just neurotransmitters?

Text Message

The specification says...

Theories of depression: Psychological explanation (influence of nurture): Negative schemas and attributions.

Description

Faulty thinking	The cognitive approach sees depression as caused by faulty or irrational thinking.
	When a person is depressed they focus on the negative and ignore positives and think in 'black-and-white' terms.
	Creates feelings of hopelessness and depression.
Negative schemas	Schemas are mental frameworks containing ideas and information developed through experience.
	Having a negative self-schema means you are likely to interpret all information about yourself in a negative way.
Attributions	Attribution means explaining causes of behaviour.
	Seligman proposed that some people have a negative attributional style.
	They have negative internal, stable and global attributions which result in depression.
The influence of nurture	Seligman suggested that a negative attributional style is learned.
	An unpleasant experience makes you try to escape but if you can't escape, you learn to give up trying. This is called 'learned helplessness'.

Evaluation

Research support	One strength is support for learned helplessness.
	Seligman has demonstrated the process of learned helplessness. Dogs learned to react to challenge by 'giving up'.
	Therefore, this research supports his explanation of depression due to negative attributions.
Real-world application	Another strength is that the cognitive explanation leads to ways of treating depression through CBT.
	People learn to replace faulty, irrational thinking with rational thinking to help relieve depression.
	Therefore, the explanation leads to successful ways to help people with depression.
EXTRA: Negative beliefs may be realistic	One weakness is that negative beliefs may simply be realistic rather than depressing.
	Alloy and Abramson found that depressed people gave more accurate estimates of the likelihood of a disaster than 'normal' people ('sadder but wiser').
	So a negative attributional style may sometimes be good.

EMPTY   FULL

Could make you feel depressed if you always see it as half empty.

APPLY IT

A magazine article explained depression as being like seeing a glass as half empty instead of half full.

• Explain how this article relates to the psychological explanation of depression. Refer to negative schemas in your answer. **[3 marks]**

Exam booster

Use alternative explanations when evaluating

You can use your knowledge of the biological causes of depression to evaluate psychological explanations and vice versa. For example, research linking depression with low serotonin levels can challenge the idea that depression is just caused by faulty thinking. But make sure you use the other explanation as an evaluation, don't just describe it.

KNOWLEDGE CHECK

1. What is meant by a 'negative schema' in relation to depression? **[2 marks]**

2. With reference to an example, explain how attributions could cause depression. **[4 marks]**

3. Outline and evaluate the psychological explanation of depression. **[9 marks]**

Put the description right

The passage below is a description of the psychological explanation of depression. Unfortunately, ten mistakes have crept into it. Your task is to identify the errors and correct them.

One explanation of depression is cognitive. According to this theory, depression is the result of faulty genes. When someone is depressed, they think in an irrational way. For example, they focus on positive things and ignore negatives. This is called red-and-white thinking. This kind of thinking causes them to feel hopeless and depressed.

People who are depressed also have negative social-schemas. A schema is a metal framework containing ideas and information developed through experience. Depressed people interpret information about themselves in a negative way.

According to Seligman, depressed people have a negative attributional style. An attribution is our way of explaining the outcome of a behaviour. Depressed people's attributions are internal, unstable and global.

Seligman believed that a negative attributional style is innate. We try to escape from negative experiences. But if you cannot escape then you learn that there is no point trying. Seligman called this learned helpfulness.

Fake news evaluation

Here are some fake news headlines for you to think about.
Rewrite them in the 2nd column to make them true statements about the psychological explanation of depression.
Then, in the 3rd column, explain your new headline by writing the first sentence of an imaginary article.

Learned helplessness 'not linked to depression', say experts.		
Cognitive theory of depression 'nothing to do with real life', claim cheeky biopsychologists.		
Negativity is a sign you're out of touch with reality.		

Description

Selective serotonin reuptake inhibitor (SSRI)	Low levels of serotonin may cause depression, so increasing serotonin levels may treat depression. • SSRIs *selectively* target serotonin at the synapse. • SSRIs *inhibit* the *reuptake* of the serotonin molecules.
Presynaptic neuron	Serotonin is stored at the end of a transmitting (presynaptic) neuron in sacs called vesicles. The electrical signal travelling through the neuron causes the vesicles to release serotonin into the synaptic cleft.
Synaptic cleft	Serotonin locks into the postsynaptic receptors, chemically transmitting the signal from the presynaptic neuron.
Reuptake	Normally serotonin is taken back into the presynaptic neuron, broken down and reused. SSRIs block this reuptake so when new serotonin is released it adds to the amount held in the synaptic cleft.

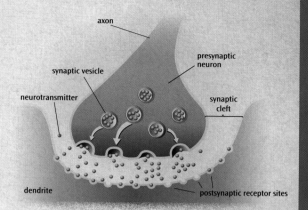

Diagram showing the reuptake of serotonin which is blocked by SSRIs.

Evaluation

Side effects	One weakness is SSRIs have serious side effects. The side effects include nausea, insomnia, dizziness, weight loss or gain, anxiety and, most seriously, suicidal thoughts. Side effects mean that people stop taking the drugs, reducing effectiveness of drug therapies.
Questionable evidence for effectiveness	Another weakness of antidepressant medication is that the evidence for the effectiveness of it is questionable. Research by Asbert shows that the serotonin levels of depressed people may not actually be that different from the normal population. This suggests that the effectiveness of the drug may not be related to serotonin. It may be a placebo effect.
EXTRA: A reductionist approach	A further weakness of antidepressant medication is that it is regarded as a reductionist explanation. Antidepressant medication targets serotonin (and sometimes noradrenaline) so focuses on only one kind of factor. This suggests that other treatments are not necessary but a more successful treatment might include both biological and psychological approaches (a holistic approach).

 Exam booster

Use reductionism and holism

These terms are in the specification so use them – but make sure you *apply* them. For example, linking depression to low serotonin levels is reductionist and could be considered a weakness but also could be a strength <u>because</u> SSRI drugs that raise serotonin levels have been found to be an effective treatment for many people who suffer from this debilitating illness.

KNOWLEDGE CHECK

1. What is meant by an 'antidepressant medication'? **[2 marks]**
2. Distinguish between reductionism and holism in relation to antidepressant medication. **[4 marks]**
3. Outline and evaluate antidepressant medication as a therapy for depression. **[9 marks]**

APPLY IT

Read the item below and then answer the question that follows.

Emma has been taking antidepressants to treat her depression for two months and they haven't made a difference. She wonders whether to continue. Her friend Nelly suggests that something as complex as depression is more than just a chemical imbalance in her brain so taking pills won't fix it especially as they can make you feel sick and give you problems with your sleep.

• Briefly evaluate antidepressants as a treatment for depression. Refer to the above conversation between Emma and Nelly in your answer. **[5 marks]**

Medication crossword

Complete the crossword to see how familiar you are with terms relating to antidepressant medication as a therapy for depression.

DOWN

1. The neuron where the neurotransmitter is stored. P_____ (11)
2. SSRIs have a S_____ action on the neurotransmitter. (9)
4. These are on the postsynaptic neuron. R_____ (9)
6. The biological explanation is at a lower level and is R_____ (criticism). (12)
8. This is the disorder treated by SSRIs. D_____ (10)
9. The neurotransmitter is stored in these sacs. V_____ (8)

ACROSS

3. SSRIs may be no more effective than a P_____. (7)
5. This is the neurotransmitter targeted by SSRIs. S_____ (9)
7. The 'R' in SSRI. R_____ (8)
10. The unintended results of taking medication. S_____ E_____ (4,7)
11. The gap between neurons. S_____ C_____. (8,5)
12. Neurotransmitters are bio-C_____. (9)

Evaluation match-up

Work out which statements in the first column best go with the statements in the second column.

1. SSRIs have some serious side effects.	A. Instead, taking antidepressants may just provide a placebo effect.
2. Side effects mean that patients may stop taking antidepressants.	B. These include nausea, dizziness, weight loss/gain and anxiety.
3. There is some research into effectiveness of antidepressants by Asbert.	C. This is because medication targets serotonin so focuses on just one kind of factor.
4. The effectiveness of antidepressant drugs may not be related to serotonin.	D. This would be a more holistic treatment.
5. Explanations based on antidepressants are reductionist.	E. This shows that serotonin levels of depressed people may not be much different from levels in non-depressed people.
6. A better treatment might combine biological and psychological approaches.	F. This means that the effectiveness of drug therapies is reduced.

Description

Cognitive	CBT focuses on what a client thinks.
	Negative, irrational or faulty thinking causes depression because people tend to catastrophise and think in all-or-nothing terms.
	Aim of therapist is to change this to rational thinking to reduce depression.
Behaviour	CBT aims to change behaviour indirectly through changing thinking.
	Behaviour also changed directly, e.g. behavioural activation where a pleasant activity is planned each day, creates more positive emotions and mood.
Therapist deals with irrational thoughts	'Disputing' is used to deal with the negative and irrational thoughts experienced by a depressed person, i.e. the thoughts are challenged.
	More rational thinking leads to greater self-belief and self-liking.
Client deals with irrational thoughts	Any negative emotions experienced are recorded in a 'thought diary', where the client also records the 'automatic' thoughts created by these emotions. The client rates how much they believe in these thoughts.
	A rational response to the automatic thoughts is then recorded and rated.

Evaluation

Lasting effectiveness	One strength of using CBT to treat depression is that it has lasting effectiveness.
	The 'tools' learned in CBT to help challenge irrational thoughts can help the client deal with future episodes of depression.
	Therefore, this therapy offers a long-term solution where the client can draw on the skills they learned in the future.
It's not for everyone	One weakness is that it takes a lot of time and thought for CBT to be successful.
	Therapy takes months, homework is expected so a lot of effort is needed in comparison to just taking a pill.
	This means that many people drop out or fail to engage enough for it to work.
EXTRA: A holistic approach	Another strength of CBT is that it is holistic.
	CBT focuses on treating the whole person and what they think/feel.
	This may be preferable because it deals with the core symptoms of depression (e.g. feeling sad).

KNOWLEDGE CHECK

1. Explain how CBT improves mental health. **[4 marks]**
2. Explain **one** criticism of using CBT to treat depression. **[4 marks]**
3. Describe and evaluate CBT as a therapy for depression. **[9 marks]**

The specification says...

> **Interventions or therapies for depression: Cognitive behaviour therapy (CBT).**
> How this improves mental health, reductionist and holistic perspectives.

Depression – not a laughing matter literally or metaphorically.

Exam booster

Apply, apply, apply

Questions relating to CBT are often asked in relation to a case study of a person who has depression and wants treatment. Remember to underline the key phrases in the case study relevant to CBT and then explain how each one links to the treatment.

APPLY IT – Research Methods

A study was carried out to see which technique proved most effective at treating depression – 200 patients with depression were treated with one of four techniques. The table below displays the number of patients who showed an improvement in their symptoms after 6 weeks.

Technique	1	2	3	4
Number of patients who improved after 6 weeks	25	30	10	48
Total number of patients	50	40	30	80

1. What percentage of those given technique 1 showed an overall improvement in their symptoms? Show your workings. **[2 marks]**
2. Which of the four techniques was the most effective treatment for depression? **[2 marks]**
3. Calculate the percentage of patients who didn't improve from any of the four techniques. Show your workings and round your answer up to the nearest whole number. **[4 marks]**

Boost your description with examples

Using examples is a great way to add detail to your descriptions. In the boxes below, write down brief outlines of the four CBT concepts for this topic. Add examples to take your outlines further.

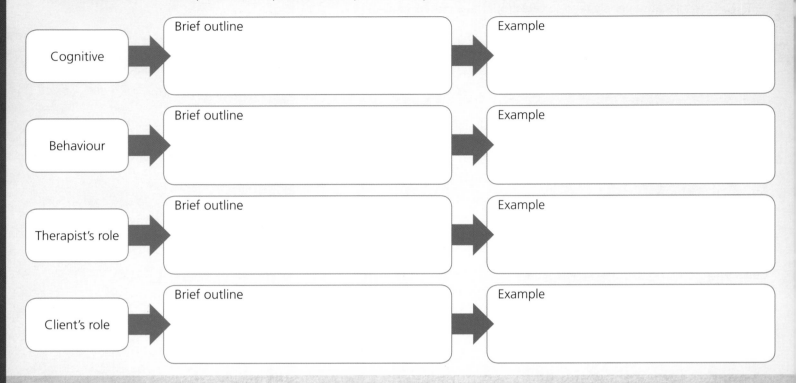

Cognitive	→	Brief outline	→	Example
Behaviour	→	Brief outline	→	Example
Therapist's role	→	Brief outline	→	Example
Client's role	→	Brief outline	→	Example

Mental health unjumble

There is an evaluation of CBT as a therapy for depression in the following sentences, but it has become jumbled up.

Put the sentences together correctly (the first half is in the first column, the second half is in the second column).

Then take the completed sentences and put them together into three elaborated points of three sentences each (Point / Explanation or Example / Conclusion).

1. For example, CBT can take …	**A.** … drop out or do not engage enough for it to be effective.
2. This is a strength because CBT offers …	**B.** … it takes a lot of time, effort and thought to be successful.
3. Another strength of CBT is that it is …	**C.** … a holistic approach to treating depression.
4. A strength of CBT is that it has …	**D.** … help to deal with future episodes of depression.
5. This is a weakness of CBT because it means that many people …	**E.** … treating the whole person and what they think and feel.
6. A weakness of CBT is that it is a therapy that does not suit everyone because …	**F.** … several months and homework is expected so a lot of effort is needed compared with just taking a pill.
7. This is a strength because it is a much better way to …	**G.** … long-term effectiveness.
8. Clients learn techniques to challenge irrational thoughts which can …	**H.** … a long-term solution as it focuses on skills the client can use.
9. This means that CBT focuses on …	**I.** … deal with the core symptoms of depression.

The specification says...

How these treatments improve mental health, reductionist and holistic perspectives.

Wiles' study of the effectiveness of CBT.

Description

Wiles' study	Only 30% of patients with depression respond fully to antidepressants, 70% are 'treatment resistant'. Treatment-resistant patients do improve with antidepressant medication plus CBT.
Aim	Wiles *et al.* set up the CoBalT trial to test a holistic approach (CBT plus antidepressants) for treating treatment-resistant depression.
Method	469 patients with treatment-resistant depression were randomly allocated to one of two groups: • Usual care (just antidepressants). • Usual care + CBT. Improvement was assessed using the Beck Depression Inventory (BDI) before and after.
Results	After six months the number who had more than 50% reduction in symptoms was 21.6% for usual care and 46.1% for usual care + CBT. After 12 months those having usual care + CBT continued to show greater levels of recovery.
Conclusion	CBT plus antidepressant medication is more effective in reducing depressive symptoms.

Evaluation

Well-designed study	One strength of the study is that extraneous variables were carefully controlled. The two groups had the same average depression score at the start and participants were randomly allocated to groups. This means that we can conclude that changes in the dependent variable (reduction in symptoms) were not affected by extraneous variables.
Assessment of depression	One weakness is the use of self-report methods to determine levels of depression. Some people might have underestimated how sad they felt, and others might have overestimated. This questions the validity of the information collected about depression.
EXTRA: Real-world application	Another strength of the study is that it is focused on developing a useful therapy. The study shows that a more holistic approach to treating depression is more successful than antidepressant medication alone. Such real-world usefulness is one of the main reasons for conducting research.

Tick one answer

☐ I do not feel sad.
☐ I feel sad.
☐ I am sad all of the time and I can't snap out of it.
☐ I am so sad or unhappy that I can't stand it.

In Wiles' study depression was assessed using the BDI (Beck Depression Inventory). On the BDI participants rate their symptoms, as in the example above, and then a score for depression is calculated.

Exam booster

Learn the key studies thoroughly

This is a named study so make sure that you know it well as you could be asked to describe it in detail in the exam. In order to make sure you get all of the marks available, you must write at least one sentence each about the aim, method, results and conclusion.

APPLY IT – Research Methods

In order to test the effectiveness of antidepressants a sample of undergraduates who had depression were either given an antidepressant or a placebo (a pill that did nothing). All assumed they were taking an antidepressant. Mood was measured before the study and again six months later to get a mood improvement score.

1. Write a null hypothesis for this study. **[2 marks]**

2. Identify **one** ethical issue in this study and explain how it could be dealt with. **[2 marks]**

3. This study used an independent groups design. Explain **one** weakness of using this type of design in this study. **[3 marks]**

KNOWLEDGE CHECK

1. Outline the method Wiles used in her study into the effectiveness of CBT. **[3 marks]**

2. Explain what Wiles' study shows about the effectiveness of CBT. **[3 marks]**

3. Describe and evaluate Wiles' study into the effectiveness of CBT. **[9 marks]**

Classic study mix-up

Describe Wiles' study of the effectiveness of CBT.

Below are some sentences that will help you answer the question above. Unfortunately, the sentences have become jumbled up so are in the wrong order.

Write down the right order in the boxes below so that the answer makes sense.

Aim	Method	Results	Conclusion

1. There were 469 patients with treatment-resistant depression in the study.
2. After 6 months, 21.6% of the antidepressant-only group had more than 50% symptom reduction.
3. Wiles was interested in finding out if CBT plus antidepressants was an effective therapy for treatment-resistant depression.

4. Wiles assessed the participants after 6 months and after 12 months.
5. The two groups in the study were usual care (antidepressants only) and usual care plus CBT.
6. A combination of CBT and antidepressants is a more effective therapy for treatment-resistant depression than antidepressants alone.
7. Wiles wanted to set up a study called the CoBalT trial.
8. After 12 months, antidepressant + CBT patients continued to show greater levels of recovery.
9. Wiles assessed symptom improvement using a questionnaire.
10. The study's participants were randomly allocated to one of two groups.
11. After 6 months, 46.1% of the antidepressant + CBT group had more than 50% symptom reduction.
12. The participants completed the Beck Depression Inventory before and after treatment.

Fill in the blanks evaluation

Complete the evaluation by filling in the missing words. Try to avoid looking back at the material in the book. But if you do get stuck, the words you need are to the right of the passage.

One strength of Wiles' study is that extraneous variables were carefully _____. For example, participants were _____ allocated to the two groups at the start so there was no bias. This is a strength because we can conclude that symptom reduction was due to the _____ and not affected by extraneous variables.

One weakness of the study is that a self-_____ method was used to assess depression. In filling in a _____, some participants may have underestimated or overestimated how depressed they were. This is a weakness because it places a question mark over the _____ of the data collected and the _____ of the study.

Another strength of the study was that it focused on developing a useful therapy. It showed that a _____ approach using CBT is more effective in treating depression than just _____ on its own. This is a strength because it is a useful real-world _____ that improves quality of life.

validity

report

medication

randomly

holistic

application

controlled

questionnaire

therapy

conclusions

What is addiction?

What is addiction?	Griffiths suggests that salience, dependence and substance abuse are key characteristics.
	Salience means the substance/activity becomes the most important thing in a person's life.
Dependence versus addiction	Dependence is a characteristic of addiction but is not the same as addiction.
	Dependence is doing something (e.g. drug taking) because of psychological reliance and to prevent withdrawal symptoms.
	Addiction is where a person is dependent on the substance/activity but also does it because of the buzz or sense of escape.
Substance misuse versus abuse	The difference between substance misuse and abuse lies in the person's intentions.
	Misuse is not following the 'rules' for usage like taking a substance more often than recommended or using it for something else.
	Abuse is using the substance to 'get high' or to escape because a person's intentions are about the outcome of taking the drug.

Diagnosing addiction

Diagnosing addiction	International Classification of Diseases (ICD-10) has a category called 'Mental and behavioural disorders due to psychoactive substance abuse disorders'.
	A diagnosis of addiction should usually be made only if three or more characteristics have been present together at some time during the previous year.
Clinical characteristics from ICD-10	1. A strong desire to use the substance.
	2. Persisting despite known harm.
	3. Difficulty in controlling use.
	4. A higher priority given to the substance.
	5. Withdrawal symptoms if substance/activity is stopped.
	6. Evidence of tolerance, i.e. needing more to achieve the same effect.

Yep, that's addiction – appears to fulfill all six characteristics.

KNOWLEDGE CHECK

1. Using an example, explain what is meant by 'dependence'. **[3 marks]**
2. Distinguish between substance misuse and substance abuse. **[3 marks]**
3. Explain how the International Classification of Diseases is used to diagnose addiction. **[4 marks]**

The specification says...

Characteristics of addiction.

The difference between addiction/dependence and substance misuse/abuse.

The use of International Classification of Diseases in diagnosing addiction (dependence syndrome), including a strong desire to use substance(s) despite harmful consequences, difficulty in controlling use, a higher priority given to the substance(s) than to other activities or obligations.

Abusing your phone, or misusing?

Exam booster

Compare rather than just describe

You may be asked to draw comparisons such as being asked to distinguish between substance misuse and abuse. It is important to select criteria in which they differ and for each, explain how. For example, misuse and abuse differ in terms of the person's intentions, with substance abuse the person intends to 'get high' whilst with misuse they intend to use the substance for something other than it was originally intended.

APPLY IT

Read the item below and then answer the question that follows.

Gary loves to drink alcohol because of the 'high' that it gives him. His job has been difficult recently so having a few drinks helps him forget the negative events of the day. He tried stopping this habit but he found he was constantly craving a drink.

- Distinguish between dependence and addiction. Refer to Gary's behaviour in your answer. **[4 marks]**

Three-column match-up

Match up the statements across the three columns.

Dependence	(1) Using a drug mainly in order to change your mood.	(5) Involves taking drugs because of psychological reliance.	(9) Another example is using the drug to escape the stresses of everyday life (become 'numb').
Substance misuse	(2) This is guided by ICD-10.	(6) This has a category called 'Mental and behavioural disorders due to psychoactive substance use'.	(10) An example is taking more sleeping tablets than the prescribed dose.
Substance abuse	(3) Feature of addiction but not the same as it.	(7) For example, using the drug to experience an intense 'high'.	(11) Also involves trying to prevent withdrawal symptoms.
Diagnosis	(4) Failing to follow the 'rules' for using a drug.	(8) For example, taking the drug more often than recommended.	(12) This diagnosis is made only if three or more features have been present together during the previous year.

Addiction cube

Make a small cardboard cube using the template on the right. Roll the cube and whichever term or phrase comes up, provide a detailed explanation of it.

You can do this on your own, but if you're with other students you can take turns to explain to each other. Keep the explanation going until everyone understands it.

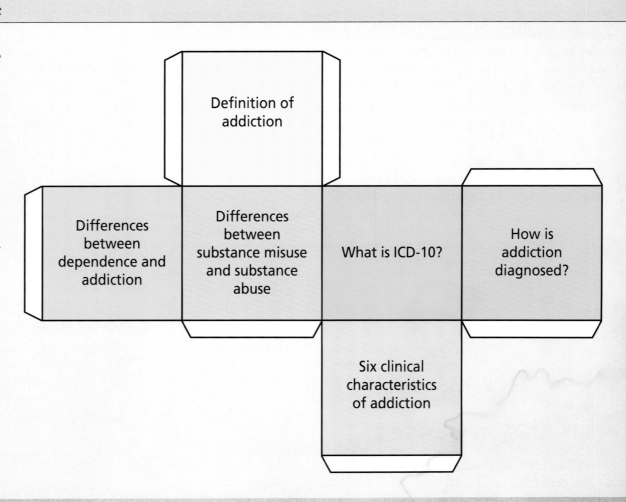

Definition of addiction

Differences between dependence and addiction

Differences between substance misuse and substance abuse

What is ICD-10?

How is addiction diagnosed?

Six clinical characteristics of addiction

The specification says...

Biological explanation (influence of nature): Hereditary factors/genetic vulnerability. Kaij's twin study of alcohol abuse.

Description

Hereditary factors	Research suggests that addictions are moderately to highly inherited.
Genetic vulnerability	Multiple genes create a vulnerability. Diathesis-stress proposes a genetic vulnerability (nature) is only expressed if a person's life stresses and experiences (nurture) are a trigger.
Kaij's twin study: Aim	To see whether alcoholism could be explained in terms of heredity, using twins.
Method	Male twins from Sweden identified from twins registered with the temperance board. Twins and close relatives were interviewed, to collect information about drinking habits. 48 identified as MZ and 126 as DZ.
Results	61% of the MZ twins were both alcoholic whereas only 39% of the DZ twins were. Twins with social problems were overrepresented among temperance board registrants.
Conclusion	Alcohol abuse is related to genetic vulnerability. If it was entirely genetic we would expect all MZ twins to be the same. If it was entirely due to environment we would expect no difference between MZ and DZ twins.

DZ twins (not identical) can be compared with MZ twins who have exactly the same genetic make-up. This helps us assess the contributions of nature and nurture to behaviour.

Evaluation

Flawed study	One weakness of Kaij's twin study is that there were flaws in the design of the study. Temperance board data only includes drinkers who made a public display of their alcohol abuse. This means that the conclusions lack validity.
Supported by later studies	One strength is support from by later research. Kendler *et al.* conducted a well-controlled study using a similar but larger sample. MZ twins were more likely to both be alcoholics than DZ twins. Research generally supports the role of heredity in alcoholism (Prescott *et al.*).
EXTRA: Misunderstanding genetic vulnerability	Another weakness with biological explanations of addiction is that they may be misleading. People assume that, if you inherit certain genes, then addiction is inevitable, ignoring nurture. It is very important to fully understand the implications of genetic research.

Exam booster

Too many names and dates

Students often worry they will be marked down in the exam for not remembering names and dates of studies but this is actually not the case. As long as the study is outlined in an accurate and detailed way that demonstrates specific knowledge and understanding of the study then you will get credit.

However you do need to recognise named studies in exam questions and know what study they refer to.

APPLY IT

Read the item below and then answer the question that follows.

Darren and his identical twin James' lives have turned out in a very different way. Darren is an alcoholic whilst his brother is not. Although they both went to the same schools when they were younger, Darren ended up being badly bullied, something that his mum reckoned had a profound effect on him. Sadly, alcoholism runs in their family and she feels that the bullying Darren experienced triggered his urge to drink.

- Use the biological explanation of addiction to explain Darren's alcoholism. **[4 marks]**

KNOWLEDGE CHECK

1. Explain how genetic vulnerability can influence addiction. **[3 marks]**
2. Describe the conclusion of **one** study that investigated alcohol abuse. **[2 marks]**
3. Outline and evaluate the biological explanation of addiction. Refer to Kaij's twin study of alcohol abuse in your answer. **[9 marks]**

Fill in the description blanks

Fill in the blanks in the following description of the biological explanation of addiction. The words are given on the right if you get stuck but try and do the activity without them first.

There are hereditary factors involved in addiction. Research studies show that the role of inherited influences in addictions is moderate to high.

Multiple _____ operate to create a vulnerability to develop an addiction. However, this genetic vulnerability (the result of _____) is only expressed if the person's life stresses and experiences (the result of _____) are a trigger. This is the _____-stress explanation.

Kaij carried out a twin study to see whether _____ addiction could be explained in terms of heredity. The participants were male twins from _____ who were registered with the temperance board. 48 MZ (identical) and 126 _____ (non-identical) twins were interviewed.

Kaij found that in _____% of the MZ pairs, both twins were addicted to alcohol. The figure for DZ twins was _____%.

Kaij concluded that alcohol addiction is related to _____ vulnerability. If it was completely genetic, then the figure for MZ twins would be _____% rather than 61%. If it was completely due to _____ factors, then there would be no difference in the figures for MZ and DZ twins.

Words:
- DZ
- alcohol
- genetic
- nature
- 100
- genes
- nurture
- 39
- environmental
- 61
- Sweden
- diathesis

Evaluate with trigger phrases

Here are some 'trigger' phrases related to the biological explanation of addiction. The first thing to do is decide which phrases go together by putting them into pairs in the table.

Then write a sentence explaining each pair of statements (or giving an example) without looking at your notes or at the previous page.

Finally, write a further sentence, to explain why your first sentence is a strength/weakness.

Trigger phrases:
- For example, Kendler *et al.*
- Biological explanations may be misleading
- Flawed design
- Misunderstands genetic vulnerability
- Data from the temperance board
- Support from later studies

Description

Peer influence	'Nurture' refers to the influence of experience from the physical and/or social environment.
	Peers are people who are equal in terms of, for example, age or education.
Social learning theory	Bandura states we learn how to behave and think by observing what others do.
	We imitate them especially if they are rewarded.
	We even more especially imitate those we identify with.
Social norms	We don't always know what behaviour is 'right'.
	We look to the behaviour of others to know what is 'normal' or acceptable (social norms).
	However, a person may overestimate social norms.
Social identity theory	You identify with your social groups (e.g. supporters of a football team, a group of students in your class).
	You want to be accepted by them, so behave like them.
	Adolescents in particular may feel 'pressure' to conform to the social norms of their peer group.
Opportunities for addictive behaviour	Peers influence addictive behaviour because they provide opportunities.
	Peers may give direct instruction about what to do.

Spot the social norms.

Evaluation

Supporting research	One strength of peer influence as an explanation of addiction is that there is research support.
	Simons-Morton and Farhat reviewed 40 studies and found that all but one showed a positive correlation between peers and smoking.
	This shows a strong relationship between peers and addiction.
It may be peer selection	One weakness is peers may not be influencers.
	Individuals may be actively selecting others who are like them rather than conforming to social norms.
	This means addictive behaviour is a consequence of addiction rather than caused by the group.
EXTRA: Real-world application	Another strength of the peer influence explanation is its real-world application.
	Social norms programmes have had more success than just teaching resistance skills (Hansen and Graham).
	Thus there is a value in peer influence explanations.

Exam booster

And nurture is ...

Make sure that you can explain how peer influence relates to nurture in shaping addictive behaviour. The key point to make is that nurture relates to how our experiences shape us so obviously your peers play a key role in this.

APPLY IT – Research Methods

A psychologist conducted a study to see whether exposure to films that glorify addiction were more likely to cause people to smoke. They selected twenty films that showed addiction in a positive light and asked people to indicate which films they had seen and also to say if they smoked and how many cigarettes a day on average. They found that the more of the selected films that people had seen, the more cigarettes they smoked.

1. Identify the **two** co-variables in this correlational study. [2 marks]
2. Explain **one** strength of using correlational analysis in this investigation. [2 marks]
3. Describe the type of correlation the researchers found. [2 marks]

KNOWLEDGE CHECK

1. What is meant by the term 'peer influence'? [2 marks]
2. Explain **one** way the psychological explanation for addiction can be evaluated. [4 marks]
3. Outline and evaluate the psychological explanation of addiction. Refer to nurture in your answer. [9 marks]

Psychological explanation true or false

Here are some sentences about the psychological explanation of addiction. Indicate whether you think each one is true or false. For the false statements, write down the true versions in the spaces provided.

		True or false?	
1.	Psychological explanations emphasise the role of nature rather than nurture.		
2.	A peer is someone who is your equal (e.g. similar age or education level).		
3.	Bandura devised social identity theory.		
4.	According to Bandura, we learn to be addicted because it's in our genes.		
5.	We are more likely to imitate someone's behaviour if we identify with them.		
6.	We always know what is the right thing to do.		
7.	Social identity theory says that we identify with groups because we want to be accepted by them.		
8.	Adolescents are especially good at ignoring social pressures to conform to the group.		
9.	Peers don't really have much influence over whether someone becomes addicted.		
10.	If peers are influential, it is always indirectly.		

Evaluation fill-in and match-up

Fill in the missing information where necessary in the sentences below. Then match the sentences up to make three full evaluation points (three sentences each).

1. A weakness of the explanation is that _____ may not be the important peer-related factor.	2. This is a weakness because it suggests that peer relationships are not a _____ of addiction but a consequence of it.	3. For example, a review by Simons-Morton and _____ found there was a positive correlation between peer influence and smoking in _____ out of 40 studies.
4. This is a strength because the research shows that peer influence is a strong factor in addiction.	5. A strength of peer influence is that it has some _____ support.	6. This is a strength because it suggests that the peer influence explanation has some validity if it can be _____ successfully.
7. For example, Hansen and _____ have showed that social _____ programmes are more successful in dealing with addiction than just resistance skills.	8. Another strength is that the peer influence explanation can be _____ to real-life situations.	9. Instead, it may be that individuals who are already prone to addiction are selecting other people who are _____ them.

The specification says...

Interventions or therapies for addiction: Aversion therapy. How this improves mental health, reductionist and holistic perspectives.

Description

Aversion therapy	Based on classical conditioning.
	Addict learns to associate their addiction with something unpleasant, and therefore avoids the addictive substance.
Treating alcoholism	A drug like *Antabuse* is taken which causes nausea.
	Just before vomiting, the addict has an alcoholic drink several times.
	• Antabuse (UCS) leads to vomiting (UCR).
	• Alcohol (NS) is associated with Antabuse (UCS).
	• Alcohol becomes a learned/conditioned stimulus (CS) producing nausea/vomiting (CR).
	Alcohol now associated with vomiting not pleasure.
Treating gambling	An addicted gambler writes phrases related or unrelated to gambling on cards.
	The gambler reads out each card and gets an electric shock for gambling-related phrases.
	• Electric shock (UCS) leads to pain (UCR).
	• Gambling-related phrase (NS) is associated with electric shock (UCS).
	• Gambling-related phrase becomes a CS producing pain (CR)
	Gambling-related behaviours associated with pain.
Treating smoking	Addicted smoker rapidly smokes in closed room.
	Disgust from smoking is associated with smoking.

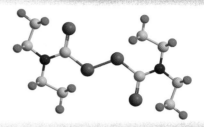

If you were an alcohol molecule that's what Antabuse would look like.

Evaluation

Treatment adherence issues	One weakness is that addicts may abandon therapy as it's unpleasant.
	Many addicts drop out before the treatment is completed because the aversive stimulus has to be negative.
	This makes it hard to assess effectiveness.
Poor long-term effectiveness	Another weakness is that benefits of aversion therapy seem to be short term rather than long term.
	In a long-term follow-up (nine years) McConaghy *et al.* found aversion therapy was no more effective than a placebo. Covert sensitisation was better.
	This suggests aversion therapy lacks effectiveness.
EXTRA: A holistic approach	One strength is that aversion therapy can be combined with CBT in a holistic way.
	Aversion therapy gets rid of immediate urge to use the addictive substance. CBT provides longer lasting support by changing a person's feelings/thinking.
	This provides a longer-term solution to the addiction.

APPLY IT

Read the item below and then answer the questions that follow.

Annie takes her netball career seriously which is why she knows she must cut out fast food from her diet. She recognises that she has an addiction and so is willing to try aversion therapy even though she has heard that it can be painful and may not be as effective as other techniques out there.

1. Briefly explain how aversion therapy would be used to treat Annie's addiction to fast food. **[3 marks]**

2. Briefly evaluate aversion therapy. Refer to the above item in your answer. **[4 marks]**

KNOWLEDGE CHECK

1. Briefly explain why aversion therapy could be used as a holistic treatment for addiction. **[2 marks]**

2. With reference to an example of an addiction, explain the way aversion therapy works as a therapy for addiction. **[4 marks]**

3. Outline and evaluate aversion therapy as a method to improve mental health. **[9 marks]**

Aversion anagrams

Here are ten anagrams of words related to this topic. There are some clues to help you if you need them.

1.	VASEIRON RATHYPE		The treatment this is all about.
2.	LILACSACS CONNINGIDIOT		The type of learning the treatment is based on.
3.	ACTIONOASIS		The link between an addiction and something unpleasant.
4.	DADCOINIT		The disorder that is being treated.
5.	SAUNABET		The name of the drug used in this treatment.
6.	MOVINGIT		What people start doing after taking the drug.
7.	NICOTINEODD		Nausea becomes a _____ response after treatment.
8.	BANGGLIM		Another costly addictive behaviour treated with this method.
9.	CREELTIC HOCKS		Used instead of chemicals to treat the above behaviour.
10.	KONGISM		Another addictive behaviour, this one involves nicotine.

Organise your answer

Here's a typical 9-mark question: Describe and evaluate aversion therapy for addiction.

An excellent way to boost your marks to such a question is to organise your answer clearly. The table below offers a way to visualise your answer.

Just identify 4 AO1 points/phrases (on left) and 3 AO3 points/phrases (on right) as triggers.

AO1 – use a different colour for each one.	AO3 – keep it brief.
1.	1.
2.	2.
3.	3.
4.	

Now use the framework above to write out your essay in full.	
For the description you should write about 25 words for each point.	For the evaluation you need to provide an explanation and a conclusion for each point.

Published in 2018 by Illuminate Publishing Ltd,
P.O. Box 1160, Cheltenham, Gloucestershire GL50 9RW
Orders: Please visit www.illuminatepublishing.com
or email sales@illuminatepublishing.com

British Library Cataloguing in Publication Data
A catalogue record for this book is available from the
British Library
ISBN 978-1-911208-06-8
Printed by Standartų Spaustuvė, Lithuania
12.18

The publisher's policy is to use papers that are natural,
renewable and recyclable products made from
wood grown in sustainable forests. The logging and
manufacturing processes are expected to conform to the
environmental regulations of the country of origin.

Every effort has been made to contact copyright holders
of material produced in this book. If notified, the publisher
will be pleased to rectify any errors or omissions at the
earliest opportunity.

Editor: Geoff Tuttle
Text design and layout: John Dickinson
Cover design: Nigel Harriss
Artwork: John Dickinson and Nigel Harriss

Unsung heroes

The authors would like to express their appreciation to all of those people who have made this book possible – it's not just writing the book that counts!

Number 1 is Rick Jackman, our publisher. He makes it all happen and is unswervingly enthusiastic and understanding, and is always a joy to work with. He has been supported at Illuminate Publishing by Clare Jackman and Peter Burton as well as Saskia Santos.

Our second big thanks goes to John Dickinson and Nigel Harriss for the design and layout of this book which we hope you agree looks fantastic.

Geoff Tuttle is our editor who has shown fanatical care in ensuring the words on the page are correct. He is our safety net.

Finally we would like to thank Dave, our man with a sense of humour, who wrote most of the captions! The good ones.

About the authors

Cara is author of many books for A level and GCSE Psychology students and a conference organiser and speaker; she is also senior editor of *Psychology Review*. She is looking forward to one day spending more time lying on a beach or climbing mountains but does manage it occasionally.

Rob was an A level Psychology teacher for more than 20 years, before turning to writing. He now has quite a lot of books under his belt, for all the major exam boards. He has also done some examining in his time. In his spare moments, Rob likes nothing better than to pluck away skill-lessly at his guitar. He is enthusiastically looking forward to *Frozen 2* coming out, even though his granddaughters couldn't care less.

Ruth and **Mark** both work as heads of Psychology in southwest Britain with Ruth working at Gordano School and Mark at SGS College. They are parents to a delightful two year boy called Ezra and 6 month old Ivy who take up most of their time when they are not teaching or writing. Ruth enjoys countryside walks and shopping in her free time which is why Ezra and Ivy are the best dressed children in the nursery (no bias of course...). Mark on the other hand loves football with Manchester United the team lucky enough to have his support.

Dave is Head of Psychology at Oldham Hulme Grammar School. When not teaching or writing he divides his time between his beloved wife and son, football, politics and *Come dine with me*. He does not share his wife's enthusiasm for shopping but will go if he is guaranteed a coffee every half hour. He has an unfortunate – but nevertheless lifelong – commitment to Leeds United Football Club.

AQA Psychology for GCSE

Revision Guide

Cara Flanagan
Dave Berry
Ruth Jones
Mark Jones
Rob Liddle

Illuminate Publishing